GOTHAM CENTRAL

BOOK ONE: **IN THE LINE OF DUTY**

KT-445-125

30131 04514888 6

London Borough of Barnet

BARNET LIBRARIES

GOSH! COMICS   2012

DAN DIDIO SENIOR VP-EXECUTIVE EDITOR
MATT IDELSON EDITOR-ORIGINAL SERIES
NACHIE CASTRO ASSISTANT EDITOR-ORIGINAL SERIES
ANTON KAWASAKI EDITOR-COLLECTED EDITION
ROBBIN BROSTERMAN SENIOR ART DIRECTOR
PAUL LEVITZ PRESIDENT & PUBLISHER
GEORG BREWER VP-DESIGN & DC DIRECT CREATIVE
RICHARD BRUNING SENIOR VP-CREATIVE DIRECTOR
PATRICK CALDON EXECUTIVE VP-FINANCE & OPERATIONS
CHRIS CARAMALIS VP-FINANCE
JOHN CUNNINGHAM VP-MARKETING
TERRI CUNNINGHAM VP-MANAGING EDITOR
ALISON GILL VP-MANUFACTURING
DAVID HYDE VP-PUBLICITY
HANK KANALZ VP-GENERAL MANAGER, WILDSTORM
JIM LEE EDITORIAL DIRECTOR-WILDSTORM
PAULA LOWITT SENIOR VP-BUSINESS & LEGAL AFFAIRS
MARYELLEN MCLAUGHLIN VP-ADVERTISING & CUSTOM PUBLISHING
JOHN NEE SENIOR VP-BUSINESS DEVELOPMENT
GREGORY NOVECK SENIOR VP-CREATIVE AFFAIRS
SUE POHJA VP-BOOK TRADE SALES
STEVE ROTTERDAM SENIOR VP-SALES & MARKETING
CHERYL RUBIN SENIOR VP-BRAND MANAGEMENT
JEFF TROJAN VP-BUSINESS DEVELOPMENT, DC DIRECT
BOB WAYNE VP-SALES

Cover by Michael Lark. Publication design by Brainchild Studios/NYC.

GOTHAM CENTRAL BOOK ONE: IN THE LINE OF DUTY
Published by DC Comics. Cover, introduction and compilation Copyright © 2008 DC Comics. All Rights Reserved.
Originally published in single magazine form in GOTHAM CENTRAL #1-10. Copyright © 2004, 2005 DC Comics.
All Rights Reserved. All characters, their distinctive likenesses and related elements featured in this publication are
trademarks of DC Comics. The stories, characters and incidents featured in this publication are entirely fictional.
DC Comics does not read or accept unsolicited submissions of ideas, stories or artwork.

DC Comics, 1700 Broadway, New York, NY 10019
A Warner Bros. Entertainment Company
Printed by Quad/Graphics, Dubuque, IA, USA. 6/17/11. Second Printing.
ISBN 13: 978-1-4012-2037-2

SUSTAINABLE
FORESTRY
INITIATIVE
Certified Chain of Custody
Promoting Sustainable
Forest Management
www.sfiprogram.org
Fiber used in this product line meets the
sourcing requirements of the SFI program.
www.sfiprogram.org SGS-SFICOC-0130

GOTHAM CENTRAL

BOOK ONE: IN THE LINE OF DUTY

Written by
ED BRUBAKER & GREG RUCKA
"In the Line of Duty"

ED BRUBAKER
"Motive"

GREG RUCKA
"Half a Life"

Art by
MICHAEL LARK

*Batman created
by* **BOB KANE**

Colors by
NOELLE GIDDINGS
MATT HOLLINGSWORTH
LEE LOUGHRIDGE

Letters by
WILLIE SCHUBERT

by
LAWRENCE BLOCK

WE ALWAYS KNEW THEY MEANT NEW YORK.

Oh, sure, they called it Gotham City. That's where the Bat Signal hung in the night sky like the moon, and where the Batmobile never had to circle the block looking for a parking space. Gotham was home to the Joker and the Riddler and the Penguin, and in its streets and upon its rooftops Batman and Robin the Boy Wonder waged their endless noble battle against the forces of evil.

That was Gotham City, all right, and that was a perfectly fine thing to call it in the alternate universe of comic book fiction. But we're not dim. We knew well and good what town we were talking about, whatever name they fastened on it, and whatever they called its streets and newspapers and citizens.

They were talking about New York.

I mean, why else call it Gotham?

The original Gotham, it may interest you to know, was in England, a village in Nottinghamshire. The name meant "goat town" in Anglo-Saxon, which would seem to suggest that some of the inhabitants kept goats and didn't care who knew it. Back in the thirteenth century, the Gothamites earned a reputation as "wise fools" by feigning insanity in order to avoid paying taxes to King John. (There was evidently something about King John that put people's backs up; it was he, you'll recall, who in 1215 inspired the peers of the realm to force upon him the Magna Carta, that Great Charter that stands as the foundation of all our freedoms, granting the citizenry such rights as trial by jury. But I digress. . .)

King John had long since gone to his reward when the Dutch bought the island of Manhattan and founded a town they called New Amsterdam. And it was almost two centuries after that, in 1807, when Washington Irving published a series of essays entitled *Salmagundi, or the Whims and Opinions of Launcelot Langstaff and Others,* wherein he referred to the city as Gotham. Irving's use of the name implied that Gothamites were self-important and foolish, but the name shrugged off its connotations and endured.

And wasn't Washington Irving the lad for naming things? *Salmagundi*, which he seems to have cobbled up out of a handful of leftover Scrabble letters, became the name of an artists' club; founded in 1871, it endures to this day, and its brownstone clubhouse boasts the only remaining stoop on Fifth Avenue. Meanwhile, Irving followed *Salmagundi* with *A History of New York,* which he wrote under the pen name of Diedrich Knickerbocker, ostensibly an embittered old codger of Dutch extraction. There's another name that's hung on, and you'll find it attached to any number of present-day New York institutions, including a group of tallish fellows who pass the time throwing a round ball through a hoop. But there I go, digressing again. . .

In 1844, Edgar Allan Poe wrote a series of satirical reports on daily life in New York, which he called *Doings of Gotham.* (He lived at various New York locations — in Greenwich Village, on

West 84th Street, and in a cottage in the Bronx that survives to this day as an Edgar Allan Poe museum.) The author of "The Raven" doesn't seem to have found New York's streets all that mean, but did trouble to call them "with rare exception, insufferably dirty." He went on to lament the $50,000 spent annually for street cleaning, and proposed a novel alternative: "Contractors might pay roundly for the privilege of cleaning the streets, receiving the sweepings for their perquisite, and find themselves great gainers by the arrangement. In any large city, a company of market gardeners would be induced to accept a contract of this character."

Believe it or not, Poe's notion never did reach the right ears, and to this day the city actually spends money to clean the streets. In some years the tab runs even higher than $50,000.

William Sydney Porter, whom you'd know as O. Henry, lived in New York from 1902 until his death in 1910. Many of his stories, especially those in *The Four Million*, were set in New York, but when he called the place Gotham he was just using a sobriquet that had long since been incorporated into the local language. He had other names he invented for the city, most notable "Baghdad-on-the-Subway." Now there's a phrase that must have resonated very differently a century ago than it does today.

• • • • •

Forget the name. Suppose they called the city something else, or nothing at all. Could it be any place but New York?

In 1939, when Bob Kane started drawing BATMAN, the urban landscape alone could have told us what town he had in mind. The high-rises and skyscrapers defined New York in an era where not many cities boasted a building much taller than the local water tower.

Things are a little different now, and you don't have to look far to find a one-horse town with a genuine skyline. But it's not just the height of the buildings that makes New York the right setting for Batman, and the perfect home for these Gotham cops — dressed, I don't doubt, in GCPD Blue — who fight the good fight in these pages.

It's not the actual meanness of the streets, either. New York, its image notwithstanding, has a lower crime rate than most of the rest of the country, and one that continues to drop. Gentrification has upgraded Harlem and made the Lower East Side unrecognizable, and you pretty much have to leave Manhattan and do some real searching to find a genuinely bad neighborhood these days.

So it's not the crime rate, and it's not the tall buildings. What is it? The answer's somewhere in the following gag: *Tourist to New Yorker: Can you tell me how to get to the Empire State Building, or should I just go #%@&#!!! myself?*

The New York energy goes beyond anything you'll find anywhere else. It's too much for some people and it grinds them down, but it lifts up and animates the rest of us.

It gives us the New York edge, which is attitude and something

more. Reggie Jackson, who had some of his best years at that ballpark in the Bronx, smiled when someone asked him how he felt about the city. "If you give a New Yorker the first line," he said, "he's got the whole page."

Hey, get a grip, will you? Can you imagine the Joker trying to make his bones by putting one over on the cops in Albuquerque? Or the Riddler trying out conundrums on Fargo's Finest? Can you picture Catwoman in Cleveland, or the Penguin in Peoria, or Two-Face in the Twin Cities? Or our villain *du jour*, the chilling Mr. Freeze, in, say, Fresno?

I didn't think so.

It's Gotham City, baby. Get used to it.

• • • • •

LAWRENCE BLOCK's novels range from the urban noir of Matthew Scudder to the urbane effervescence of Bernie Rhodenbarr, while other characters include the globe-trotting insomniac Evan Tanner and the introspective assassin Keller. He has published articles and short fiction in *American Heritage*, *Redbook*, *Playboy*, *Cosmopolitan*, *GQ*, and *The New York Times*, and *84* of his short stories have been collected in *Enough Rope*. Larry is a Grand Master of Mystery Writers of America, and a past president of both MWA and the Private Eye Writers of America. He has won the Edgar and Shamus awards four times each and the Japanese Maltese Falcon award twice, as well as the Nero Wolfe and Philip Marlowe awards, and, most recently, a Life Achievement award from the Private Eye Writers of America. In France, he has been proclaimed a Grand Maitre du Roman Noir and has twice been awarded the Societe 813 trophy. Larry and his wife Lynne are enthusiastic New Yorkers and relentless world travelers.

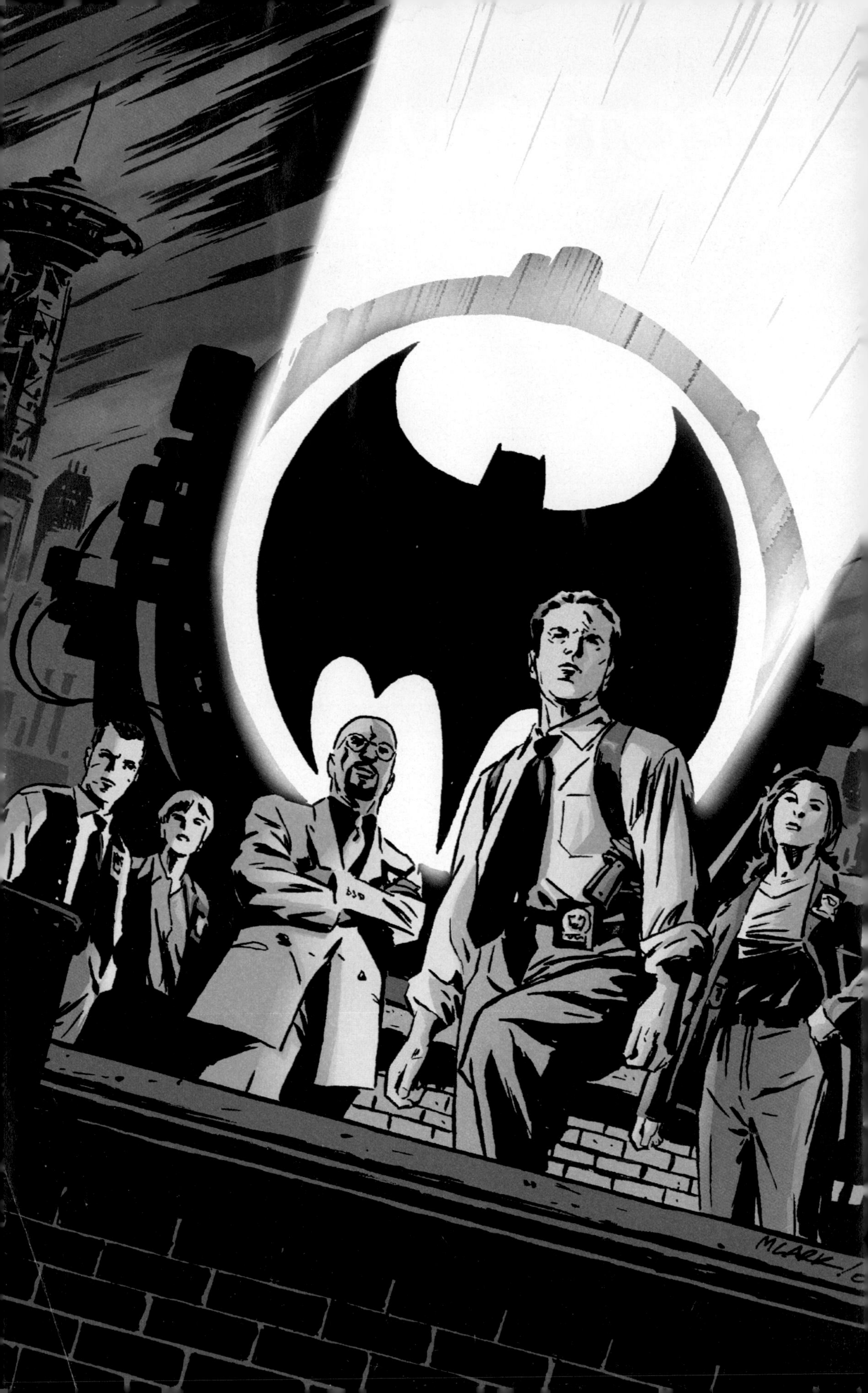

JUNE 23rd -- 6:02 a.m. ...

YOU'RE WASTIN' MY *TIME*, MARCUS. I MEAN IT. WHAT'S THE LIKELIHOOD THAT SOME JUNKIE SNITCH IS GONNA GIVE US A *SERIOUS LEAD* ON THE LEWIS THING?

WHAT, ZERO-TO-NONE?

THAT'S RIGHT, ZERO-TO-NONE...

YET, HERE I AM, *AFTER* OUR SHIFT, WHEN I COULD BE CRAWLING INTO BED WITH MY WIFE FOR THOSE FEW HOURS WHEN WE'RE BOTH ASLEEP...

HEY, IF YOU *WANT*, I CAN CHECK INTO THIS BY MYSELF.

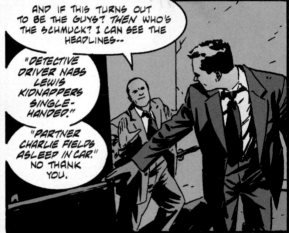

AND IF THIS TURNS OUT TO BE THE GUYS? *THEN* WHO'S THE SCHMUCK? I CAN SEE THE HEADLINES--

"DETECTIVE DRIVER NABS LEWIS KIDNAPPERS SINGLE-HANDED."

"PARTNER CHARLIE FIELDS ASLEEP IN CAR." NO THANK YOU.

IT'S A FOURTEEN-YEAR-OLD-GIRL BEEN GRABBED, CHARLIE... SURE IT'S *PROBABLY* NOTHING, BUT WHAT DID THAT SNITCH SAY...? THESE GUYS'VE BEEN HIDING OUT AND ACTING *SUSPICIOUS* IN THIS $#!%#@! FOR A *WEEK*.

THE *TIMING'S* RIGHT, AT LEAST.

TIMING'S RIGHT FOR ME TO GET SOME *SLEEP*, TOO...

THEN WE GOT THAT *CEREMONY* TONIGHT, WHICH'LL PROBABLY BE *MANDATORY ATTENDANCE*...

YEAH YEAH, CRY ME A RIVER. YOU'LL PROBABLY BE HOME IN *TEN* MINUTES.

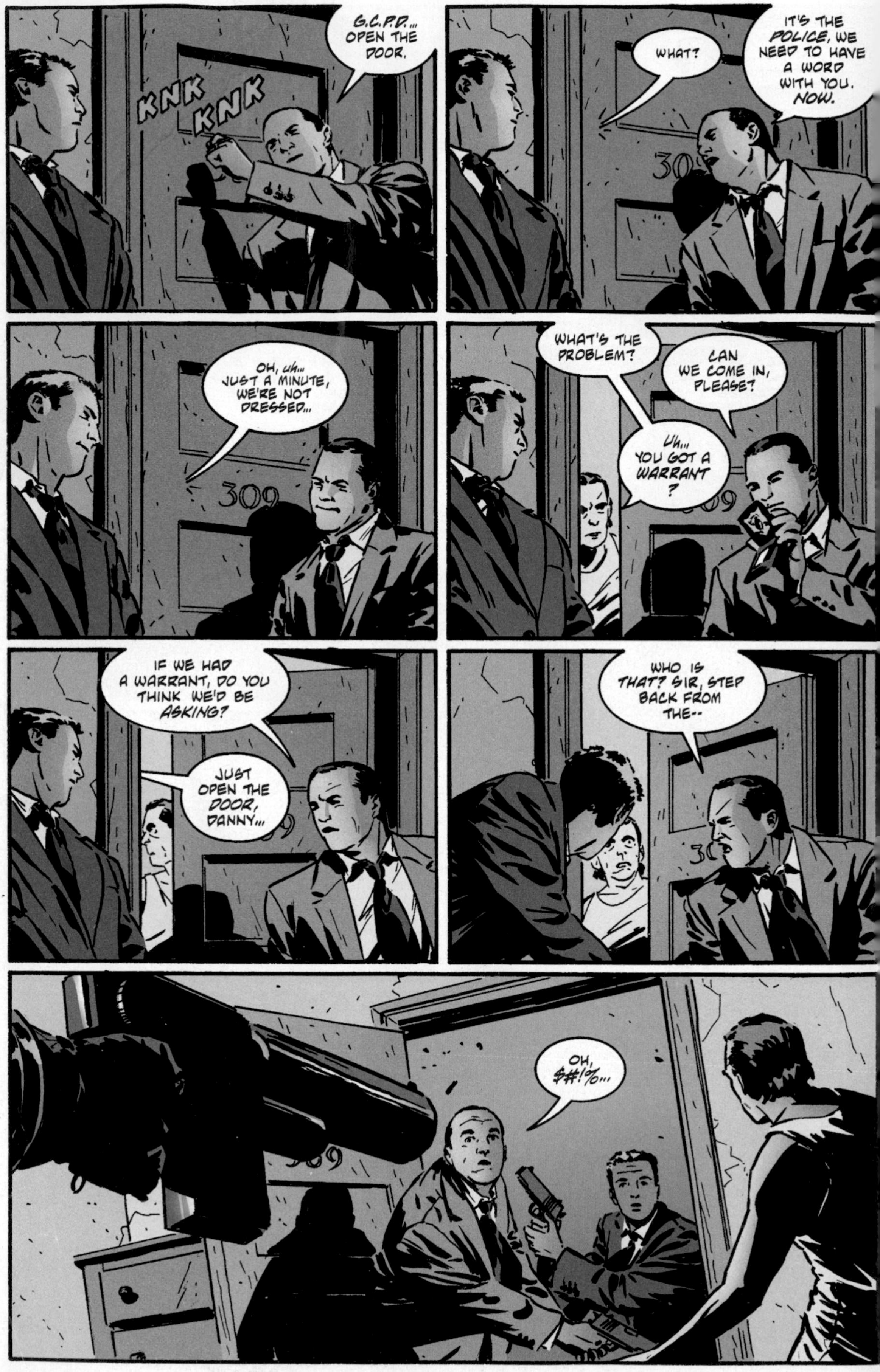
KNK KNK
G.C.P.D.... OPEN THE DOOR.
WHAT?
IT'S THE POLICE, WE NEED TO HAVE A WORD WITH YOU. NOW.
OH, UH... JUST A MINUTE, WE'RE NOT DRESSED...
WHAT'S THE PROBLEM?
CAN WE COME IN, PLEASE?
UH... YOU GOT A WARRANT?
IF WE HAD A WARRANT, DO YOU THINK WE'D BE ASKING?
JUST OPEN THE DOOR, DANNY...
WHO IS THAT? SIR, STEP BACK FROM THE--
OH, $#!%...

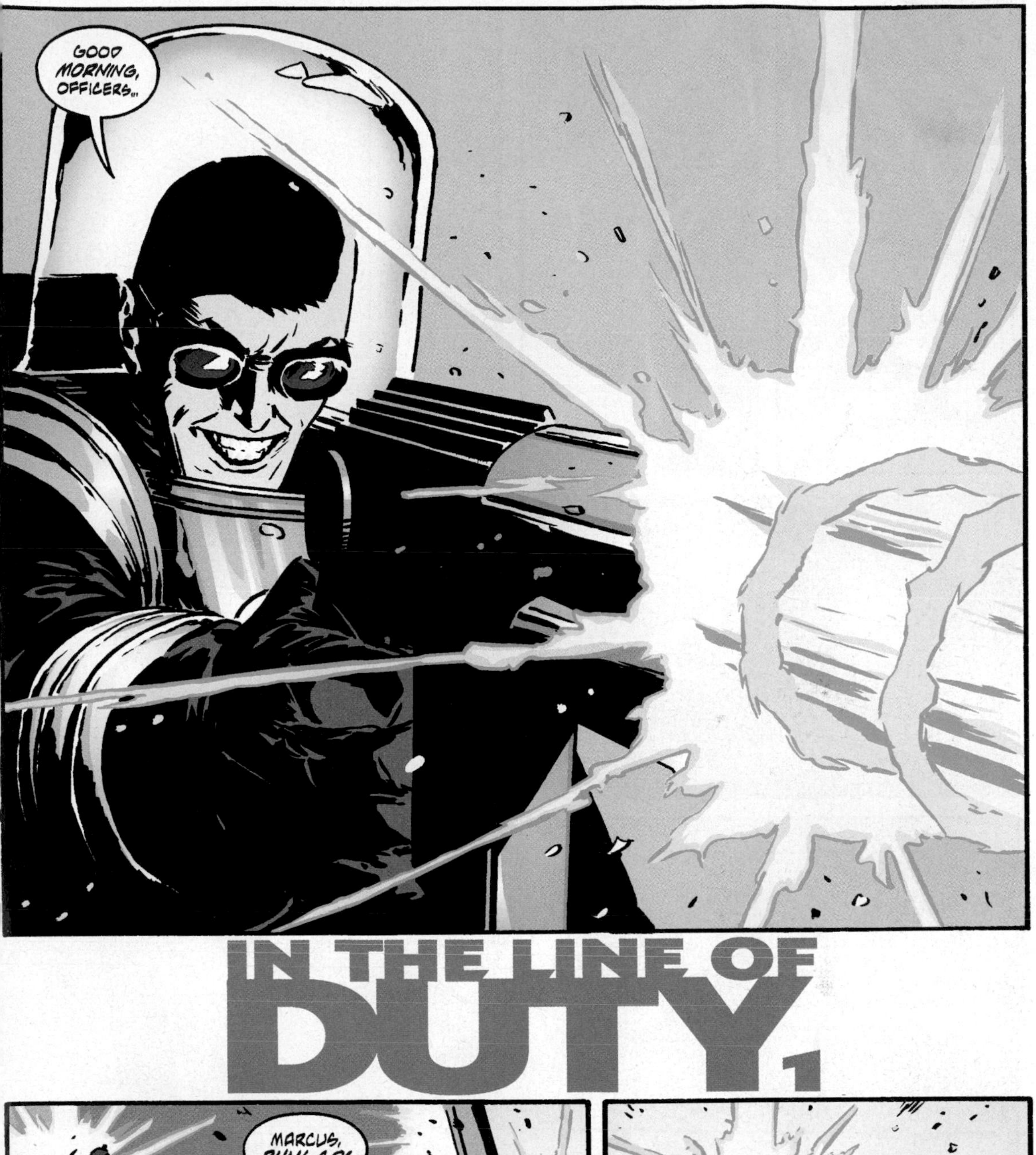
GOOD MORNING, OFFICERS...

IN THE LINE OF DUTY 1

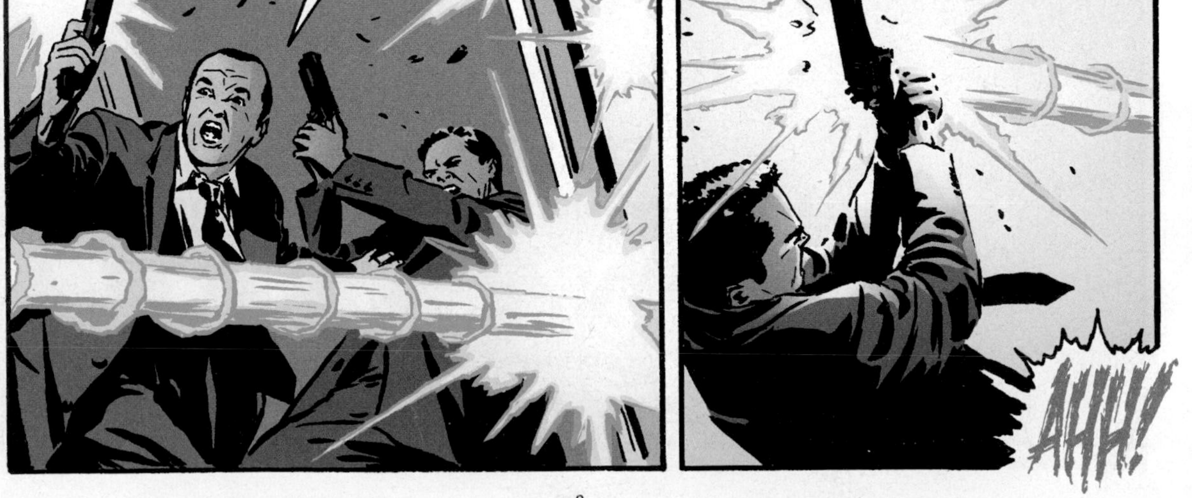
MARCUS, RUN! GO!
AHH!

BLAM!
BLAM!

CHARLIE...?

YOU OKAY?

NO... I'M AFRAID "OKAY" ISN'T A WORD CHARLIE WILL BE USING ANY LONGER...

NOW THEN...

AAAAH!

OH PLEASE... STOP. YOUR PARTNER DIDN'T COMPLAIN AT ALL...

NOW, HOW DID YOU FIND ME?

THE HELL WITH YOU, YOU %@&#$% PSYCHO...

YOU KNOW, I'VE ALWAYS FOUND THE GOTHAM POLICE TO BE AN INCREDIBLY UNEDUCATED LOT...

LET ME GIVE YOU A LESSON, DETECTIVE.

chrnk... krrk

SHALL I CONTINUE, OR DO YOU WANT TO ANSWER MY QUESTION?

WEREN'T AFTER YOU...

WHAT? THE HELL YOU SAY?

TRUE...W-WE HAD A *TIP*, LOOKING FOR KIDNAPPERS...

...THINK WE'D WALK INTO A ROOM WITH...Y-YOU IN IT... WITH NO B-BACKUP?

WELL, IT APPEARS YOU HAD SOME *BAD LUCK* THIS MORNING THEN, DIDN'T YOU?

OF COURSE, I KNOW ABOUT BAD LUCK...THAT'S ONE OF THE LESSONS THAT GOTHAM TEACHES US ALL, EVENTUALLY.

HEY, *uh*, DON'T YOU THINK WE'D BETTER GET *OUTTA HERE*, FREEZE? SOMEONE MUSTA CALLED IN THAT GUNFIRE.

PLACE'LL BE SWARMIN' WITH *COPS* SOON...

IN A *MINUTE*, DANNY...

...I JUST WANT TO INSTRUCT OUR FRIEND HERE IN GOTHAM'S MORE *ADVANCED CURRICULUM*... THE *TRAGEDY OF SURVIVING LOSS*...

...AS A PREVIEW OF *THINGS TO COME*.

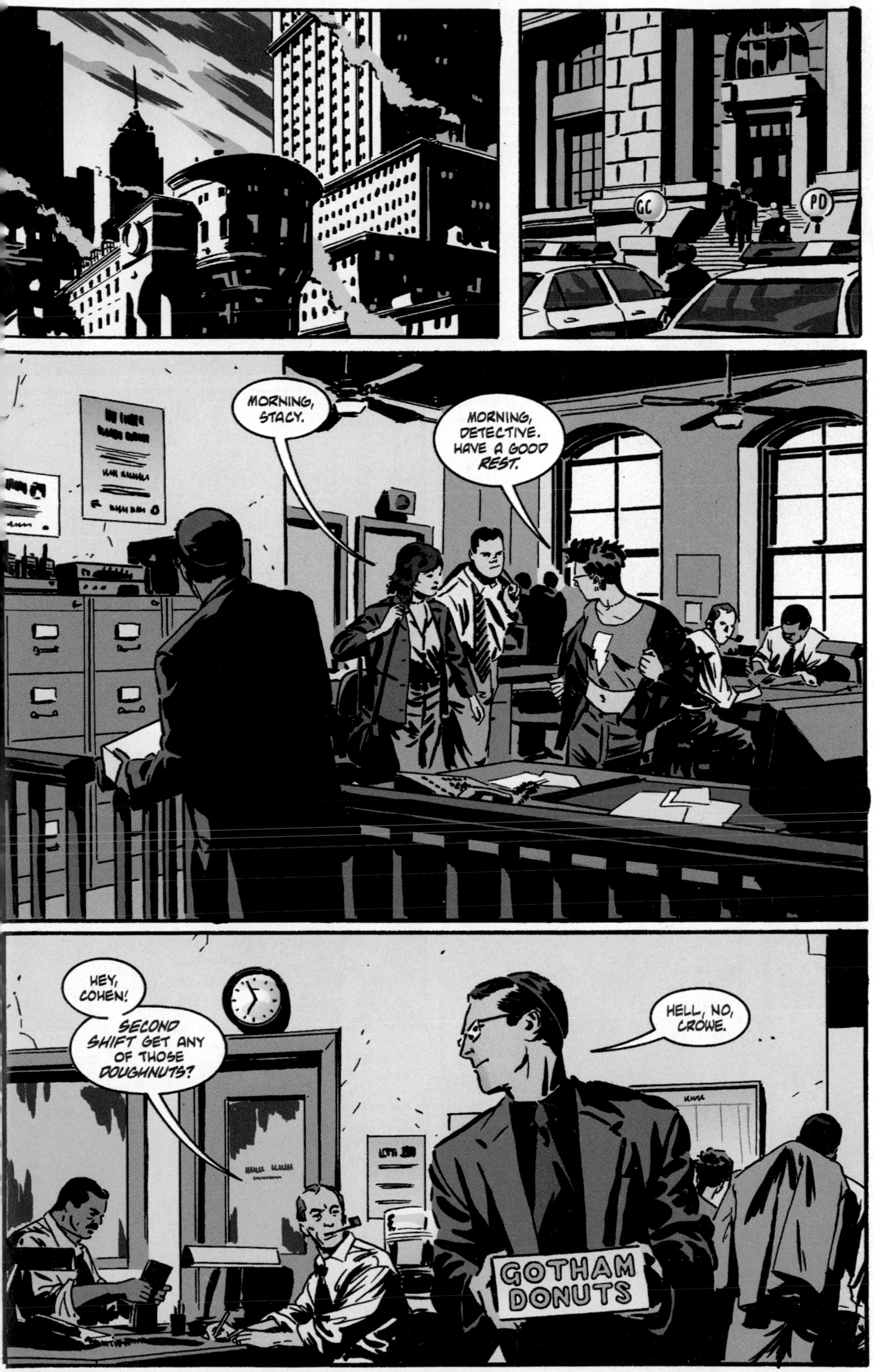
GC
PD
MORNING, STACY.
MORNING, DETECTIVE. HAVE A GOOD REST.
HEY, COHEN!
SECOND SHIFT GET ANY OF THOSE DOUGHNUTS?
HELL, NO, CROWE.
GOTHAM DONUTS

WE DONE?

YEAH, WE'RE FINISHED...

--THINK THE POLITICAL SITUATION IN THIS CITY IS GOING TO *CHANGE*, RENEE, THEN YOU'RE *NOT* PAYING *ATTENTION*.

ALL I ASKED WAS IF YOU WERE GOING *TONIGHT*, CHRIS, THAT'S ALL...

...WENT *LAST NIGHT*?

PRETTY *QUIET*, MUST BE THE *HEAT*. GONNA BE A *LONG SUMMER*.

HEY! WHICH ONE OF YOU LEFT YOUR *DINNER* ON MY *DESK*?

CAPTAIN SAYWER.

LIEUTENANT PROBSON.

THOUGHT YOU'D HAVE GONE ALREADY.

FINISHING UP O.T.S.

ANYTHING I SHOULD KNOW?

NAH, IT WAS *DEAD* LAST NIGHT. ALL *MY* KIDS ARE ACCOUNTED FOR.

FIELDS AND DRIVER ARE STILL *OUT.* FOLLOWING UP ON A TIP BEFORE THEY GO OFF-SHIFT.

THAT THE *LEWIS* THING?

YEAH. STILL *NOTHING.* THEY'RE GRASPING AT STRAWS.

YOU WANT ANY OF *MINE* TO LOOK INTO IT?

PROCJNOW AND BURKE ARE *CLEAR--*

IT'S *COVERED* CAPTAIN, WE'VE GOT IT. WE DON'T NEED *YOUR* HELP.

IT BOTHERS YOU *THAT* MUCH? THAT I GOT THE *PROMOTION*?

OR MAYBE IT'S *SOMETHING* ELSE THAT'S EATING YOU, *LIEUTENANT*?

YOU'RE NOT *CATCHING* ME IN SOME *HARASSMENT* THING--

CAPTAIN!

ARGARET AWYER

CH COMMANDER

JUST CAME *IN,* OFFICER DOWN--

--IT'S DETECTIVES DRIVER AND *FIELDS,* CAPTAIN...

DETECTIVE DRIVER...?

...I'M SORRY... DETECTIVE...

WE'RE GONNA TRY AND *MOVE* YOU NOW...

OH, UH... YEAH, SURE... OKAY...

IS THIS OKAY? CAN YOU MOVE YOUR ARMS?

YEAH, JUST NOT MY HANDS...

THEY'VE GOT A CREW DOWNSTAIRS THAT'LL TAKE CARE OF THAT FOR YOU, SIR... YOU'RE GOING TO BE *FINE*.

MAN... HOW THE &@$% ARE THEY GONNA GET THIS GUY TO THE MORGUE? IN A COUPLE OF FREEZER BAGS?

SHUT UP, TODD... OKAY?

WHAT, WHAT'D I SAY?

16

DRIVER! *THERE YOU ARE...* WHERE'S *CHARLIE?* WHAT THE HOLY HELL IS *GOING ON* HERE?

DID HE--

--OH, *GOD...* YOUR *HANDS.* WHAT HAPPENED TO YOUR *HANDS?*

CHARLIE'S *DEAD,* LIEUTENANT...

CHARLIE... *DAMN...*

WELL--WHAT ARE YOU STANDING *HERE* FOR! GET THIS MAN SOME *MEDICAL ATTENTION* AND THEN GET HIM BACK TO CENTRAL...

I WAS ON MY *WAY,* SIR.

HANG IN THERE, DRIVER... JUST HANG IN THERE.

SORRY ABOUT THAT.

HE'S *MY* BOSS, NOT YOURS...

WELL, STILL...

HOW COME YOU ALWAYS GIVE ME THE JUICY ONES, CAPTAIN?

BECAUSE YOU'RE MY FAVORITE, CRIS.

EXCEPT THIS TIME, YOU'RE NOT.

THIS ONE'S YOURS, RENEE...

...PUT IT DOWN.

I'LL CALL IN BOTH SHIFTS, THEY'LL BE AT YOUR DISPOSAL.

MARCUS.

I'M SORRY.

YEAH. IT WAS FREEZE.

I HEARD.

WE'LL TALK WHEN I GET BACK TO THE SQUADROOM, OKAY?

I'LL TAKE YOUR *STATEMENT* THEN.

SURE.

...KNOW ABOUT FREEZE?

JUST WHAT I'VE READ.

HAS A SUIT. NEEDS IT TO LIVE. CAN'T STAND HEAT.

A LITTLE SIMPLE, BUT YEAH...

...MOTHER OF GOD...

PARTNER?

RENEE?

20

THEY DO STANDARD ENTRY, RIGHT?

WHAT?

PROBSON SAID THAT FIELDS AND DRIVER WERE JUST CHECKING OUT A *TIP* ON THE LEWIS KIDNAPPING.

AND THEY'RE FIGURING IT'S A *BOGUS* TIP TOO, BECAUSE THEY DON'T EVEN HAVE A *BACK-UP.*

RIGHT, THEY'RE NOT *EXPECTING* ANY KIND OF REAL TROUBLE.

SO THEY KNOCK ON THE DOOR AND *FREEZE* JUST GOES *BOOM.*

WHY?

WHY DOESN'T HE JUST *HOOF* IT WHEN THEY *DECLARE...*

JUST GO OUT THE *WINDOW* HERE?

...HE WANTS TO KNOW HOW THEY *FOUND* HIM?

FREEZE DOESN'T *CARE* ABOUT THAT, C'MON...

...HE COULD'VE KILLED THEM *BOTH,* WE'D NEVER HAVE *KNOWN* UNTIL DRIVER AND FIELDS DIDN'T SHOW UP TONIGHT.

BUT FREEZE LEAVES MARCUS *ALIVE.*

WHY?

MARCUS...?

HEY, SARGE... YOU ALL GET CALLED IN?

YEAH, I'M JUST THE FIRST TO ARRIVE, KID... GUESS NONE OF US'RE SLEEPIN' *TODAY*...

YOU WANNA TELL ME WHAT WENT DOWN?

NOT MUCH TO TELL. KNOCKED ON THE WRONG DOOR...

YOU KNOW WHAT THIS *MEANS*, RIGHT?

YEAH, I KNOW...

DAMN... YOU KNOW WHAT'S FUNNY?

FUNNY?

NO, WHAT?

WHEN CHARLIE FIRST CAME OVER TO THE M.C.U., HE THOUGHT IT'D BE A REAL BIG JOKE TO PUT THE BAT UP ON THE BOARD, LIKE HE WAS PART OF THE SQUAD, TOO.

HE WAS TRYIN' TO SHAME US ALL BY SHOWIN' HOW MUCH HIGHER THAT FREAK'S CLEARANCE RATE WAS THAN OURS.

THING IS, WE LEFT HIS NAME UP THERE, AND WHENEVER THE JOKER OR TWO-FACE OR WHOEVER KILLED SOMEBODY, AND WE COULDN'T CLOSE IT...

...WE'D PUT THE VIC'S NAME UNDER THE BAT'S, LIKE IT WAS HIS CASE NOW.

THEN THE PROBE TOOK OVER 2nd SHIFT AND MADE US ERASE IT... SAID IT WAS DEMORALIZING TO THE SQUAD.

AND CHARLIE, HE SAYS, "WELL, THAT'S THE POINT, LIEUTEN-ANT."

HE WANTED THAT CONSTANT REMINDER THAT IF WE DIDN'T DO OUR JOB, SOME-ONE ELSE WOULD...

...CHARLIE WAS JUST FUNNY THAT WAY.

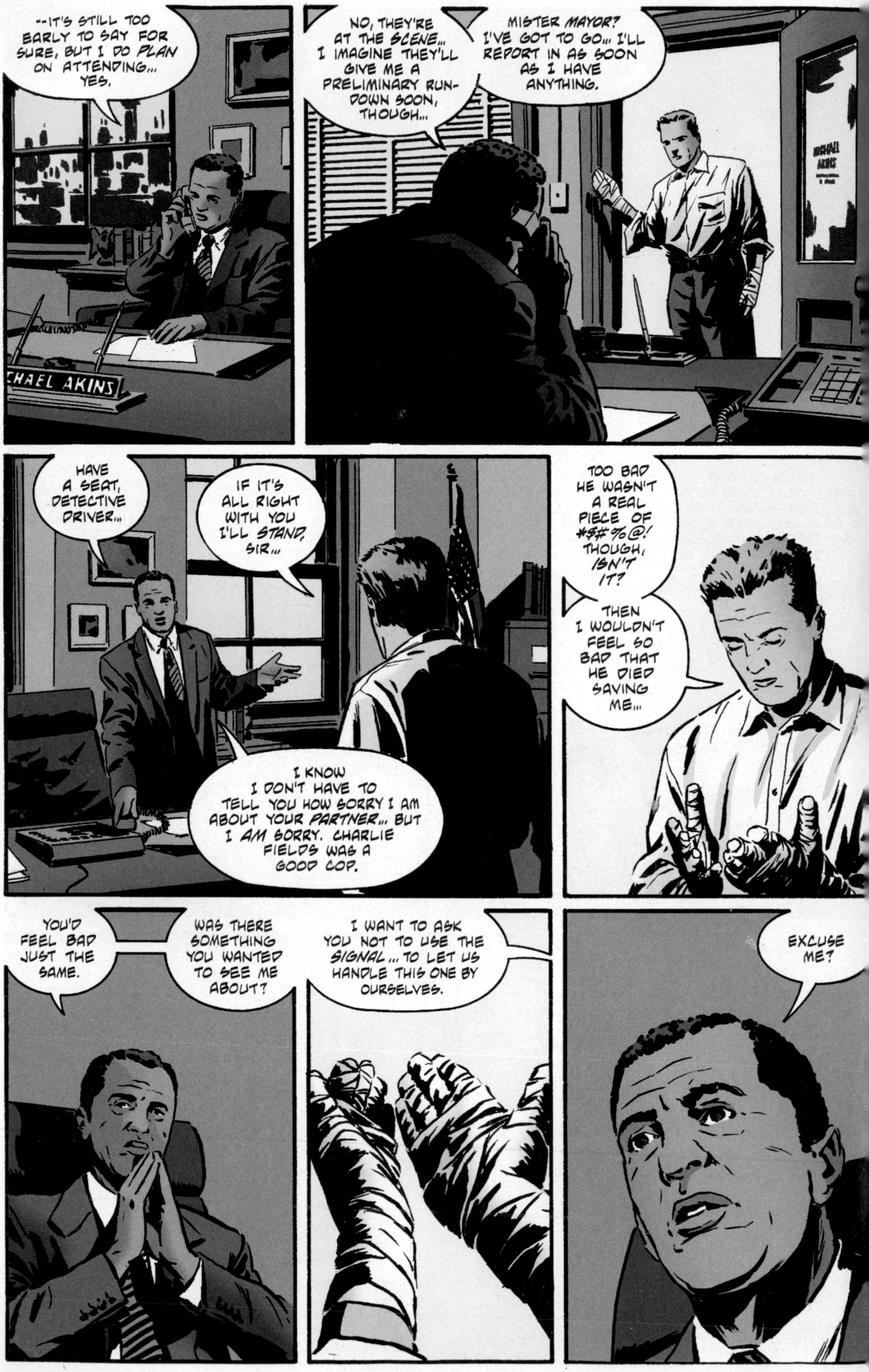
--IT'S STILL TOO EARLY TO SAY FOR SURE, BUT I DO PLAN ON ATTENDING... YES.
CHAEL AKINS
NO, THEY'RE AT THE SCENE... I IMAGINE THEY'LL GIVE ME A PRELIMINARY RUN-DOWN SOON, THOUGH...
MISTER MAYOR? I'VE GOT TO GO... I'LL REPORT IN AS SOON AS I HAVE ANYTHING.
HAVE A SEAT, DETECTIVE DRIVER...
IF IT'S ALL RIGHT WITH YOU I'LL STAND, SIR...
I KNOW I DON'T HAVE TO TELL YOU HOW SORRY I AM ABOUT YOUR PARTNER... BUT I AM SORRY. CHARLIE FIELDS WAS A GOOD COP.
TOO BAD HE WASN'T A REAL PIECE OF *$#%@! THOUGH, ISN'T IT?
THEN I WOULDN'T FEEL SO BAD THAT HE DIED SAVING ME...
YOU'D FEEL BAD JUST THE SAME.
WAS THERE SOMETHING YOU WANTED TO SEE ME ABOUT?
I WANT TO ASK YOU NOT TO USE THE SIGNAL... TO LET US HANDLE THIS ONE BY OURSELVES.
EXCUSE ME?

WE **NEED** TO BRING THIS FREAK DOWN ON **OUR OWN.** HE TOOK CHARLIE AND MADE HIM INTO **ICE CUBES,** COMMISSIONER, AND WE NEED TO TAKE HIM DOWN WITHOUT HELP...

...FOR CHARLIE'S SAKE IF NOT FOR OURS...

I **AGREE** WITH YOU... BUT MISTER FREEZE IS IN GOTHAM, WHICH MEANS THERE'S **MORE** AT STAKE HERE THAN OUR **PRIDE,** DETECTIVE.

BESIDES, DO YOU **REALLY** THINK I COULD **STOP** BATMAN JUST BY NOT ASKING HIM TO HELP?

I DON'T **KNOW...** PROBABLY NOT. BUT MAYBE YOU COULD MAKE HIM UNDERSTAND WHAT IT **MEANS** TO US TO HAVE TO TURN ON THAT **DAMN** SIGNAL.

ALL I KNOW IS, WE **CAN'T** TURN IT ON TODAY... WE **CAN'T...**

YOU'VE GOT A ROOM FILLING UP WITH COPS OUT THERE... KNOWING IF THEY DON'T GET THIS GUY BY **DARK...** THEN... I MEAN...

...IT'S JUST NOT **FAIR,** SIR...

IF IT MAKES YOU FEEL ANY BETTER, I DON'T PLAN TO CALL FOR HIM UNLESS I ABSOLUTELY **HAVE TO.** I WANT **US** TO DO THIS AS MUCH AS YOU DO.

KN K
KN K

SORRY TO DISTURB YOU, COMMISSIONER... BUT DETECTIVES **ALLEN** AND **MONTOYA** ARE BACK, AND THEY NEED TO TALK TO DETECTIVE **DRIVER...**

OKAY, STACY. TELL THEM HE'LL BE RIGHT THERE...

WE'LL CONTINUE THIS CONVERSATION LATER, DETECTIVE. YOU GO DO YOUR JOB NOW, OKAY?

LET **ME** WORRY ABOUT THE REST...

YES, SIR, THANK YOU...

YOU UP TO THIS, MARCUS? YOU WANT ANYTHING BEFORE WE START?

NO, LET'S JUST GET ON WITH IT...

...I HAVE TO MEET NORA AT THE MORGUE IN A COUPLE MINUTES.

WON'T TAKE US LONG.

YOU WANT ME TO TELL IT?

I THINK WE'VE GOT MOST OF IT.

IS IT POSSIBLE, THIS INFORMANT OF YOURS, HE WAS SETTING YOU TWO UP?

NO. THIS GUY WAS JUST SOME JUNKIE TRYIN' TO EARN A FEW BUCKS.

HE JUST GAVE US THE ROOM NUMBER AND SAID IT MIGHT BE OUR GUYS. I FIGURED IT WAS WORTH A LOOK, CHARLIE WANTED TO GO HOME...

I JUST CAN'T FIGURE OUT WHY...

...WHY HE LEFT YOU ALIVE, MARCUS.

HE HAD TO KNOW WE'D PULL OUT ALL THE STOPS TO FIND HIM.

INCLUDING THE BAT.

MAYBE HE'S TRYING TO GET BATMAN'S ATTENTION.

MAYBE, BUT AGAIN, WHY?

COULD WE LEAVE THE BAT OUT OF THIS FOR NOW?

YOU THINK? MAYBE?

SURE, DETECTIVE.

I UNDERSTAND.

I DON'T *KNOW* WHY. HE'S *CRAZY*, RENEE. YOU'VE READ THE *FILE*.

FREEZE WANTS PEOPLE TO *HURT*. NOT *PHYSICALLY*. EMOTIONALLY.

TAKE TWO *COPS*, KILL A *PARTNER...*

...INSTANT GRIEF.

...SEE... IT DOESN'T *FIT* THE PROFILE.

JOKER, I'D *BELIEVE* THAT.

BUT *FREEZE* IS SMARTER THAN HE IS *CRAZY*.

SO, HE'S GOTTA BE SENDING SOME KIND OF *MESSAGE* IF HE LET YOU LIVE...

TRYING TO LET US KNOW HE'S *SMARTER* THAN US.

IF YOU *SAY* SO...PERSONALLY--

GUYS, WE GOT A CALL COMING IN YOU *MIGHT* WANNA TAKE...

SERGEANT, WE'RE IN THE MIDDLE OF--

JUST *TRUST ME*, OKAY?

WHAT IS IT?

UNIFORM JUST CALLED IN, HE'S ON LINE TWO, SOUNDS PRETTY *SHOOK UP*...

...LONG AND SHORT OF IT, THOUGH, IS WE GOT ANOTHER *FROZEN BODY.*

THIS IS DETECTIVE *MONTOYA,* WHO AM I SPEAKING TO?

ALL *RIGHT,* OFFICER DUMFY... WE'VE GOT PEOPL ON THE WAY *RIGHT NOW,* DON' *WORRY.*..

OKAY, DETECTIVE... BUT TELL THEM TO *HURRY.* IT LOOKS LIKE SOMEBODY FROZE THIS GUY FROM THE INSIDE OUT...

...AND NO OFFENSE, MA'AM... BUT I *DON'T* WANT TO BE STANDIN' HERE IF HE DECIDES TO COME *BACK*...

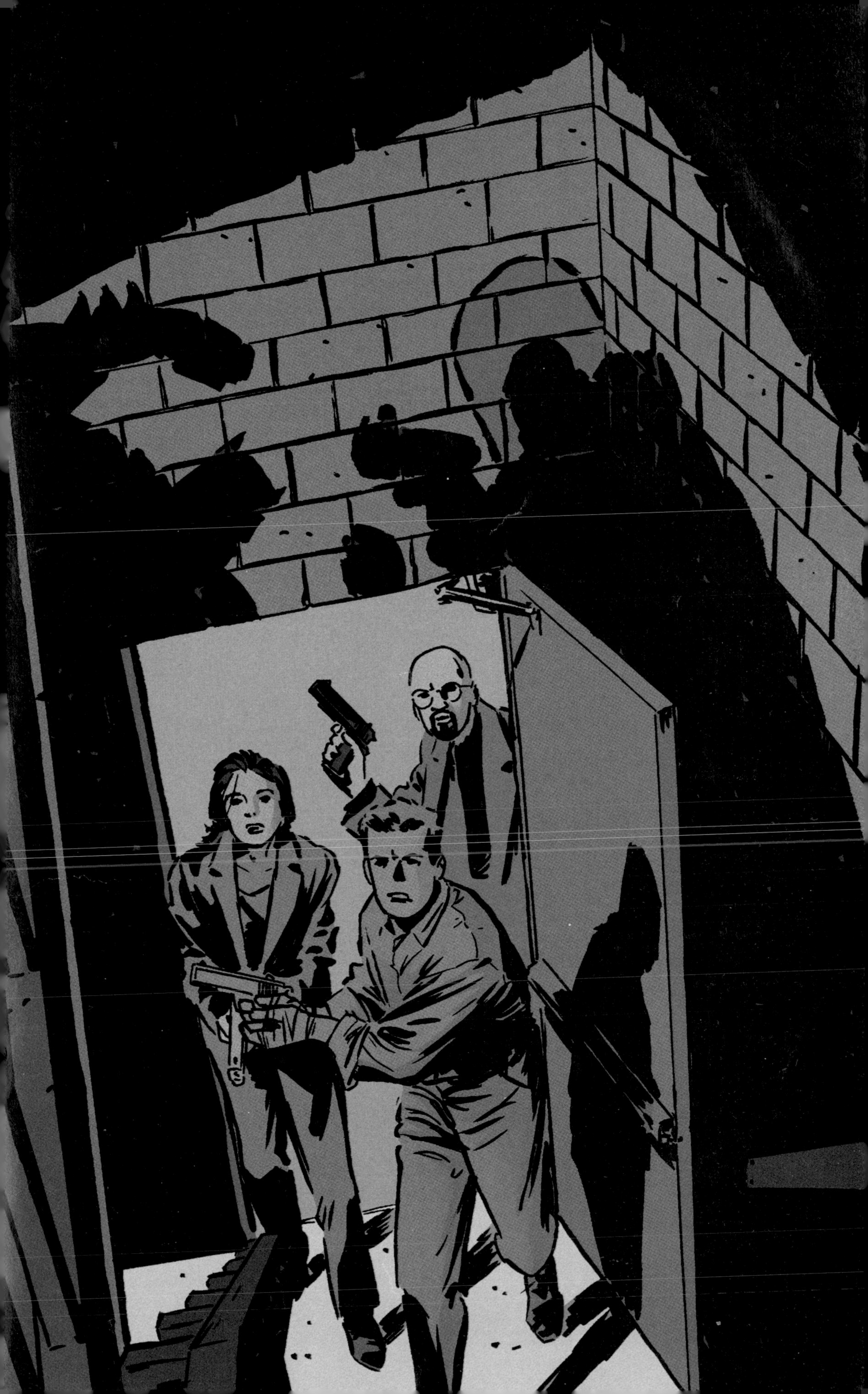

JUNE 23rd -- 1:37 p.m. ...

ANY IDEA *HOW* LONG HE'S BEEN LIKE *THIS?*

NAH, WE'RE NOT GETTING *ANYTHING* USEFUL FROM A GUY WHO'S BEEN FROZEN FROM THE INSIDE OUT LIKE THIS...

HAVE TO GET TIME OF DEATH ON THIS ONE FROM *WITNESSES*--

--OR MAYBE WE'LL GET LUCKY WITH SOMETHING IN THE CAR...

HEY, *CAREFUL* NOT TO BREAK HIM...

LIKE WE'VE GOT A *CHOICE*...

Krak

OH, MAN...

I *KNOW*...

SO, WHAT DO YOU THINK?

SAME AS *YOU*--

FREEZE PUT HIS GUN RIGHT IN THAT POOR #@$%'S MOUTH, TURNED IT ON FULL BLAST...

PROBABLY HURT LIKE HELL.

YOU *THINK?*

SO, MARCUS, YOU'RE ABSOLUTELY SURE THAT WAS THE GUY WHO WAS WORKIN' WITH FREEZE?

YEAH, EXCEPT FOR THE BULGING EYES AND BLUE LIPS, HE'S THE SPITTING IMAGE.

WELL, THAT'S NOT GOOD AT ALL, THEN, IS IT?

OBVIOUSLY, WHATEVER HE NEEDED BACKUP FOR HAS BEEN DONE.

AND I DON'T LIKE THE LOOKS OF THAT TRUCK EITHER... THEY WERE HAULING SOMETHING SOMEWHERE...

GOD, THIS DAY JUST GETS BETTER, DOESN'T IT?

YEAH, I'M AFRAID IT DOES...

HANG ON... I'LL RIDE WITH YOU...

WHAT, YOU HEADED TO THE MORGUE?

YEAH, I AM...

IN THE LINE OF DUTY 2

LISTEN... ARE YOU SURE YOU'RE UP TO THIS, NORA?

I WORK IN THIS MORGUE, MARCUS, AND MY HUSBAND IS--WAS-- A COP...

KANE COUNTY MORGUE

I DON'T HAVE ANY ILLUSIONS ABOUT LIFE AND DEATH.

I KNOW, BUT... THIS IS DIFFERENT... HE'S NOT... UH--

I KNOW THAT, TOO. CAPTAIN SAWYER TOLD ME...

BECAUSE YOU DON'T HAVE TO IDENTIFY HIM, OFFICIALLY, WE KNOW WHO HE IS... AND I REALLY DON'T THINK YOU--

--LOOK, I HAVE TO SEE HIM... IT'S NOT GOING TO BE REAL UNTIL I SEE HIM, OKAY?

I LOOK AT DEAD PEOPLE ALL DAY LONG AND EVERY NIGHT I WAIT FOR THE PHONE TO RING OR SOMEONE TO KNOCK ON THE DOOR... TO TELL ME...

AND-- AND... IT JUST DOESN'T FEEL REAL SOMEHOW...

IT'S OKAY, NORA...

SO I DON'T CARE WHAT THEY DID TO HIM, OKAY?...

I HAVE TO SEE...

OH, UH... NORA... I, UH... I'M--

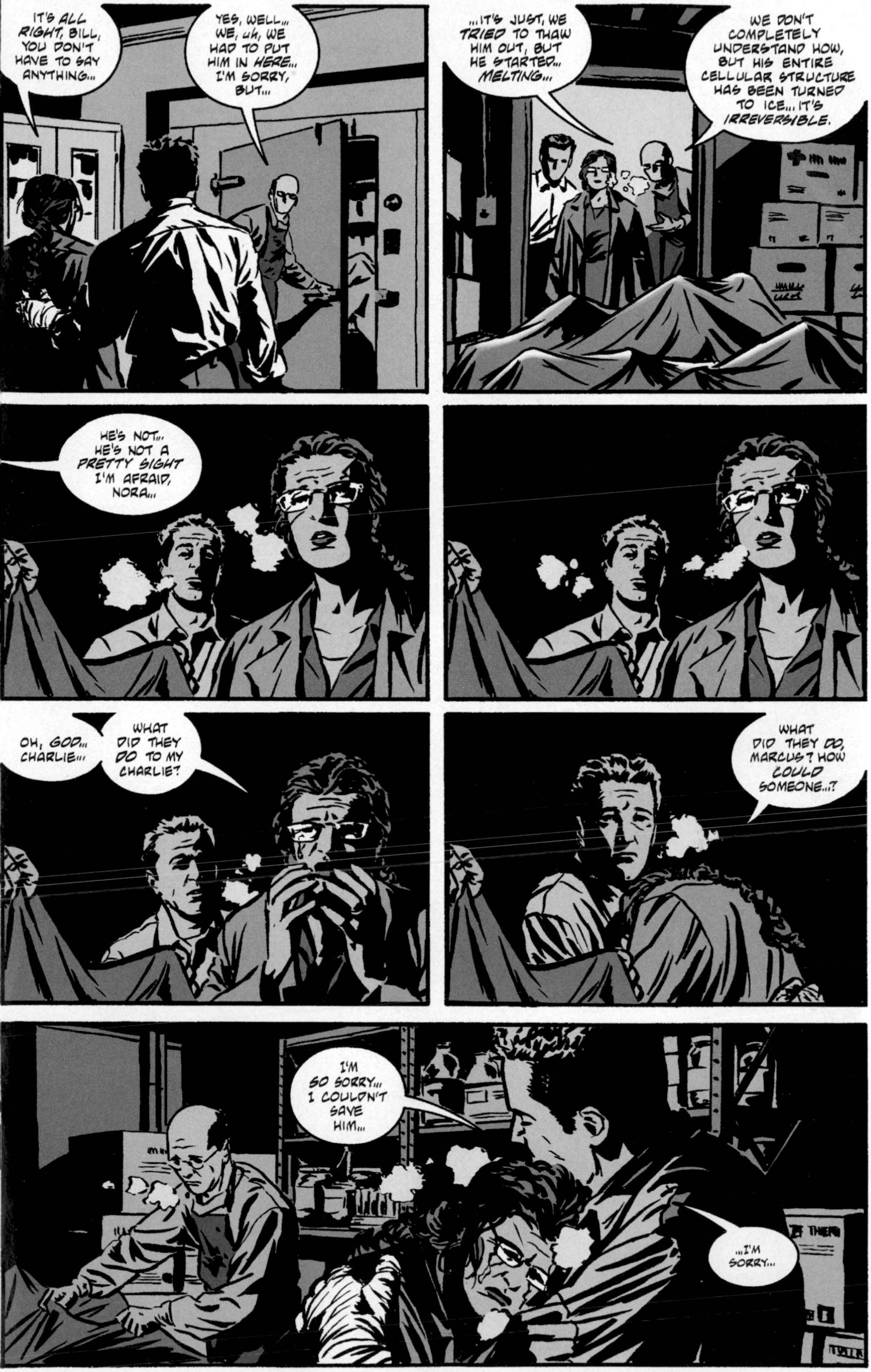
IT'S ALL RIGHT, BILL, YOU DON'T HAVE TO SAY ANYTHING...
YES, WELL... WE, uh, WE HAD TO PUT HIM IN HERE... I'M SORRY, BUT...
...IT'S JUST, WE TRIED TO THAW HIM OUT, BUT HE STARTED... MELTING...
WE DON'T COMPLETELY UNDERSTAND HOW, BUT HIS ENTIRE CELLULAR STRUCTURE HAS BEEN TURNED TO ICE... IT'S IRREVERSIBLE.
HE'S NOT... HE'S NOT A PRETTY SIGHT I'M AFRAID, NORA...
OH, GOD... CHARLIE...
WHAT DID THEY DO TO MY CHARLIE?
WHAT DID THEY DO, MARCUS? HOW COULD SOMEONE...?
I'M SO SORRY... I COULDN'T SAVE HIM...
...I'M SORRY...

...LISTEN UP, PEOPLE!

DETECTIVE MONTOYA?

THANKS, CAPTAIN.

OKAY... TO MAKE SURE EVERYONE'S ON THE SAME PAGE I'M GOING TO HIT THESE POINTS AGAIN IN BRIEF.

AT APPROX OH-SIX THIS MORNING DETECTIVES FIELDS AND DRIVER WENT TO QUESTION SOME MEN AT THE WHARFSIDE INN ON A TIP IN CONNECTION WITH THE LEWIS KIDNAPPING.

AT THE HOTEL THEY ENCOUNTERED VICTOR FRIES WITH AN UNIDENTIFIED ASSOCIATE KNOWN ONLY AS "DANNY."

FRIES SUBDUED BOTH DETECTIVES, THEN MURDERED DETECTIVE FIELDS. SOMETIME IN THE NEXT FEW HOURS HE ALSO APPARENTLY KILLED DANNY...

AND NOW YOU KNOW EVERYTHING WE DO.

DETECTIVE AZEVEDA?

ANY CHANCE FREEZE IS CONNECTED TO THE LEWIS GRAB?

NO...

...IT WAS JUST ROTTEN %.$&^ING LUCK, JOSH.

THE LEWIS KIDNAPPING HAS BEEN HANDED TO THE F.B.I. FOR THE TIME BEING...

...DETECTIVE FIELDS' MURDER IS OUR ONLY PRIORITY RIGHT NOW.

34

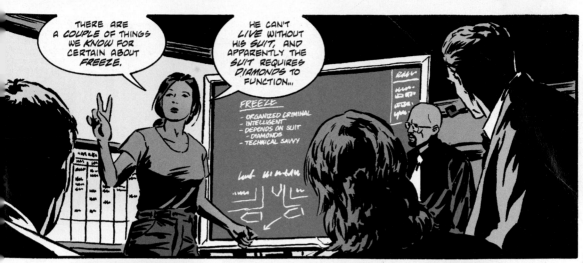

THERE ARE A *COUPLE* OF THINGS WE *KNOW* FOR CERTAIN ABOUT *FREEZE*.

HE CAN'T *LIVE* WITHOUT HIS *SUIT*, AND APPARENTLY THE *SUIT* REQUIRES *DIAMONDS* TO FUNCTION...

FREEZE
- ORGANIZED CRIMINAL
- INTELLIGENT
- DEPENDS ON SUIT
- DIAMONDS
- TECHNICAL SAVVY

...AND HE STRIKES AT THE *HEART* OF HIS VICTIMS.

HE LIKES PEOPLE TO SUFFER.

WE DON'T KNOW *WHAT* HE'S PLANNING OR *WHERE*.

PROBABLY SOMETHING *BIG*-- DANNY'S CORPSE WAS FOUND WITH AN *EMPTY* TRUCK--LOOKS LIKE THEY WERE *HAULING* SOMETHING--

--AND IT'S GOT TO BE *SOON*, BECAUSE *FREEZE* KNOWS AS WELL AS *WE DO*, AS SOON AS THE *SUN* GOES DOWN...HE'S GOING TO HAVE A *BAT* UP HIS $%@#.

OKAY, CHRIS HAS THE *ASSIGN- MENTS*...

35

FREEZE?

YOU'RE KIDDING ME, RIGHT?

YEAH, HE'S *REAL* BIG ON KEEPIN' IN TOUCH, AIN'T HE?

THINK I JUST GOT A *POSTCARD* FROM HIM THE OTHER DAY...

RIGHT...

I DUNNO NUTHIN', MAN...

BUT IF HE'S PLANNIN' SOMETHING *BIG*, YOU MIGHT WANNA STAY OUTTA HIS WAY...

'CAUSE, LIKE I SAID, I AIN'T IN ON *ANY* OF HIS ACTION ANYMORE...

...BUT THAT *MOTHER* IS NOT TO BE *MESSED* WITH...

WELL... *THAT* WAS PRODUCTIVE. HOW DID WE END UP WITH THE KNOWN-ASSOCIATE DETAIL?

I GUESS ALLEN MUST'VE HEARD HOW THE SMELL OF *HOLDING CELLS* BRINGS BACK MEMORIES OF THOSE *BOARDING SCHOOL* DAYS FOR YOU, TREY...

YES, THAT *MUST'VE* BEEN IT...

...THOUGH I CAN'T HELP BUT THINK MY EXPERIENCE WOULD'VE COME IN A LITTLE MORE HANDY QUESTIONING THE CITY'S *DIAMOND MERCHANTS.*

WHAT, YOU DON'T THINK SARGE HAS A LIGHT ENOUGH TOUCH FOR THOSE *POWDERPUFFS?*

WHAT I'M TELLING YOU IS I HAVE A *DEAD COP*--

--AND THE GUY WHO KILLED HIM NEEDS DIAMONDS JUST TO *BREATHE!*

SO, I DON'T CARE ABOUT YOUR TAXES OR YOUR INSURANCE, I JUST WANT YOU TO ANSWER THE QUESTION.

NO, I DON'T KNOW OF *ANY* DIAMOND THEFTS OF ANY REAL CONCERN IN THE PAST FEW MONTHS... I *CERTAINLY* HAVEN'T HAD ANY GO MISSING.

OKAY, WELL, WHAT ABOUT ANY OFF-THE-BOOKS DEALS?

YOU HEAR ABOUT ANY BLACK MARKET STONES THAT'VE GONE MISSING LATELY?

BLACK MARKET?

I'M NOT SURE I UNDERSTAND YOUR IMPLICATION, OFFICER...

WHAT BLACK MARKET ARE YOU TALKING ABOUT?

CROWE, I SWEAR TO GOD I'M GONNA DECK THIS @$$#%!#...

BAD MOVE SWINGING ON MY PARTNER THERE, RICO.

DIDN'T YOU KNOW ROMY HAD THE BLACK BELT?

DAMN, THINK I BROKE MY HAND, NATE...

NOW ARE YOU GONNA TELL US ABOUT THOSE DIAMONDS, OR NOT?

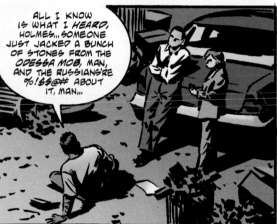

ALL I KNOW IS WHAT I HEARD, HOLMES... SOMEONE JUST JACKED A BUNCH OF STONES FROM THE ODESSA MOB, MAN, AND THE RUSSIANS'RE %!$$@# ABOUT IT, MAN...

WHAT KIND OF WEIGHT ARE WE TALKING ABOUT?

WHAT I HEARD HEAVY WEIGHT...

LOOKIN' AT TWENTY MIL...

HAD SOME FOREIGN BUYER ALL LINED UP OR SOMETHIN'...

WE BETTER CALL DAVIES...

TWENTY MILLION IN DIAMONDS COULD DO A LOT OF DAMAGE IN MISTER FREEZE'S HANDS...

HEARTFELT
MEDICAL SUPPLIES

"...WELL, TO KEEP ICE FOR A START.

LIKE IN ORGAN TRANSPLANTS?

WELL, WE DON'T HANDLE STUFF LIKE THAT HERE.

WE SUPPLY SOME STUFF TO HOSPITALS, BUT NOTHING LIKE THAT.

THANKS FOR YOUR TIME--

YOU KNOW SOMETHING? I JUST THOUGHT OF SOMETHING...

THERE'S A PLACE JUST OPENED, KINDA A QUACK THING, CALLED...uh, WHAT IS IT...

"...SOMETHING CRYOGENICS... LIKE CHATTER OR uh FROSTY OR...

shiver

"...ANY PROBLEMS WITH MATERIAL GOING MISSING OR ANYTHING LIKE THAT?

"...I'M SORRY, WHAT WAS THAT, DETECTIVE?

DETECTIVE PROCJNOW WAS ASKING IF YOU'RE MISSING ANYTHING.

OH, NO. NOTHING LIKE THAT, AT LEAST.

WELL, MAYBE WE COULD SEE YOUR INVENTORY LISTS?

IF YOU'RE NOT TOO BUSY...

OH, SURE. HERE THEY ARE.

I COULD HELP YOU GO THROUGH THEM, IF YOU LIKE...

MOVE A LOT OF THESE, DO YOU?

THESE? NAW, WE'VE ONLY EVER SOLD TWO OF THEM.

REALLY? WHO BOUGHT THEM?

YEAH, SEE, I REMEMBER THEM BOTH 'CUZ IT'S SO RARE THAT WE SELL THEM AT ALL.

WE SOLD ONE TO WAYNE, YOU KNOW, BEFORE HE WENT CRAZY... RIGHT AFTER N.M.L....

...AND THE OTHER TO THE GOVERNMENT FOR THE NATIONAL GUARD BARRACKS.

AH, WELL.... THANKS FOR YOUR HELP.

...NOT SAYING IT'LL BE ANYTHING BUT IT'S BETTER THAN DOING NOTHING.

YOU AND I BOTH KNOW THIS IS GOING TO END UP IN THE BAT'S HANDS, RENEE.

I UNDERSTAND DRIVER'S CONCERN, BUT WE'RE NOT TALKING ABOUT SOME STREET SKEL HERE.

MAYBE IT'S TIME TO USE A BIG GUN, YOU KNOW?

FALL'S FURNACE AND FAN

I REMEMBER WHEN YOU FIRST SHOWED UP HERE, YOU WERE NOT DOWN WITH BATMAN AT ALL.

TIMES CHANGE.

ANYTHING?

NOTHING.

LET'S HEAD BACK...

...PRACTICALLY BLOWING IN MY PARTNER'S *EAR*, THERE.

LEAVING *ME* TO DO THE *DETECTIVE* WORK, I MIGHT ADD.

HE GET A PHONE *NUMBER*?

YOU THINK HE'S GONNA *SHARE* WITH *YOU*, DETECTIVE PATTON?

I THOUGHT YOU HAD A THING FOR *CHANDLER*, ANYWAY--

HEY, LISTEN, *PROCJNOW*--

ALL RIGHT, LET'S *HEAR* IT...

...*WHAT* DO YOU GOT?

DETECTIVE *HARTLEY*?

NOTHING FROM THE *KNOWN* ASSOCIATES.

THEY DON'T SPEAK *HIGHLY* OF FREEZE AS AN *EMPLOYER*.

SURPRISING, WE *KNOW*.

NO REPORTED *THEFTS* FROM THE *LEGIT* BUSINESSES AT LEAST.

BUT ROMY AND NATE GOT SOMETHING *INTERESTING*...

"...YEAH, SOMEONE HIT THE *ODESSA* BOYS FOR *20 MIL* IN *ICE.*

THAT'S *WORD* ON THE *STREET,* THOUGH, SO TAKE IT FOR WHAT IT'S *WORTH.*

WELL, WHATEVER *FREEZE* USES, IT'S *CUSTOM.*

MEDICAL SUPPLY DOESN'T HAVE ANYTHING EVEN *CLOSE.*

TWENTY MIL IN *DIAMONDS.*

HOW MANY DOES THIS GUY NEED TO MAKE HIS *GIZMOS* GO?

WELL, *INTERESTING* THAT YOU WOULD *ASK* THAT, *RENEE*...

...AS MY *PARTNER* GOT A *CRASH COURSE* IN THE ART AND SCIENCE OF THE *DEEP FREEZE.*

WAY IT WORKS, DOESN'T ACTUALLY TAKE *SO* MUCH ENERGY TO FREEZE SOMETHING.

KEEPING IT *FROZE,* THAT'S THE TRICK.

SO SOME- THING *BIG.*

BUT WE DON'T KNOW *WHERE.* WE DON'T KNOW *WHEN.*

ALLEN AND I *CHECKED* THE PLACE BY THE *INN*...

..."IT'S AN *ABANDONED* HEATING PLACE. USED TO SELL *FURNACES* AND *OIL HEATERS.*

AND *AIR CONDITIONERS.*

GOD, IT'S *HOT* IN HERE...

OKAY, LET'S GO OVER IT *AGAIN*...

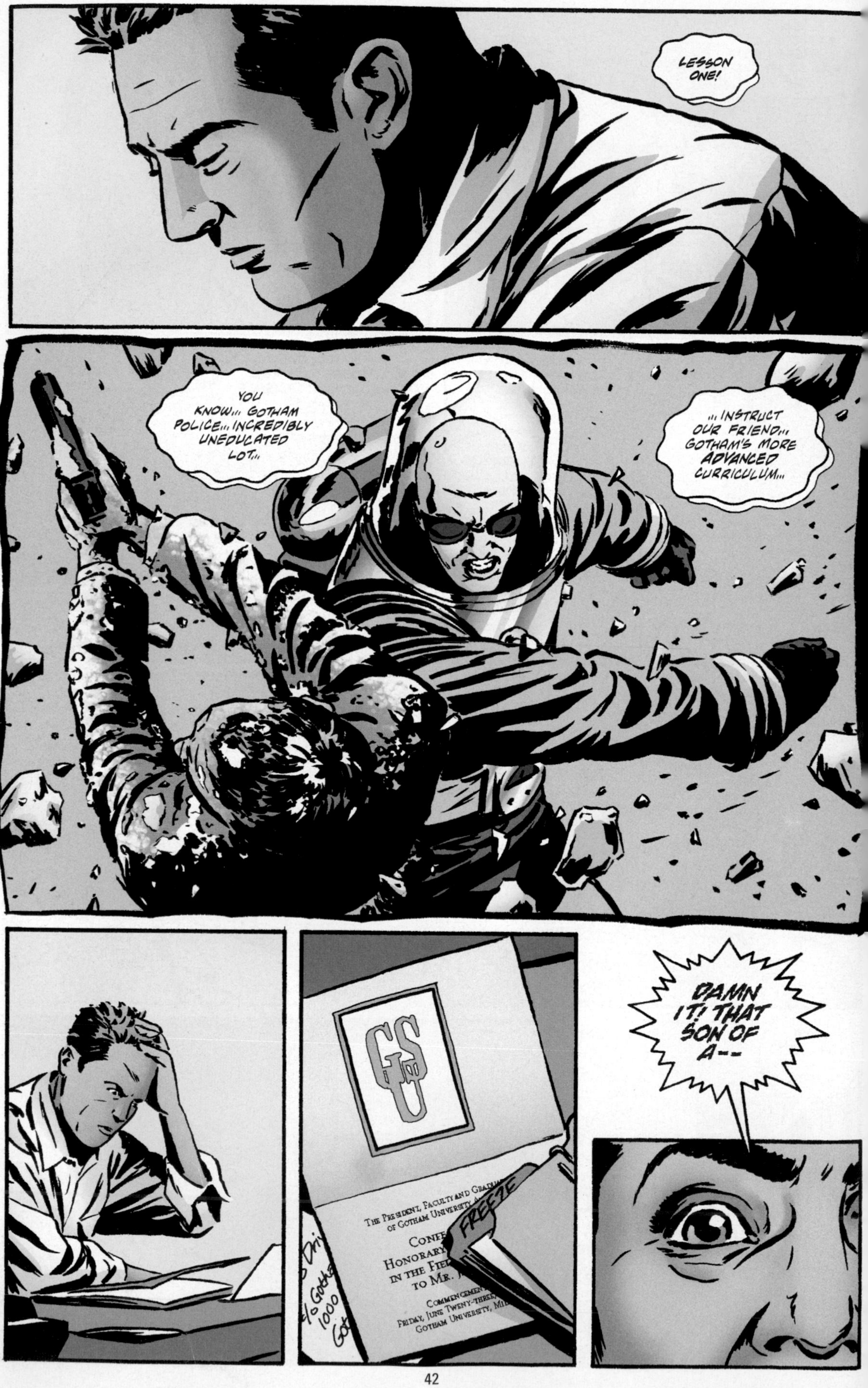
LESSON ONE!
YOU KNOW... GOTHAM POLICE... INCREDIBLY UNEDUCATED LOT...
...INSTRUCT OUR FRIEND... GOTHAM'S MORE ADVANCED CURRICULUM...
FREEZE
DAMN IT! THAT SON OF A--

MARCUS?

IT'S BEEN RIGHT IN FRONT OF US ALL *DAMN DAY*...

THE SICK #$@!%# PRACTICALLY GAVE US A HAND-WRITTEN INVITATION...

...EXCEPT WE ALREADY GOT THE *PRINTED VERSION* A WEEK AGO.

OH MY GOD...

IT'S LIKE THE WHOLE DAY IS JUST *ONE BIG JOKE*... ISN'T IT?

COMMISSIONER, WE *HAVE* TO TURN ON THE *SIGNAL*, RIGHT NOW!

WHAT? I THOUGHT YOU--

THERE'RE TOO MANY LIVES INVOLVED NOW, SIR...

IT'S TOO BIG FOR US.

...UNDERCOVER! REMEMBER!

WE DON'T WANT TO START A PANIC!

USE YOUR EARPIECES. STAY ON THE NET.

BUT NOBODY MOVE UNTIL WE'VE GOT Q.R.T. IN PLACE!

YOU SUPERVISE THE FLOOR UNTIL I GET THERE.

I'LL TALK TO HENELLY, FOLLOW THEM OUT.

GOT IT.

LIEUTENANT HENELLY?

CAPTAIN SAWYER IN THE M.C.U. ...

"...GET Q.R.T. MOBILIZED AND DOWN TO G.S.U.--

THAT'S RIGHT, WE THINK FREEZE IS GOING FOR THE CEREMONY...

The President, Faculty and Graduating Class of Gotham State University Announce the

CONFERRING OF THE HONORARY DEGREE OF DOCTOR IN THE FIELD OF CRI

Friday, June Twenty Gotham State Univ

44

IF YOU DON'T MIND, COMMISSIONER, I'D LIKE TO DO IT MYSELF...

I'M AFRAID I CAN'T ALLOW THAT...

THE G.C.P.D. CAN'T OFFICIALLY TOUCH THE BAT-SIGNAL, OR IN *ANY WAY* ACKNOWLEDGE THE EXISTENCE OF BATMAN.

SO WE'RE CALLING HIM IN TO TAKE DOWN MISTER FREEZE, BUT WE CAN'T ADMIT HE'S *REAL*?

IT'S A FINE LINE, I KNOW.

GO AHEAD, STACY...

SO YOU'RE OKAY WITH THIS THEN?

NO... BUT I'M A COP IN GOTHAM.

I CAN'T *AFFORD* TO LIVE IN DENIAL...

I'VE NEVER ACTUALLY *BEEN HERE* FOR THIS...

HOW LONG DOES IT USUALLY TAKE FOR HIM TO SHOW?

WITH HIM, IT'S ALWAYS SOONER THAN YOU THINK...

TALK.

"...IN POSITION OUTSIDE, WHERE ELSE?"

WELL, HE'S NOT GOING TO BE IN THE CROWD.

YOU THINK HE'S JUST GOING AFTER HIM?

MAYBE HE WANTS TO GET THE WHOLE DAMN ROOM?

MILLER AUDITORIUM
Gotham State University

THAT'S A COMFORTING THOUGHT...

"...KEEP ME WARM AT NIGHT."

THAT'S VERY FUNNY, ROMY--

THIS IS HENELLY, EVERYONE SHUT UP.

ROOF ACCESS

THANK YOU.

THIS IS Q.R.T. LEADER. ALL POSTS, CONFIRM POSITIONS. GREEN TEAMS?

GREEN ONE, GOOD. SOUTH ENTRANCE SECURE.

GREEN TWO, GOOD. PARKING LOT SECURE.

GREEN THREE, GOOD. BACKSTAGE SECURE.

CONFIRMED.
RED TEAMS?

RED TWO,
ROOFTOP
SECURE.

**EAST
STAIRWELL**
AUTHORIZED
PERSONNEL
ONLY

RED ONE,
GROUND
SECURE.

RED
THREE,
SUBLEVEL
SECURE.

CONFIRMED.
NO SIGN OF
FREEZE...

...WHERE
THE *HELL*
IS HE?

THIS IS
SAWYER.

THEY'RE
STARTING THE
CEREMONY.

LADIES AND GENTLEMEN, WELCOME TO THE FORTY-THIRD *COMMENCEMENT* OF GOTHAM STATE UNIVERSITY.

WE WILL BEGIN WITH *REMARKS* FROM THIS YEAR'S *DISTINGUISHED GUEST*...

...A MAN KNOWN TO US ALL AS A *DEDICATED PUBLIC SERVANT*.

HE IS THIS YEAR'S *RECIPIENT* OF THE J.K. MANNING AWARD FOR SERVICE TO THE COMMUNITY...

"...AND HAS JUST BEEN CONFERRED AN HONORARY DOCTORATE IN THE FIELD OF CRIMINOLOGY..."

"...MAY 1 PRESENT TO YOU GOTHAM CITY'S FORMER COMMISSIONER OF POLICE...."

JAMES GORDON.

CLAPCLAP PC CLAPCLA

ANYTHING?

CLAPCLAPLA

NOTHING.

NOTHING AT ALL.

CLAPCLAPCLA

49

THANK YOU, THANK YOU VERY MUCH...

IT'S A HELL OF A NICE WAY TO BE WELCOMED *HOME,* I'LL TELL YOU *THAT.*

I DON'T HAVE *MUCH* TO SAY, I'M AFRAID, SO YOU *KIDS* ARE GETTING OFF EASY. I'M GOING TO BE *BRIEF.*

BIG DAY FOR YOU. GOING OUT AFTER THIS, YOU'LL HAVE *PARTIES,* YOU'LL CELEBRATE YOUR ACCOMPLISHMENTS.

YOU SHOULD. YOU'VE *EARNED* IT.

GONNA GO OUT IN THE *WORLD* AND MAKE A *DIFFER-ENCE.*

WHATEVER YOU *DO,* REMEMBER THAT. YOU'RE GOING TO MAKE A *DIFFER-ENCE.*

A LOT OF TIMES IT WON'T BE *HUGE,* IT WON'T BE *VISIBLE,* EVEN.

BUT IT WILL MATTER, JUST THE SAME.

DON'T DO IT FOR *PRAISE* OR *MONEY,* THAT'S WHAT I WANT TO TELL YOU.

EXIT

DO IT BECAUSE IT *NEEDS* TO BE *DONE.* DO IT TO MAKE YOUR *WORLD* BETTER.

IT'S *FINISHED.*

...JUST A *LITTLE* AT A *TIME...*

HE'S ON THE *ROOF.*

HE WON'T BE A *PROBLEM.*

--FOUND HIM ON THE *ROOF* TRYING TO ALTER THE *AIR CONDITIONER,* FREEZE EVERYONE PRESENT. YOU-KNOW-WHO STOPPED HIM.

OKAY, RENEE... THANKS... I'M GOING *HOME* NOW.

THERE'S SOMETHING ELSE.

THE *FEDS* CALLED... THEY FOUND THE *LEWIS* KID.

SHE DIDN'T *MAKE* IT.

...HELL...

YEAH.

...DAMN IT ALL TO HELL...

...AND *DAMN* YOU, TOO.

The END

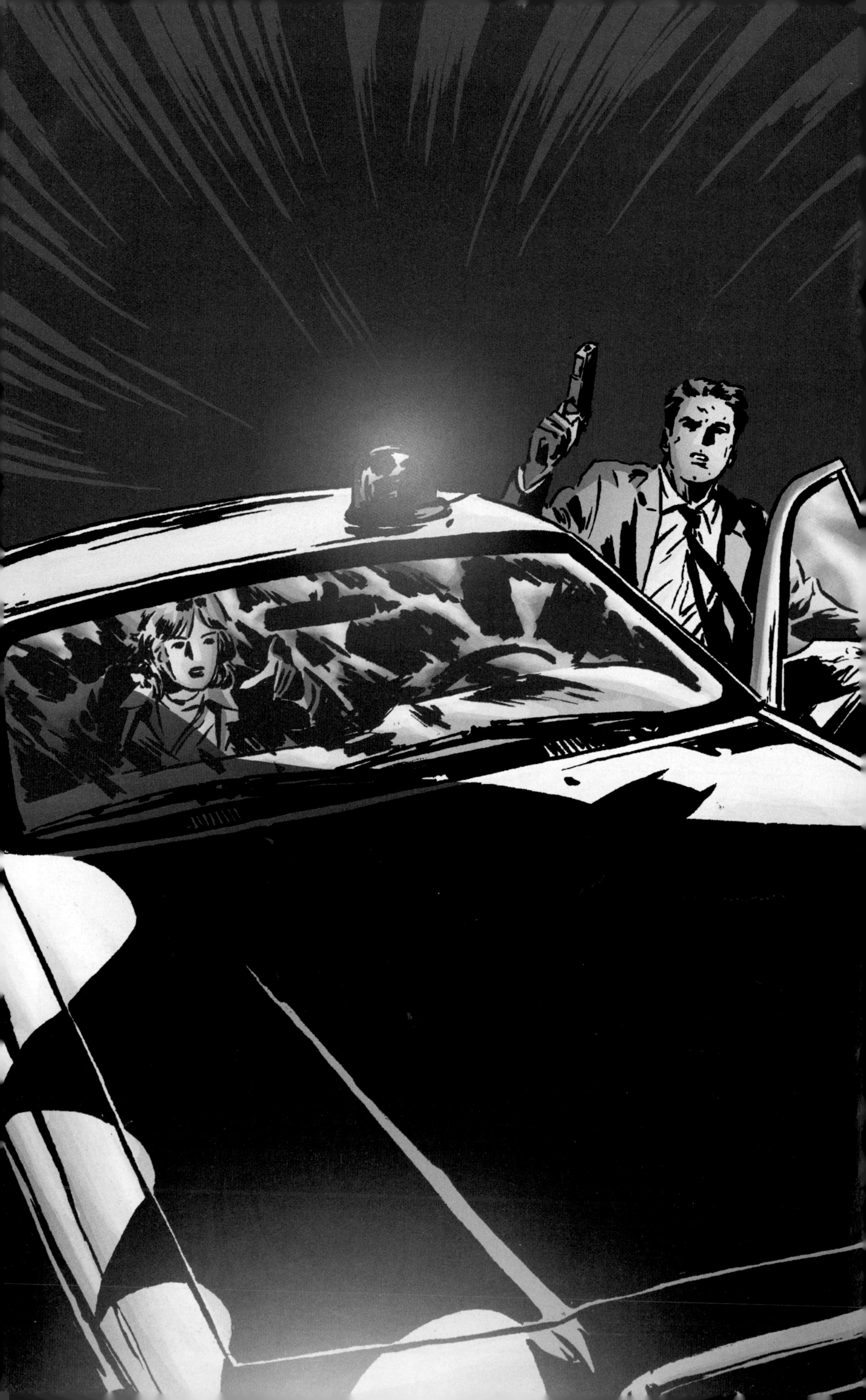

JUNE 24th-- 6:45 p.m...

--NO, NO... I'M NOT FEEDING YOU A LINE OF BULL HERE...

YOU'VE BEEN A COP FOR OVER 20 YEARS AND YOU DON'T *BELIEVE* THE BAD GUYS ARE EVIL?

SO, THAT GUY WE BUSTED LAST WEEK FOR RAPING HIS DAUGHTER, *THAT GUY*--

YOU'RE TWISTING MY WORDS, JOSH... WHAT I *SAID* IS-- I DON'T THINK THE BAD GUYS, FOR THE MOST PART, *THINK* THAT THEY'RE ACTUALLY EVIL...

MOST PEOPLE THINK THEY'RE DOING THE RIGHT THING, NO MATTER *HOW* SICK IT IS...

LIKE THE GUY WITH HIS DAUGHTER... I WANTED TO BOUNCE HIM FROM THE ROOF TO THE SIDEWALK, BUT...

HE THOUGHT HE *LOVED* HER, AND THIS WAS HIS WAY OF *SHOWING* IT.

I DON'T *BUY* IT, SARGE... WHAT ABOUT GUYS LIKE *TWO-FACE*?

HE SURE AS $#!% KNOWS THE DIFFERENCE BETWEEN RIGHT AND WRONG...

NO $#!%, SHERLOCK, DENT'S A %#&@ING *SCHIZO* THOUGH... I'M TALKING ABOUT YOUR REGULAR SKELS, NOT THE FREAKS AND SERIAL MURDERERS...

OKAY, SO THEN *HITLER*... HE THOUGHT *GENOCIDE* WAS THE RIGHT THING?

THAT'S IT... END OF DISCUSSION.

WHAT?

YOU KNOW THE *RULE*-- ALL DEBATE ENDS WHEN IT GETS TO HITLER...

OH, YEAH, I FORGOT...

LIKE HELL YOU DID.

--JUST *DON'T* LIKE IT, THAT'S ALL, WE'RE A *TEAM* AND--

IT'S TWO OR THREE DAYS, NATE... *BUCK UP,* OKAY?

DRIVER HERE ALREADY?

YEAH, HE'S TALKING TO THE *PROBE* RIGHT NOW.

Hunh... YOU'D THINK HE'D TAKE AT LEAST A *DAY...*

--DON'T MIND TELLING YOU, DETECTIVE, IF I HAD *MY WAY* YOU'D BE ON *PERSONAL TIME* FOR A FEW *WEEKS...*

BUT YOU'VE GOT THE *COMMISSIONER* BACKING YOU ON THIS ONE, SO...

...YOU'VE GOT THE *CASE.*

GOOD, WHO'M I PARTNERING WITH?

IT'S YOU AND ROMY CHANDLER, SHE'S GOOD AT *LIAISONING* WITH THE *FEDS...*

CROWE'S OUT SICK, SO I'M PAIRING PATTON WITH *SARGE* ON THIS *FIREBUG* CASE...

I THOUGHT THAT WAS BACK-BURNED *WEEKS* AGO. NO LEADS...

IT *WAS,* THEN TODAY'S PAPER CAME OUT...

SOME *TOURIST* SNAPPED A *PICTURE* LAST NIGHT, WHILE *WE* WERE ALL BASKING IN THE GLORY OF THE FREEZE TAKE-DOWN...

SO NOW WE GOT THE *MEDIA* UP OUR BUTT ON THIS FREAK, AND THE MAYOR WANTS IT BACK TO *TOP PRIORITY.*

FIREBUG IS BACK

MOTIVE PART ONE

IT'S ALWAYS *SOMETHING,* ISN'T IT?

I'M BEGINNING TO THINK SO...

HOW ARE YOUR HANDS?

SORE... BUT THEY'RE HEALING...

I REALLY *DO* WISH YOU'D TAKE SOME TIME, MARCUS...LOSING A *PARTNER,* IT--

I KNOW... I JUST NEED TO DO THIS ONE CASE, AND THEN *I WILL,* LIEUTENANT.

I MEAN IT.

SO, YOU GOT THE WORD?

JUST BEFORE YOU DID... YOU READY TO ROLL?

JUST LET ME CHANGE REAL QUICK...

THE FEEBS ARE HOLDING A COPY OF THE FILE FOR US AT THE SCENE...

TRY NOT TO ACTUALLY CALL THEM THAT WHEN WE GET THERE, OKAY?

YOU WATCH HER BACK ON THIS, DRIVER... ROMY'S MY PARTNER.

I'LL MEET YOU IN THE CAR.

REAL THOUGHTFUL, BUTTHEAD!

HEY! I DIDN'T MEAN IT LIKE THAT...

YOU DON'T HAVE TO BE SUCH AN IDIOT ALL THE TIME, NATE...

AW, ROMY, I DIDN'T...

...DAMN IT.

OBSON		2002	
	FIELDS	DRIVER	WARRANTS
20	016 LEWIS	009 LEVITZ	SCHRECK
Y		023 CARLIN	IDELSON
S		167 KAHN	CASTRO
		178 LUTES	BOND
AS		233 JOHNS	BENOIS
A		246 CHANG	DENNIS
		268 HART	STEWART
		285 GAUDIANI	
		298 PHILIPS	

I SHOULD'VE COME STRAIGHT OUT LAST NIGHT WHEN THEY FOUND HER.

DAMN FEDS... I CAN'T TELL JACK FROM THESE PICTURES...

WE CAN GO BACK TO CENTRAL AND WATCH THE CRIME SCENE VIDEO...

LATER.

SO, YOU WANNA GET ME UP TO SPEED? YOU AND FIELDS WERE WORKING THIS AS A *KIDNAPPING*, RIGHT?

YEAH, CAUGHT IT EARLY LAST FRIDAY NIGHT.

BONNIE LEWIS, AGE FOURTEEN, DISAPPEARED ON THE WAY HOME FROM A BABY-SITTING GIG THE NIGHT BEFORE.

HALFWAY THROUGH THE NEXT DAY HER DAD GETS *FAXED* A RANSOM NOTE...

KIDNAPPERS WANT *HALF A MILLION DOLLARS* IF HE WANTS TO SEE HIS *DAUGHTER* AGAIN...

THEN NOTHING...

WHAT DO YOU MEAN?

THEY NEVER MADE CONTACT AGAIN.

WHO FOUND THE BODY?

LET'S SEE... TWO TEENAGERS...

APPARENTLY THEY WERE USING THE SEWER SYSTEM AS A SHORT CUT TO THE WHARF...

SO, WHAT'D YOU *THINK*? THE KIDNAPPERS KILL HER BY ACCIDENT AND JUST *DUMP* HER?

MAYBE... THOUGH IT SEEMS LIKE THEY'D STILL GO FOR THE *RANSOM* ANYWAY...

TRUE.

WERE YOU GUYS ABLE TO TRACK THE RANSOM FAX AT ALL?

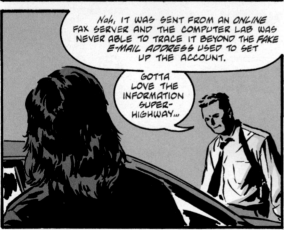

Nah, IT WAS SENT FROM AN *ONLINE* FAX SERVER AND THE COMPUTER LAB WAS NEVER ABLE TO TRACE IT BEYOND THE *FAKE E-MAIL ADDRESS* USED TO SET UP THE ACCOUNT.

GOTTA LOVE THE INFORMATION SUPER-HIGHWAY...

SO WHAT *NOW?* YOU LEARN ANYTHING HERE?

I JUST WANTED TO GET A LOOK AT THE SCENE... SEE IF IT MEANT ANYTHING.

SEEMS LIKE IT'S JUST AN *OUT OF THE WAY* SPOT, LIKE A MILLION OTHERS IN THE CITY...

LET'S GO SEE THE M.E.

GET SOME FACTS!

KANE COUNTY MORGUE

--AND FINALLY, HERE'S WHAT *DID* IT...

...YOU CAN SEE IT PRETTY *CLEARLY*...

BLUNT FORCE TRAUMA TO THE *BACK* OF THE HEAD.

YEAH, *ick*...

ANY *IDEA* WHAT SHE WAS HIT WITH?

SOMETHING *METALLIC*, HARD...

NOT *SURE* WHAT, BUT WE PULLED A COUPLE OF MICROSCOPIC FRAGMENTS OUT OF HER *SCALP* AND SENT THEM FOR ANALYSIS...

...WHATEVER IT WAS, THE *EDGE* WAS ROUNDED...

ANY CHANCE SHE *FELL?* WHACKED HER HEAD ON SOMETHING?

AN ENGINE BLOCK OR SOMETHING?

NO, THE *ANGLE* IS *WRONG*... UNLESS SHE WAS DOING A *BACK FLIP* AT THE TIME.

NO, YOU'RE LOOKING FOR SOMEONE *STRONG*, BETWEEN FIVE AND SIX FEET TALL...

BETWEEN FIVE AND SIX FEET?

CAN YOU *NARROW* IT DOWN A LITTLE MORE, BILL?

SORRY, BEST I CAN DO BECAUSE OF THE ANGLE OF THE BLOW.

OKAY, YOU GOT A *TIME* OF *DEATH*, AT LEAST?

YES, I JUST GOT THE REPORT FROM ENTOMOLOGY...

BASED ON THE *GROWTH* CYCLE OF THE FLY LARVAE FOUND ON THE BODY, WE'RE LOOKING AT...

...SOMEWHERE BETWEEN *TEN P.M.* ON THURSDAY, AND *NOON*, LAST FRIDAY, THE 16th...UNLESS THE BODY WAS KEPT IN AIRTIGHT STORAGE FIRST, THEN IT'S ANYBODY'S *GUESS.*

YOU HAD TO USE *BUGS* TO FIX A *TIME?*

THESE LITTLE FLESH-EATERS ARE *ALMOST* AS GOOD AS A TIME-STAMP, MARCUS...

SO, YOU TALK TO *NORA*, TODAY?

YEAH, SHE'S TAKING A WEEK OFF...

HEY, *DRIVER*, YOU SAID THE FATHER GOT THE *RANSOM NOTE* THAT FRIDAY *AFTERNOON*, RIGHT?

YEAH...

I THINK WE'VE GOT A SMALL *PROBLEM* HERE, THEN...

SO, WHAT DOES *THAT* MEAN?

THAT SHE WAS ALREADY DEAD *BEFORE* HER DAD GOT THE RANSOM FAX.

SO, IT'S LIKELY THE FAX WAS JUST A *DIVERSION*, TO THROW US OFF IN THE WRONG DIRECTION.

ESPECIALLY SINCE THEY NEVER SENT A FOLLOW-UP WITH THE MONEY DROP DETAILS.

SO, WHAT IS IT, THEN? CRIME OF PASSION?

I DON'T KNOW... THE M.E. SAYS THERE WAS NO SIGN OF RAPE. IT LOOKS LIKE SOMEONE JUST KILLED HER AND DUMPED HER.

SO, BASICALLY, WE'RE BACK AT SQUARE ONE...

ANY CHANCE THAT THE *FATHER* SENT THIS RANSOM NOTE *HIMSELF?*

MY GUT SAYS *NO*... BUT WE'RE GONNA MEET WITH THE PARENTS AGAIN TO-MORROW...

IF THIS *WAS* A MURDER FROM THE START WE NEED TO LOOK AT HER *PERSONAL* LIFE HARDER.

61

ALL RIGHT, KEEP ME POSTED...

SERGEANT DAVIES, ANY PROGRESS ON THE FIREBUG CASE?

YESSIR, LIEUTENANT, COLLARED HIM AN *HOUR* AGO... HE COPPED TO THE WHOLE SHEBANG...

I FORGET TO TELL YOU?

YOU COPS ARE *SUCH* COMEDIANS.

YOU REALLY *SHOULD* CUT THAT OUT...

CAN *I* HELP IT IF HE'S SUCH AN EASY TARGET?

JUNE 25th -- 6:10 p.m. ...

I'M AFRAID I DON'T UNDERSTAND ...?

THERE *WAS* NO KIDNAPPING?

THAT'S WHAT IT LOOKS LIKE RIGHT NOW...

SO, WE NEED TO ASK YOU SOME MORE QUESTIONS ABOUT YOUR DAUGHTER, AND HAVE ANOTHER LOOK AT HER ROOM...

OF COURSE, BUT... I THOUGHT...

SO DID *WE*, THAT'S WHAT THE KILLER WANTED.

WAS THERE ANY- ONE IN YOUR DAUGHTER'S LIFE THAT SHE WAS HAVING PROBLEMS WITH? OR MAYBE SCARED OF?

YOU THINK IT WAS SOMEONE WHO SHE *KNEW?*

MOST MURDERS *AREN'T* COMMITTED BY *STRANGERS,* MISTER LEWIS...

BUT... BONNIE WAS *POPULAR.* EVERYBODY LIKED HER...

...NO...

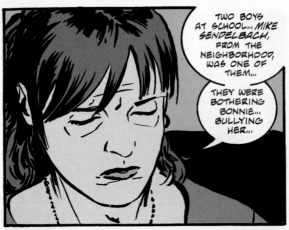

TWO BOYS AT SCHOOL... *MIKE SENDELBACH,* FROM THE NEIGHBORHOOD, WAS ONE OF THEM...

THEY WERE BOTHERING BONNIE... BULLYING HER...

SHE CAME HOME CRYING ABOUT IT A FEW WEEKS AGO...

WHAT? I NEVER HEARD ABOUT THIS...

IT DIDN'T SEEM LIKE ALL THAT BIG A DEAL... KIDS GET BULLIED...

DID BONNIE KEEP A *DIARY,* OR A JOURNAL? IF SO, WE'LL NEED IT...

NO, SHE WASN'T THE--

YES.

I'LL SHOW YOU WHERE SHE KEPT IT...

I'M REALLY SORRY, MISTER LEWIS... FOR HOW THIS TURNED OUT...

WE... WE NEVER SHOULD'VE LET HER *WALK HOME* FROM HER SITTING JOBS... IT'S JUST...

...THIS IS USUALLY SUCH A SAFE NEIGHBOR-HOOD...

SO, WHERE IS THIS PLACE BONNIE WAS WALKING *FROM?* THE COMBSES' HOUSE?

IT'S ABOUT A THREE-BLOCK WALK, JUST ON THE OTHER SIDE OF THE PARK...

I'LL SHOW YOU... I WANT TO TALK TO THEM AGAIN ANYWAY.

WHAT'D YOU GET FROM THE BEDROOM?

DIARY, SCHOOL YEARBOOK A COUPLE PHOTO ALBUMS...

JUST COVERING THE BASES...

THIS REALLY IS A PRETTY NICE NEIGHBORHOOD, Y'KNOW?

A BIT OUT OF YOUR PRICE RANGE, I THINK, ROMY...

$#!%... WHAT *ISN'T?*

Ah...WHO WANTS TO LIVE NEXT TO A BUNCH OF *INTERNET MILLIONAIRES,* ANYWAY?

DON'T EVEN GET ME STARTED...

IS THIS YOU?

OH, THAT... YES, THAT'S AT A FEW THOUSAND FEET. HAVE YOU EVER DONE ANY SKY-DIVING, DETECTIVE CHANDLER?

I'M A POLICE OFFICER, MISTER COMBS. THAT'S DANGEROUS ENOUGH FOR ME...

IT'S *QUITE* A RUSH, HONESTLY.

SO, NOW, WHAT DID YOU WANT TO KNOW, DETECTIVE DRIVER? I CAN'T IMAGINE THAT WE HAVE MUCH TO ADD TO OUR ORIGINAL STATEMENTS...

WELL, WE'RE APPROACHING THE CASE FROM A DIFFERENT ANGLE NOW, SO I'M AFRAID I'LL HAVE TO TAKE A LITTLE MORE OF YOUR TIME...

BONNIE'S FATHER SAID SHE ALWAYS WALKED HOME FROM BABY-SITTING. DO YOU KNOW WHAT PATH SHE TOOK?

AS I SAID BEFORE, SHE WENT THROUGH THE PARK...

AND THAT NIGHT SHE LEFT AT *WHAT* TIME?

WELL, AT WE GOT HOME A LITTLE AFTER NINE, SO IT WAS A FEW MINUTES AFTER THAT. AROUND 9:15...

AND YOU DIDN'T THINK THAT WAS A LITTLE *LATE* FOR A FOURTEEN-YEAR-OLD GIRL TO BE TAKING A WALK IN THE PARK?

NOT *ESPECIALLY*...

THIS ISN'T THE EAST END, AFTER ALL...

THE PARK ONLY EVEN HAS *ONE* HOMELESS PERSON, AND BONNIE WAS *FRIENDS* WITH HIM. SHE USED TO BRING HIM FOOD.

IS *THAT* RIGHT? YOU GOT A NAME FOR THIS *HOMELESS* PERSON?

I'M SURE I'VE *HEARD* IT BEFORE, BUT I WOULDN'T KNOW...

DID BONNIE *EVER* TALK TO YOU ABOUT HER *PERSONAL* LIFE? PROBLEMS AT SCHOOL, OR...?

OF COURSE NOT. SHE WAS OUR *SITTER*, SHE DIDN'T *CONFIDE* IN US.

I REALLY DON'T SEE HOW THIS CAN POSSIBLY--

SOMEONE SMASHED IN THE BACK OF BONNIE LEWIS' SKULL NOT LONG AFTER SHE WALKED OUT YOUR DOOR, MISTER COMBS...

NOW, I'M SORRY IF IT'S AN INCONVENIENCE TO YOU, BUT I'M TRYING TO FIND OUT WHO THAT WAS.

I JUST DON'T SEE HOW WE CAN HELP...

BONNIE... SHE WAS JUST GOOD WITH JOHNATHAN... SHE WAS A GOOD SITTER...

LOOK, IF THERE'S NOTHING ELSE... WE REALLY DO HAVE TO GET TO JOHNATHAN'S CHESS MATCH...

HOW LONG ARE WE GOING TO WAIT FOR THIS SUPPOSED HOMELESS GUY, MARCUS?

WHAT? YOU DOUBT HIS EXISTENCE?

CONSIDERING MARIE COMBS IS THE SOURCE, I'D BE *SURPRISED* IF HE WASN'T JUST SOME *HIPPIE* WHO COMES BY TO FEED PIGEONS...

SHE SEES SOME GUY WITH LONG HAIR, ASSUMES HE'S A *BUM* LIVING IN THE PARK.

YEAH, FOR THE LAST PEOPLE TO SEE THE GIRL *ALIVE,* THEY DON'T SEEM TOO SHOOK UP ABOUT IT...

PROBABLY MORE WORRIED ABOUT FINDING A NEW SITTER FOR LITTLE BOBBY FISHER...

WISH THEY COULD'VE BEEN MORE HELP, ANYWAY...

BEEN OVER A WEEK, AND WE STILL HAVE *NO IDEA* WHY ANYONE WOULD WANT TO *HURT* THIS LITTLE GIRL.

OH, MY GOD...

WHAT? WHAT'D YOU FIND?

OH, *SORRY.* I JUST CAN'T BELIEVE KIDS STILL WRITE, *"HAVE A BITCHIN' SUMMER"* IN YEARBOOKS.

THAT'S LIKE WRITING *"WARMEST REGARDS"* OR SOMETHING... IT'S SO SAD...

I'M *REALLY GLAD* I SURVIVED HIGH SCHOOL.

WHAT?

NOTHING.

OH, HEY, CHECK IT *OUT*... HERE'S THAT LITTLE JERK BONNIE'S *MOM* WAS TALKING ABOUT...

LEMME SEE...

WHAT DO YOU *THINK*? A YOUNG TED BUNDY?

LIKE WE'RE GONNA GET *THAT* LUCKY...

~~~ZZt~~~ ALL UNITS RESPOND...

ARSON FIRE AT 45TH AND SPRANG... SUSPECT *FIREBUG* BEING PURSUED BY OFFICERS... ALL UNITS RESPOND...

THAT'S LIKE, TWO MINUTES FROM HERE...

I KNOW...

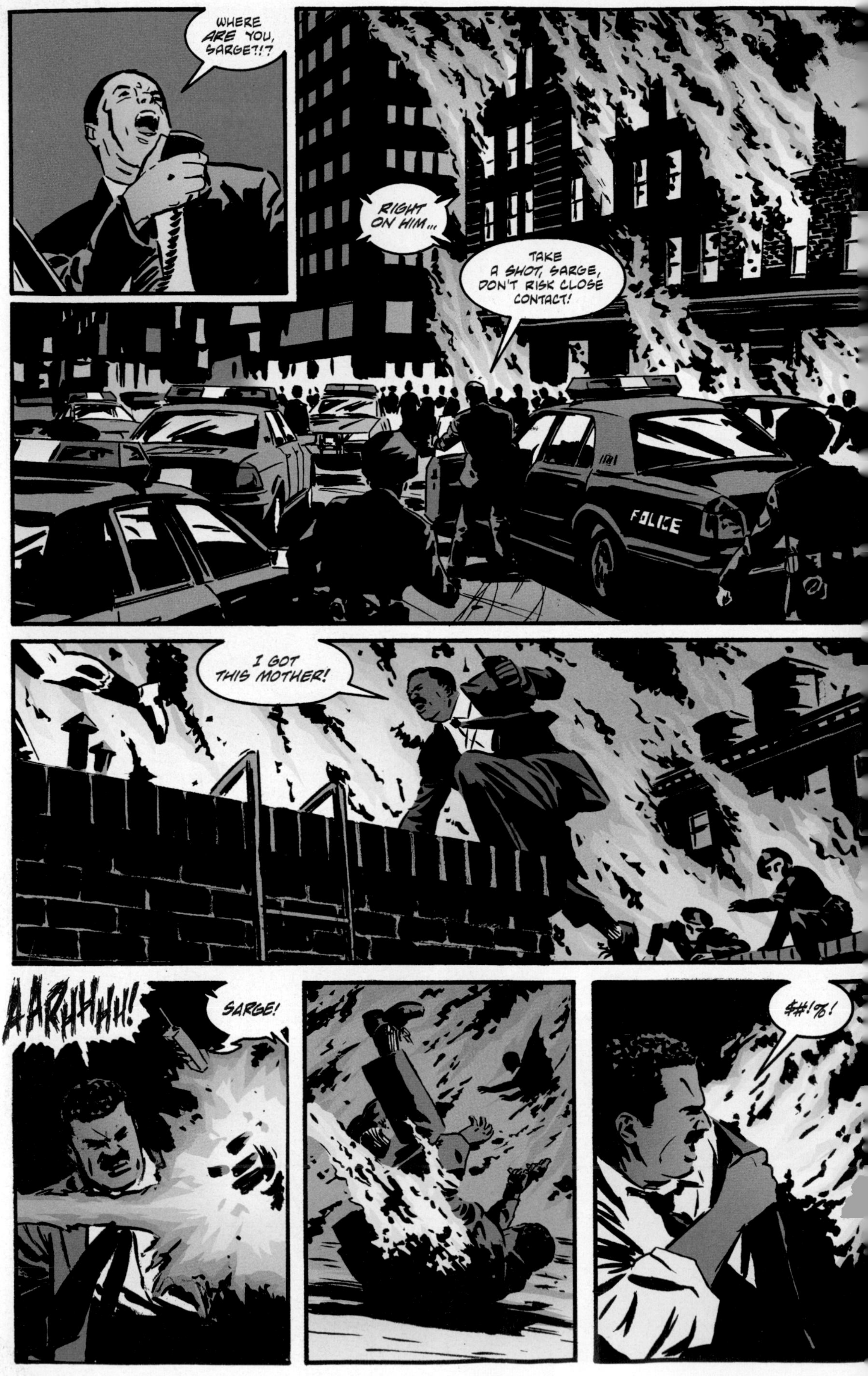
WHERE ARE YOU, SARGE?!?
RIGHT ON HIM...
TAKE A SHOT, SARGE, DON'T RISK CLOSE CONTACT!
POLICE
I GOT THIS MOTHER!
AARHHHH!
SARGE!
$#!%!

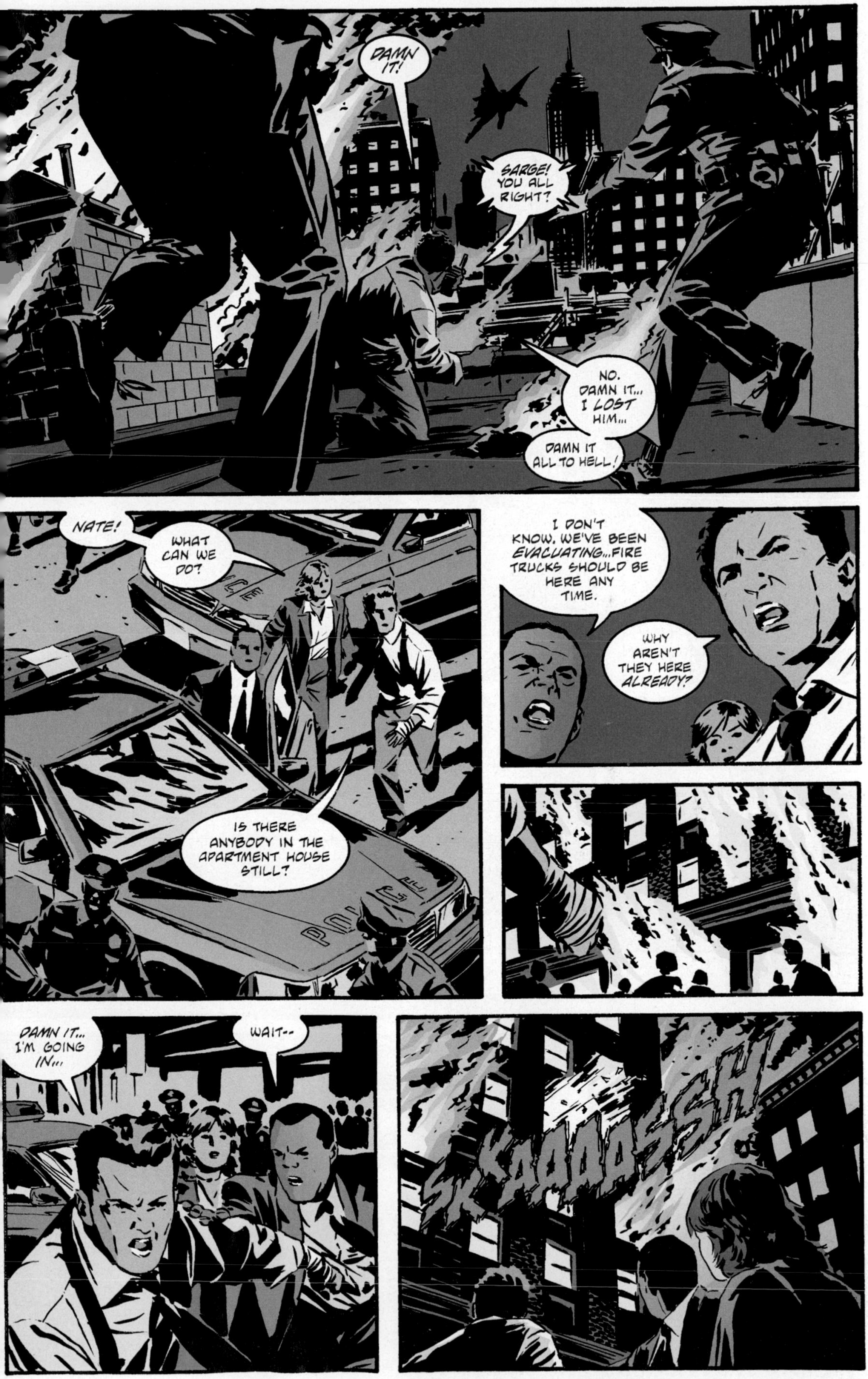
DAMN IT!
SARGE! YOU ALL RIGHT?
NO. DAMN IT... I LOST HIM...
DAMN IT ALL TO HELL!
NATE!
WHAT CAN WE DO?
IS THERE ANYBODY IN THE APARTMENT HOUSE STILL?
I DON'T KNOW. WE'VE BEEN EVACUATING...FIRE TRUCKS SHOULD BE HERE ANY TIME.
WHY AREN'T THEY HERE ALREADY?
DAMN IT... I'M GOING IN...
WAIT--
SKRAAAASSH!

WHAT THE HELL...?

THNNK

YOU'RE OKAY. NOW GO TO THE OTHER SIDE OF THE STREET.

DETECTIVE DRIVER...

THAT'S THE LAST OF THE TENANTS...

WHO *WAS* THAT MASKED MAN?

STOP IT.

FINALLY...

I GOTTA FIND SARGE, I THINK HE MIGHT'VE GOT *HURT*...

YOU WANNA HELP?

SURE...

CAN YOU HOLD DOWN THE FORT HERE, DRIVER?

YEAH, DON'T SWEAT IT.

I'LL FIND YOU TWO LATER.

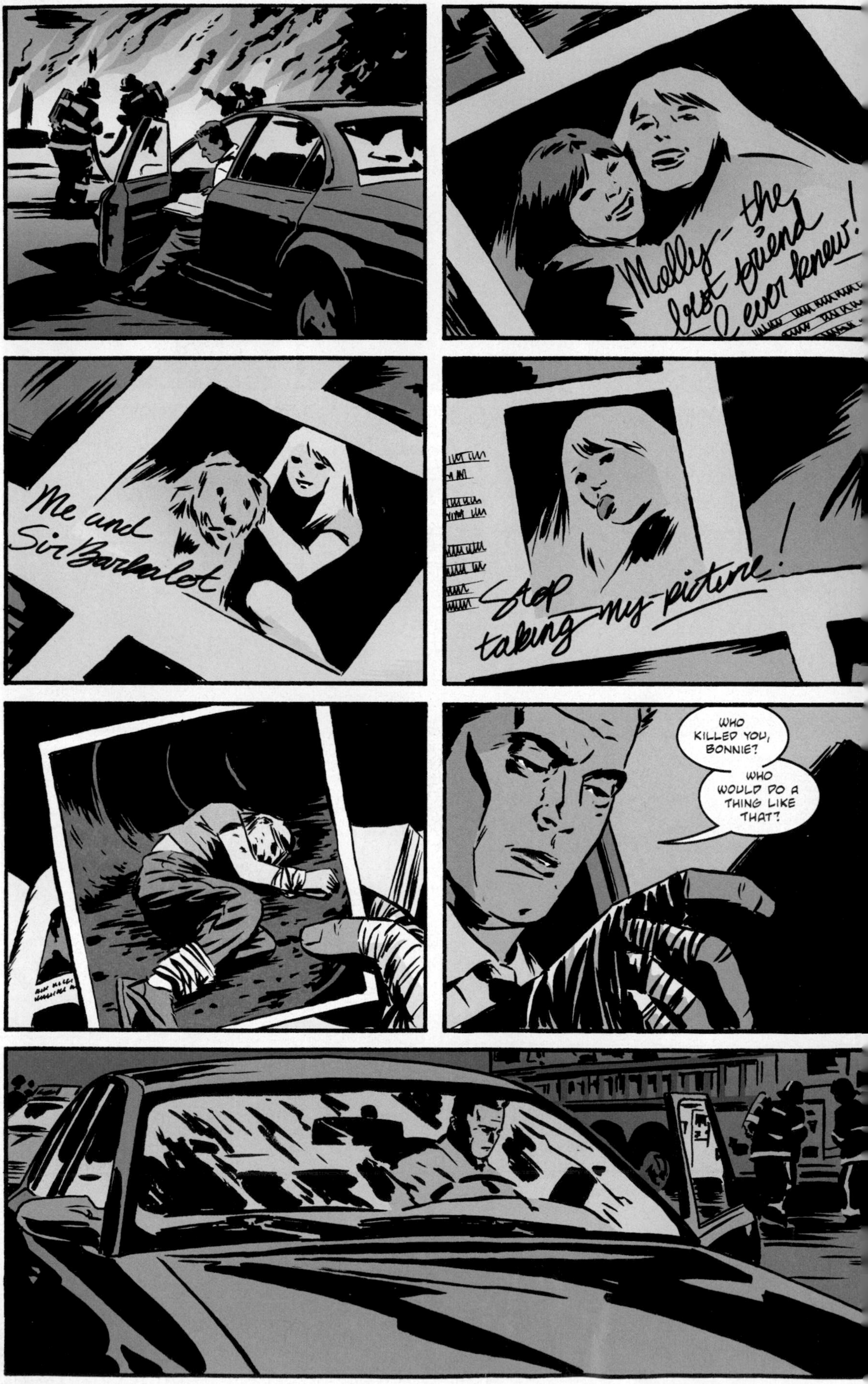
Molly - the best friend I ever knew!
Me and Sir Barkalot
Stop taking my picture!
WHO KILLED YOU, BONNIE?
WHO WOULD DO A THING LIKE THAT?

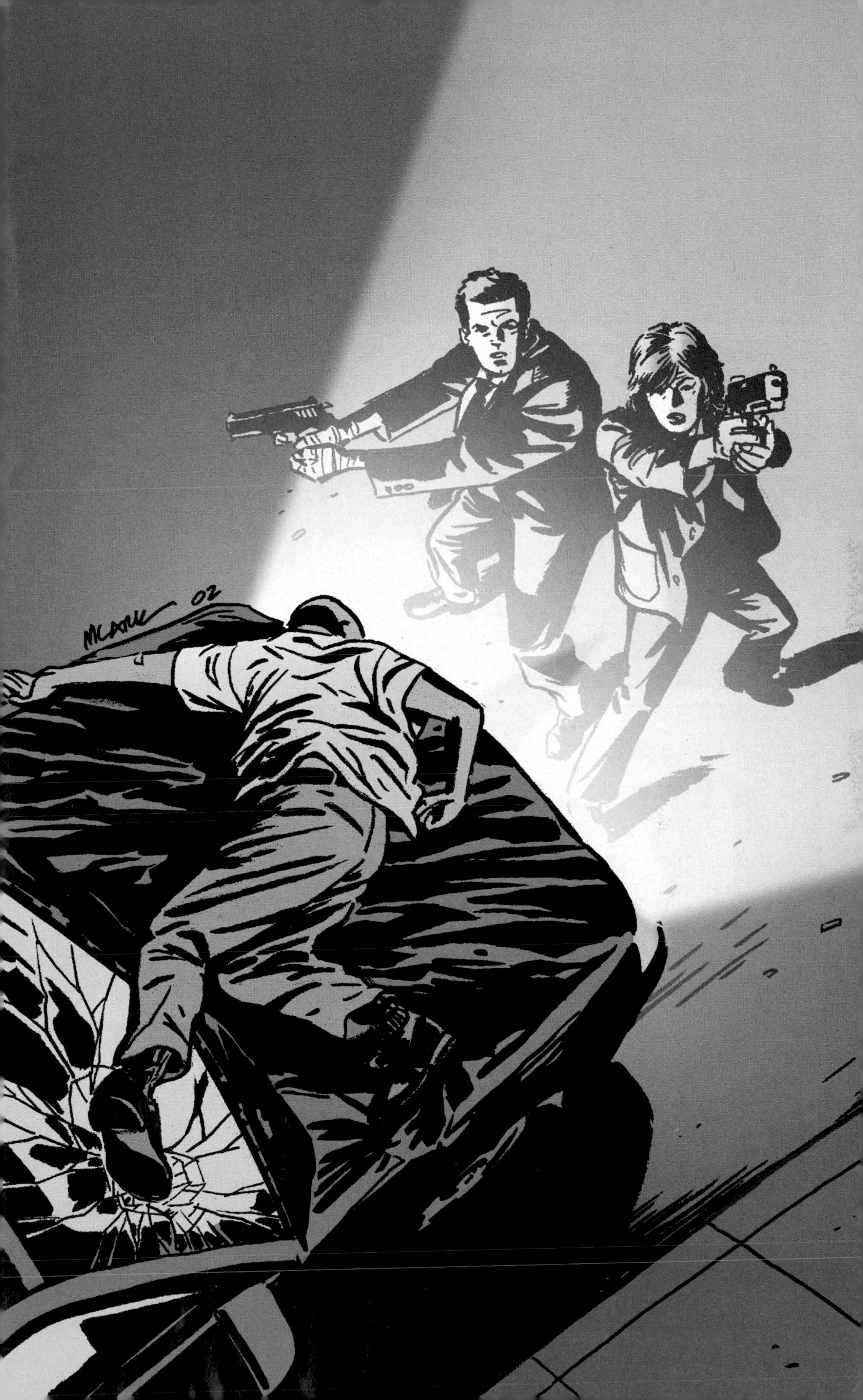

JUNE 26th, 6:03 p.m....

...IN SUDDENLY SHE'S ALL UPTIGHT.

"DON'T SWEAR IN FRONT OF MY CHILDREN."

AND I'M LIKE, LADY, THAT AIN'T EVEN SWEARING...

WELL, MAYBE SHE WAS CATHOLIC.

PROBABLY, BUT, I MEAN, THAT WASN'T EVEN HIS REAL NAME... HIS NAME WAS JOSHUA...

SHE'S ALL IN MY FACE ABOUT A GREEK TRANSLATION.

HIS NAME WAS JOSH CHRIST?

NAW, HE WAS LIKE JOSH LIPSHITZ OR SOMETHING, SOME JEWISH NAME...

CHRIST JUST MEANS MESSIAH...

HMM... HOW DO YOU KNOW ALL THIS, SERGEANT DAVIES?

BECAUSE I'M A DETECTIVE, I INVESTIGATE THINGS.

IT'S MY NATURE.

DON'T LISTEN TO HIM, STACY... HE'S JUST BONING UP FOR THINGS TO TALK ABOUT WHEN HE'S SPENDING ETERNITY IN A LAKE OF FIRE...

LIKE ALL LAPSED CATHOLICS.

YEAH, *RIGHT...* I'LL SEND YOU A POSTCARD WHEN I GET THERE, AZEVEDA...

ALL RIGHT... GUESS I'M NOT GONNA WAIT FOR *PATTON* ANYMORE.

GOTTA GIVE *THE PROBE* AN UPDATE ON THIS FIREBUG FIASCO...

ANYTHING HAPPENING?

NOT SINCE I GOT MY *BEST JACKET* TOASTED LAST NIGHT...

HAVE A GOOD *SHIFT,* DETECTIVES...

SEE YA, STACY...

HEY, STACY...

OH, HI, NATE...

SARGE WAS JUST LOOKING FOR YOU.

YEAH, I STOPPED TO GRAB SOME CHINESE...

ROMY UP THERE?

NO, SHE AND DETECTIVE DRIVER ALREADY CAME AND WENT... THEY GOT A LEAD ON THE *LEWIS* CASE, I THINK...

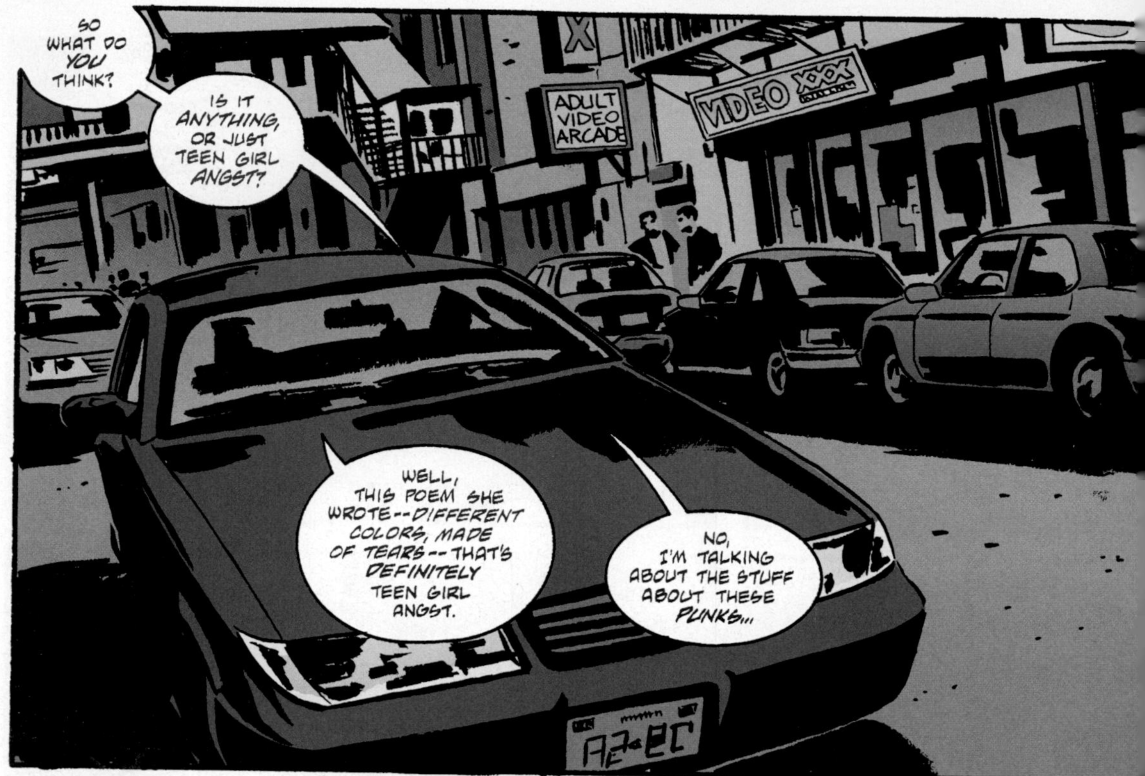
SO WHAT DO YOU THINK?
IS IT ANYTHING, OR JUST TEEN GIRL ANGST?
ADULT VIDEO ARCADE
VIDEO XXX
WELL, THIS POEM SHE WROTE--DIFFERENT COLORS, MADE OF TEARS--THAT'S DEFINITELY TEEN GIRL ANGST.
NO, I'M TALKING ABOUT THE STUFF ABOUT THESE PUNKS...

MOTIVE PART TWO

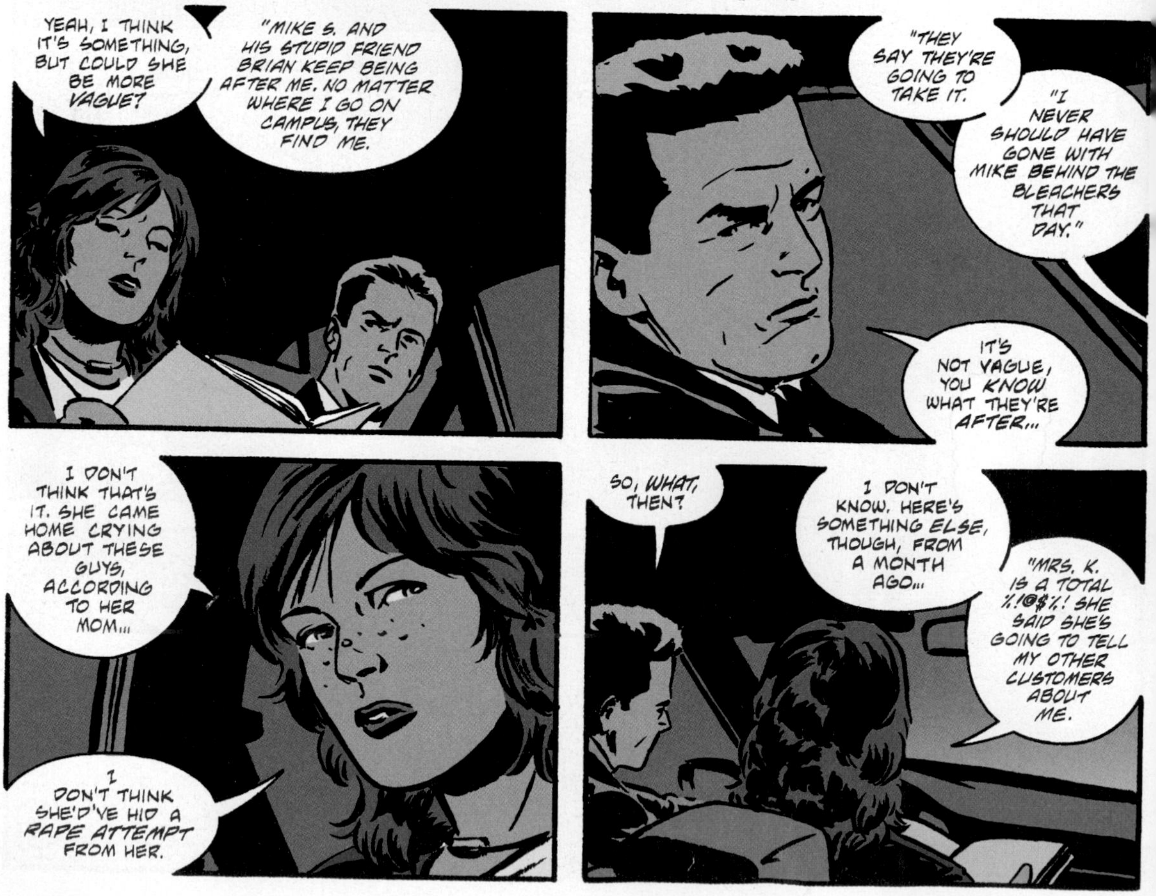
YEAH, I THINK IT'S SOMETHING, BUT COULD SHE BE MORE VAGUE?
"MIKE S. AND HIS STUPID FRIEND BRIAN KEEP BEING AFTER ME. NO MATTER WHERE I GO ON CAMPUS, THEY FIND ME.
"THEY SAY THEY'RE GOING TO TAKE IT.
"I NEVER SHOULD HAVE GONE WITH MIKE BEHIND THE BLEACHERS THAT DAY."
IT'S NOT VAGUE, YOU KNOW WHAT THEY'RE AFTER...
I DON'T THINK THAT'S IT. SHE CAME HOME CRYING ABOUT THESE GUYS, ACCORDING TO HER MOM...
I DON'T THINK SHE'D'VE HID A RAPE ATTEMPT FROM HER.
SO, WHAT, THEN?
I DON'T KNOW. HERE'S SOMETHING ELSE, THOUGH, FROM A MONTH AGO...
"MRS. K. IS A TOTAL %!@$%! SHE SAID SHE'S GOING TO TELL MY OTHER CUSTOMERS ABOUT ME.

"I TOLD HER I'D TELL THEM ABOUT *HER* IF SHE DID. MOLLY WAS SO PROUD OF ME."

YEAH, I SAW THAT, TOO... WHAT'D YOU THINK?

SOUNDS LIKE MAYBE OUR LITTLE ANGEL WASN'T SO SWEET AFTER ALL...

THEY NEVER ARE, ROMY...

YO! TOSS THAT PILL, DOG! I'M OPEN!

OKAY, THERE'S MIKE SENDELBACH...

YOU GOT A LIKELY BRIAN?

YEAH...

HEY, BRIAN!

THAT'S HIM...

NICE.

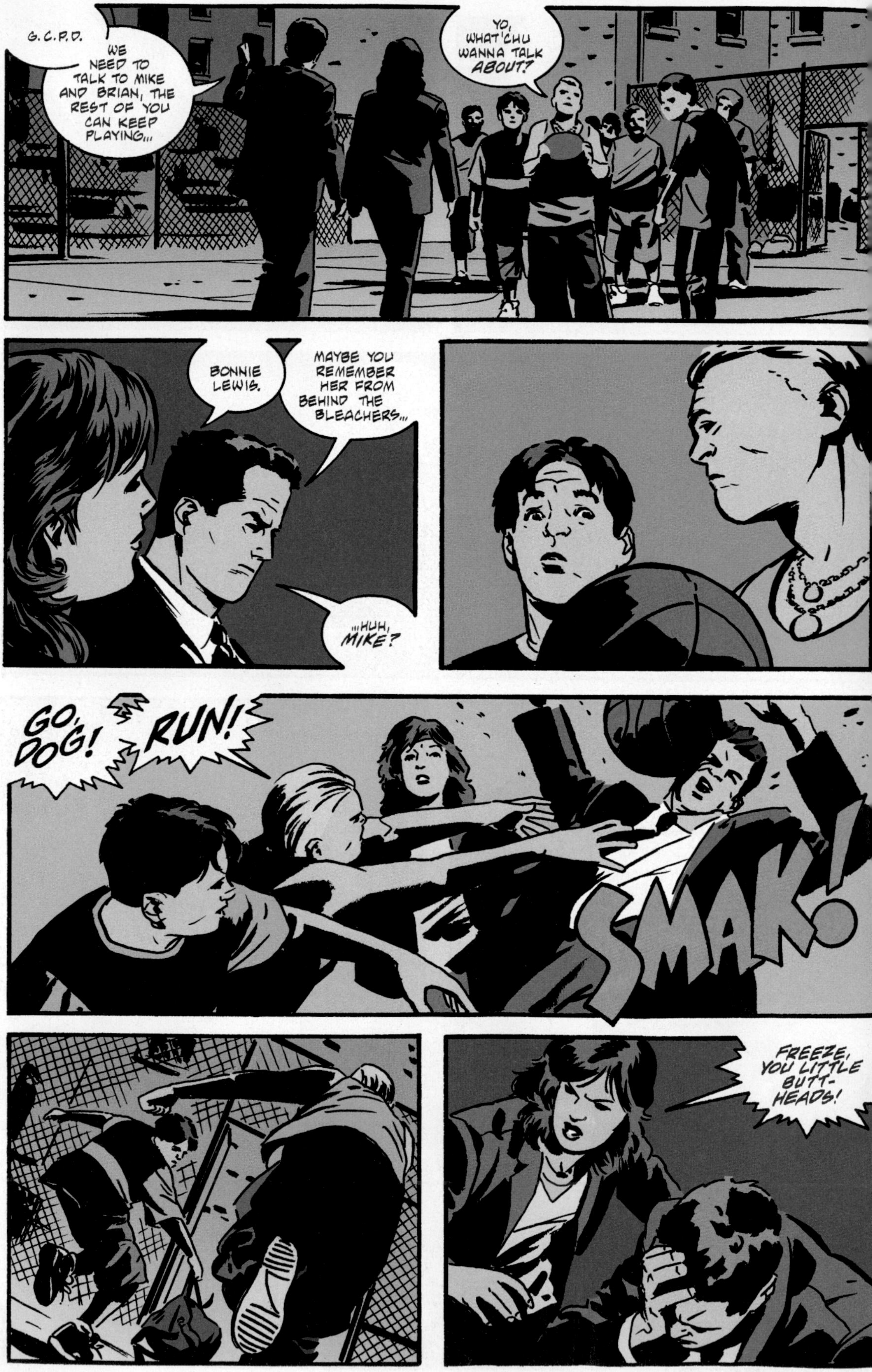
G.C.P.D.
WE NEED TO TALK TO MIKE AND BRIAN, THE REST OF YOU CAN KEEP PLAYING...
YO, WHAT'CHU WANNA TALK ABOUT?
BONNIE LEWIS.
MAYBE YOU REMEMBER HER FROM BEHIND THE BLEACHERS...
...HUH, MIKE?
GO, DOG!
RUN!
SMAK!
FREEZE, YOU LITTLE BUTT-HEADS!

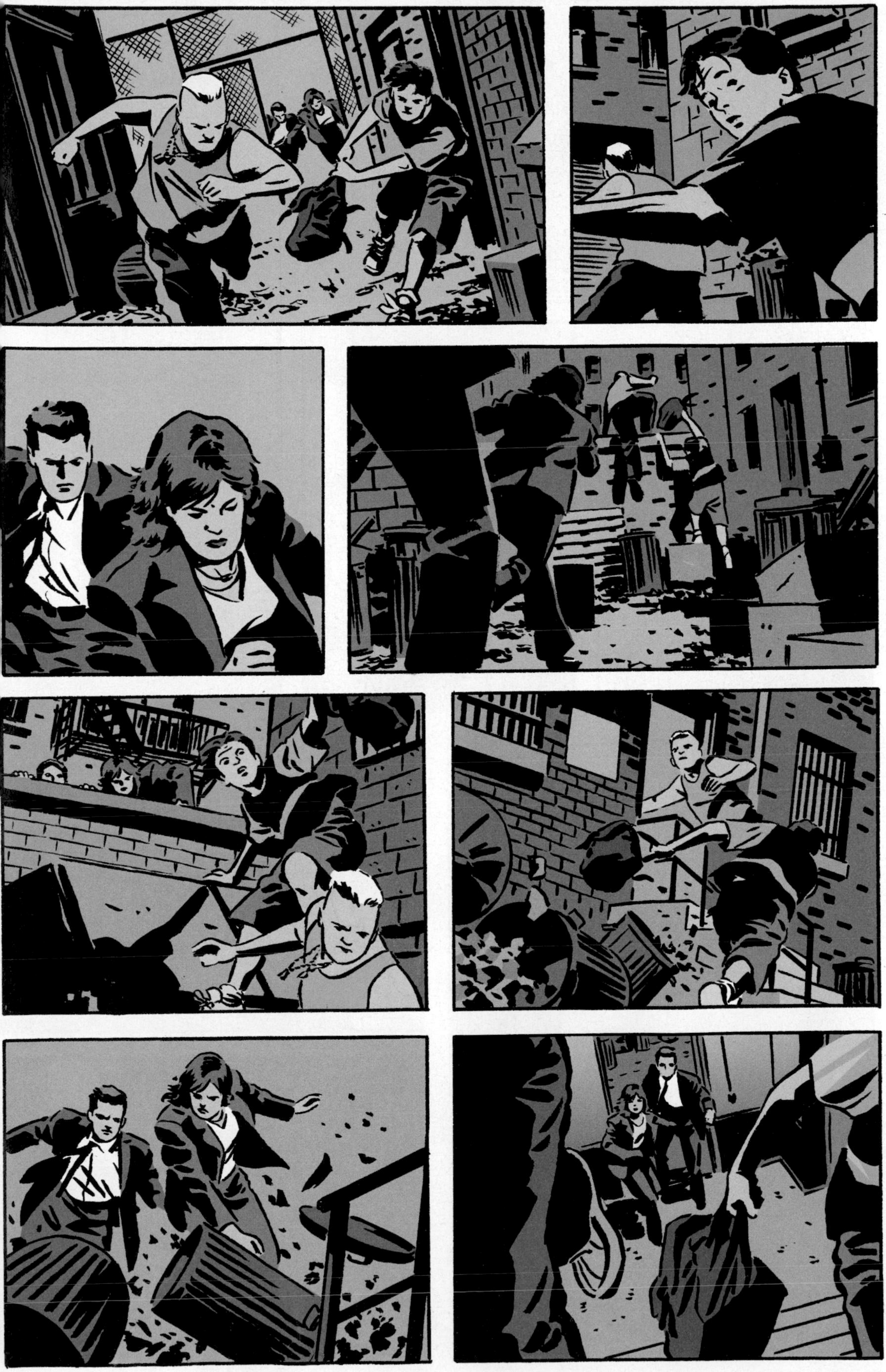

YOU OKAY?

YEAH... ...NEVER WAS TOO GOOD AT DODGE-BALL.

WHATTAYA THINK? HEADING FOR THE ROOF?

WHAT ELSE?

KIDS.

ROOF

ROOF

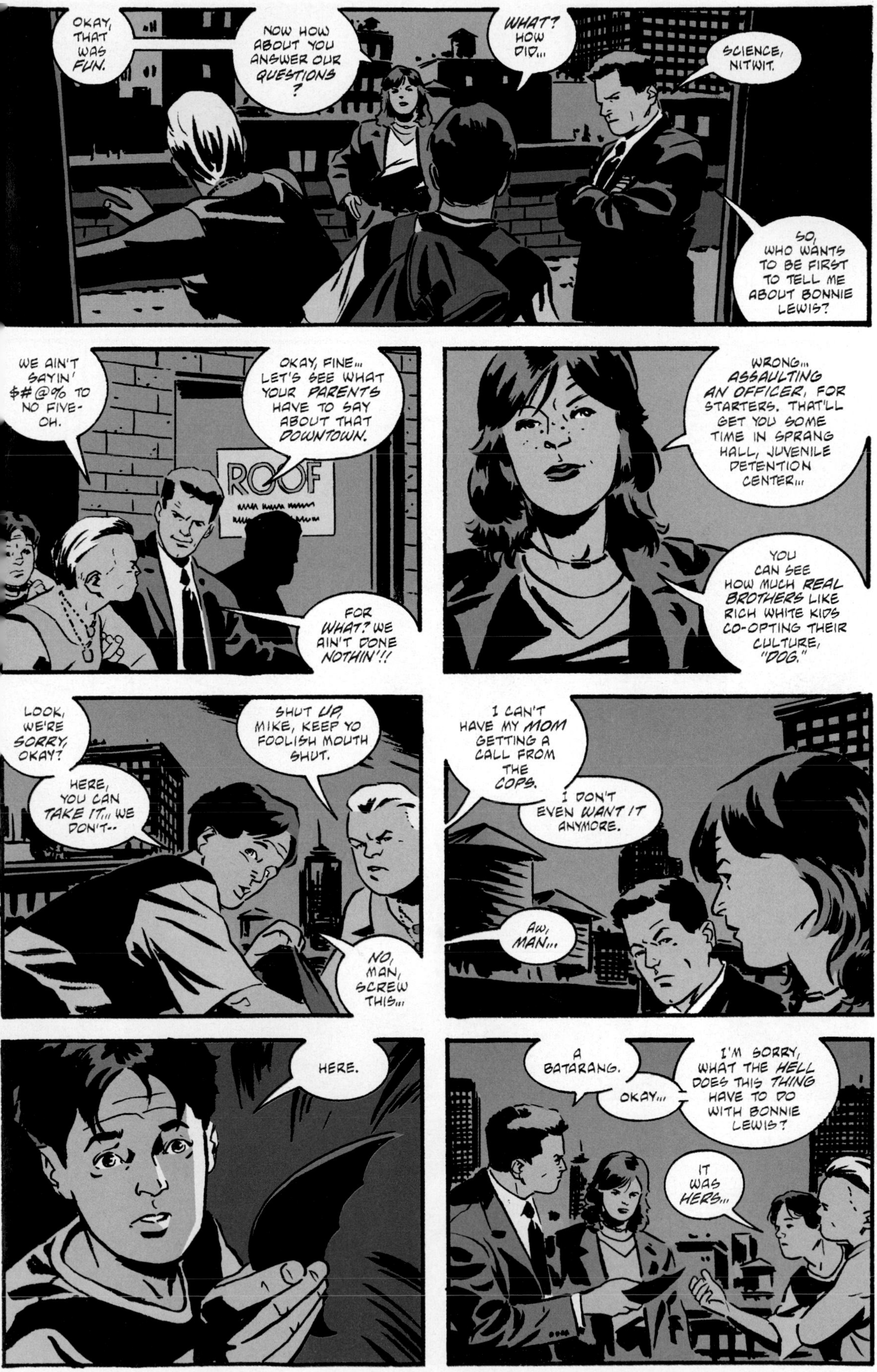
OKAY, THAT WAS FUN.
NOW HOW ABOUT YOU ANSWER OUR QUESTIONS?
WHAT? HOW DID...
SCIENCE, NITWIT.
SO, WHO WANTS TO BE FIRST TO TELL ME ABOUT BONNIE LEWIS?
WE AIN'T SAYIN' $#@% TO NO FIVE-OH.
OKAY, FINE... LET'S SEE WHAT YOUR PARENTS HAVE TO SAY ABOUT THAT DOWNTOWN.
ROOF
FOR WHAT? WE AIN'T DONE NOTHIN'!!
WRONG... ASSAULTING AN OFFICER, FOR STARTERS. THAT'LL GET YOU SOME TIME IN SPRANG HALL, JUVENILE DETENTION CENTER...
YOU CAN SEE HOW MUCH REAL BROTHERS LIKE RICH WHITE KIDS CO-OPTING THEIR CULTURE, "DOG."
LOOK, WE'RE SORRY, OKAY?
HERE, YOU CAN TAKE IT... WE DON'T--
SHUT UP, MIKE, KEEP YO FOOLISH MOUTH SHUT.
NO, MAN, SCREW THIS...
I CAN'T HAVE MY MOM GETTING A CALL FROM THE COPS.
I DON'T EVEN WANT IT ANYMORE.
AW, MAN...
HERE.
A BATARANG.
OKAY...
I'M SORRY, WHAT THE HELL DOES THIS THING HAVE TO DO WITH BONNIE LEWIS?
IT WAS HERS...
BATARANG

WELL, IT WAS *ROBIN'S* REALLY, BUT BONNIE SNAGGED IT.

WE'RE TALKING ABOUT ROBIN THE BOY *WONDER*, ROBIN? OF *BATMAN* AND...?

YEAH...

"A COUPLE OF MONTHS AGO ROBIN THREW DOWN WITH *KILLER CROC* AT OUR SCHOOL, ROBINSON HIGH...

"SOME PEOPLE THINK ROBIN ACTUALLY GOES TO ROBINSON, EXCEPT THERE WAS A BASEBALL GAME THAT DAY, SO HE *MIGHT* BE FROM SPRINGER LATIN...

"ANYWAY, IN ALL THE ACTION, HE BOUNCED A BUNCH OF BATARANGS OFF THAT SCALY MOTHER...

"IT WAS *WICKED* COOL!

AND I DON'T KNOW WHEN, 'CAUSE I NEVER SAW IT, BUT BONNIE GRABBED ONE OF THEM WHEN NO ONE WAS LOOKING...

"HER AND MOLLY WERE WALKING AROUND ACTING ALL *BIG* AFTER THAT, FOR NO REASON... THEN BONNIE TAKES ME BEHIND THE BLEACHERS AND SHOWS IT TO ME AND I WAS ALL, *'DAMN'*..."

JUST TO EVEN BE ABLE TO *TOUCH IT,* Y'KNOW?

AND YOU JUST *HAD* TO HAVE IT AFTER THAT, HUNH?

YO, IT'S A *BATARANG!*

KNOW HOW MUCH YOU C'N GET FOR THAT SUCKA ON G-BAY?

WE *WEREN'T* GONNA SELL IT...

IT'S JUST, SHE WAS A *GIRL,* Y'KNOW? WHAT'S SHE NEED A PIECE OF BATMAN FOR?

LEMME SEE IF I'VE GOT THIS...

YOU LITTLE *JERKS KILLED* SOMEONE FOR A *SOUVENIR?*

KILLED? WAIT A MINUTE...

--AND HITS DRIVER SMACK IN THE FACE.

Tino's BAR & GRILL

OPEN

OUCH.

ROMY TELLS IT BETTER.

NO, IT'S JUST NOT THAT *FUNNY*, NATE.

LUCKY THEY DIDN'T HAVE A *GUN*. KIDS TODAY.

OKAY, I GOT WHAT WE NEEDED FROM THE *BEST FRIEND*.

SHE GAVE IT UP ON THE *PHONE*?

SHE WANTS A COP COMING BY HER HOUSE TONIGHT INSTEAD? I DON'T *THINK* SO...

SO, WHAT'S THE SCOOP?

MRS. K. IS MRS. KURTZBAUM, LIVES AROUND THE CORNER FROM THE COMBS.

APPARENTLY, SHE CAUGHT BONNIE GOING THROUGH HER *CLOSET* ONE NIGHT.

BABY-SITTERS.

WHAT'D SHE FIND?

SECRETS. MRS. K. WAS IN THE *CLOSET* HERSELF, IT SEEMS, ALONG WITH SEVERAL PICTURES OF HER AT SOME OF GOTHAM'S SEAMIER NIGHTCLUBS...

WE TALKING ABOUT *BLACK-MAIL*?

COULD BE. WE'LL HAVE TO TALK TO THE WOMAN, OBVIOUSLY, SEE IF THERE WAS A GRUDGE.

SO, WAIT, THESE *KIDS* WEREN'T THE *KILLERS*.

NAH, JUST A COUPLE OF JERKS.

STOLE HER BATARANG.

SO, WHAT'S UP WITH THE *FIREBUG?* ANY WORD?

YEAH, SARGE IS GRABBING A DRINK WITH *HARVEY BULLOCK,* OF ALL PEOPLE... I GUESS BULLOCK'S GOT A SOURCE MIGHT BE ABLE TO TIP US TO THIS SKEEZE'S WHEREABOUTS...

PHHFFT-- HARVEY...

WE BETTER GET BACK OUT THERE.

YEAH, WE'VE GOT A *PARK* TO STAKE OUT...

THEY COULD BE KIND OF A *CUTE COUPLE,* DON'T YOU THINK?

WHAT?

WHAT?

--YOU DON'T *REALLY* THINK THAT, DO YOU?

AH, I DON'T KNOW... I GUESS *NOT.*

CHARLIE WAS LIKE THAT, THOUGH... WOULDN'T LISTEN TO *ANYTHING* RECORDED AFTER 1968...

...EXCEPT FOR THAT ONE SONG, *"OOOH CHILD..."*

WELL... THAT *IS* A GREAT SONG.

SO, I HEARD THEY GOT A NEW *CHICK* COMING UP, SOME BLACK GIRL WITH AN IRISH NAME...

FIRST PERSON ON THE M.C.U. THAT WASN'T HAND-PICKED BY *JIM GORDON...*IT'S THE END OF AN ERA...

I GUESS SO...

HEY, WAIT, YOU WERE THE *LAST* PERSON PICKED BY GORDON, WEREN'T YOU?

YEAH, ABOUT A MONTH OR SO BEFORE HE... BEFORE HE *RETIRED...*

CHARLIE WAS WORKING A MULTIPLE MURDER THAT CROSSED OVER WITH A ROBBERY 1 WAS ON, SO WE WORKED THEM TOGETHER...

TEAMED UP TO *FIGHT CRIME,* HUH?

OR AT LEAST *WHINE* ABOUT IT.

ANYWAY, HE RECOMMENDED ME TO GORDON AFTER THAT.

HEY, I THINK I SAW SOMETHING OVER THIS WAY.

C'MON...

ANYTHING?

HUHH. THOUGHT I SAW SOME *RUSTLING*... I GUESS IT COULDA BEEN A BIRD OR SOMETHING.

THIS IS A WILD-GOOSE CHASE, MARCUS...

THERE IS NO HOME-LESS GUY...

YOU'RE SO *SURE?*

WELL, WHERE THE HELL *IS* HE?

DOES HE HAVE A *JOB?*

WORK THE *LATE SHIFT?*

WELL, WHAT ELSE ARE WE GONNA *DO?*

WE GOT NOTHING...

THIS GIRL'S JUST *DEAD,* AND *NOTHING* JUMPS OUT AT ME AND SAYS *WHY...*

I SAY WE GO DRAG *MRS. K.* OUT OF THE CLOSET AND SEE WHAT *SHE* HAS TO SAY ABOUT IT.

MAYBE WE *SHOULD*... I DUNNO...

HEY...

WHAT THE HELL IS *THIS?*

LOOKS LIKE IT WAS SOME KIND OF *FORT* OR SOMETHING...

YEAH... EMPHASIS ON WAS...

LOOK AT THIS... SOMEBODY WAS LIVING HERE... A BOOK... SOME CLOTHES.

THINK MAYBE THE LOCALS GOT TIRED OF THEIR OWN LITTLE HOMELESS PROBLEM?

THE TIMING'S KIND OF WEIRD, THOUGH, RIGHT AFTER THE GIRL GETS--

HEY-- HOLD IT!

UHHH...

GET OUTTA MY HOUSE!

WHAK

AH!

GET OFFA ME!

MARCUS, COVER YOUR FACE!

MY HOUSE!

SHHPPT

AARRHH!

BURNS! EVERYTHING BURNS!

KRAK

YOU REALIZE THAT WE'VE GOTTA *CARRY* THIS WALKING URINAL CAKE TO THE CAR NOW, *RIGHT?*

I DON'T THINK HE WOULD'VE GONE *VOLUNTARILY* ANYWAY...

AW, GOD, ROMY... HE'S DROOLIN' SNOT ALL OVER THE SEAT...

WHAT DO YOU WANT *ME* TO DO ABOUT IT?

THAT *HARLAN COMBS* JERK JUST ZOOMED BY IN AN S.U.V.

THE HELL'S *HE* GOIN' IN SUCH A HURRY THIS TIME OF NIGHT?

THAT GUY...

I WISH I COULD THINK OF A GOOD REASON TO *BOTHER* HIM AGAIN...

SOMETHING ABOUT HIM AND HIS WIFE JUST GETS UNDER YOUR *SKIN*, Y'KNOW?

FIRST SELF-CENTERED YUPPIES YOU EVER MET, MARCUS?

DETECTIVE CAR TWELVE COME IN....

DETECTIVE 12 HERE...

ROMY. IT'S *NATE*... WE'RE PUTTING TOGETHER A UNIT TO TAKE DOWN THIS FIREBUG DIRTBAG. YOU GUYS WANT *IN*?

YEAH SURE...

JUST GOTTA DROP OFF A *PACKAGE* AT CENTRAL FIRST...

...WASN'T TRYIN' TO START A FIGHT, I WAS JUST *ASKING*.

YEAH, I'M JUST GETTING *TIRED* OF THE *QUESTION*, I GUESS...

SO, I'LL TAKE THAT AS A *NO*...

TAKE IT HOWEVER YOU *WANT*, MARCUS.

EVADING THE QUESTION JUST MAKES ME THINK THERE *IS* SOMETHING GOING ON...

HE'S MY *PARTNER*, MARCUS...YOU REALLY THINK I'D SLEEP WITH MY PARTNER?

I DON'T KNOW...IT WOULDN'T BE THE *FIRST* TIME.

YOU EVER SLEEP WITH ANY OF *YOURS*?

WELL, MINE WERE ALL *GUYS*, SO...

BIGOT.

WHERE ARE WE SET UP?

THIRD FLOOR, APARTMENT C.

GOOD, YOU'RE *HERE*, WE WERE GETTING TIRED OF WAITING...

WHAT'S THE *DEAL*? WHERE IS THIS GUY?

HE'S RIGHT DOWN THE HALL, IN G.

LIGHTS ARE OFF, BUT THE TV'S ON SO HE'S PROBABLY UP...

SO, BULLOCK'S TIP WAS GOOD?

YEAH, HARVEY KNEW A GUY WHO KNEW A GUY WHO KNEW WHERE THIS SUCKER WAS HOLED UP...

THAT WAS *ALWAYS* HARVEY'S PROBLEM, KNEW A FEW *TOO MANY* GUYS WHO KNEW A GUY...

SHUT YOUR MOUTH!

RIGHT NOW.

93

I DIDN'T MEAN NOTHIN'... I SWEAR, SARGE...

HEY... ISN'T THIS PLACE KIND OF A *DUMP* FOR A FREAK WHO'S BEEN TAKIN' DOWN *SERIOUS* BANK THE LAST FEW WEEKS?

YEAH, THAT CROSSED MY MIND...

NEVER KNOW WHERE THESE SICKOS ARE GONNA HIDE OUT, THOUGH...

ENOUGH SMALL TALK...

LET'S GO BUST THIS DIRTBAG.

REMEMBER, THIS MOTHER IS *NOT* TO BE TRIFLED WITH...

HE MAKES A MOVE FOR ONE OF HIS FLAME-THROWERS... *SHOOT HIM.*

STRIKE TEAM IN POSITION, ALL UNITS MOVE IN.

WHUMP!

KRSH!

G.C.P.D.!

JOSEPH RIGGER, YOU'RE UNDER ARREST!

PLACE YOUR HANDS SLOWLY BEHIND YOUR HEAD!

DON'T BE AN IDIOT, MAN...

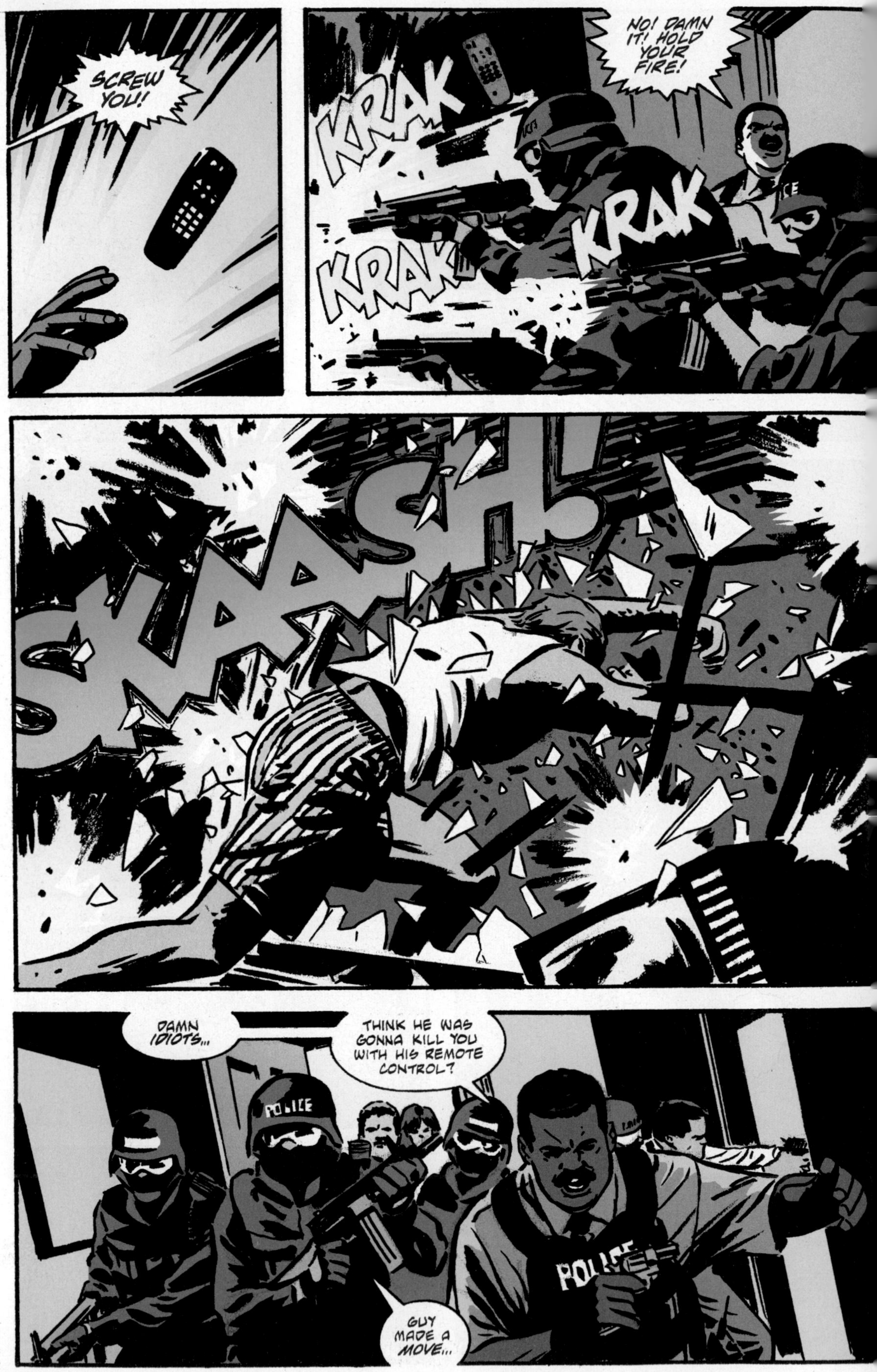
SCREW YOU!
KRAK
NO! DAMN IT! HOLD YOUR FIRE!
KRAK
KRAK
SMASH!
DAMN IDIOTS...
THINK HE WAS GONNA KILL YOU WITH HIS REMOTE CONTROL?
GUY MADE A MOVE...
POLICE
POLICE

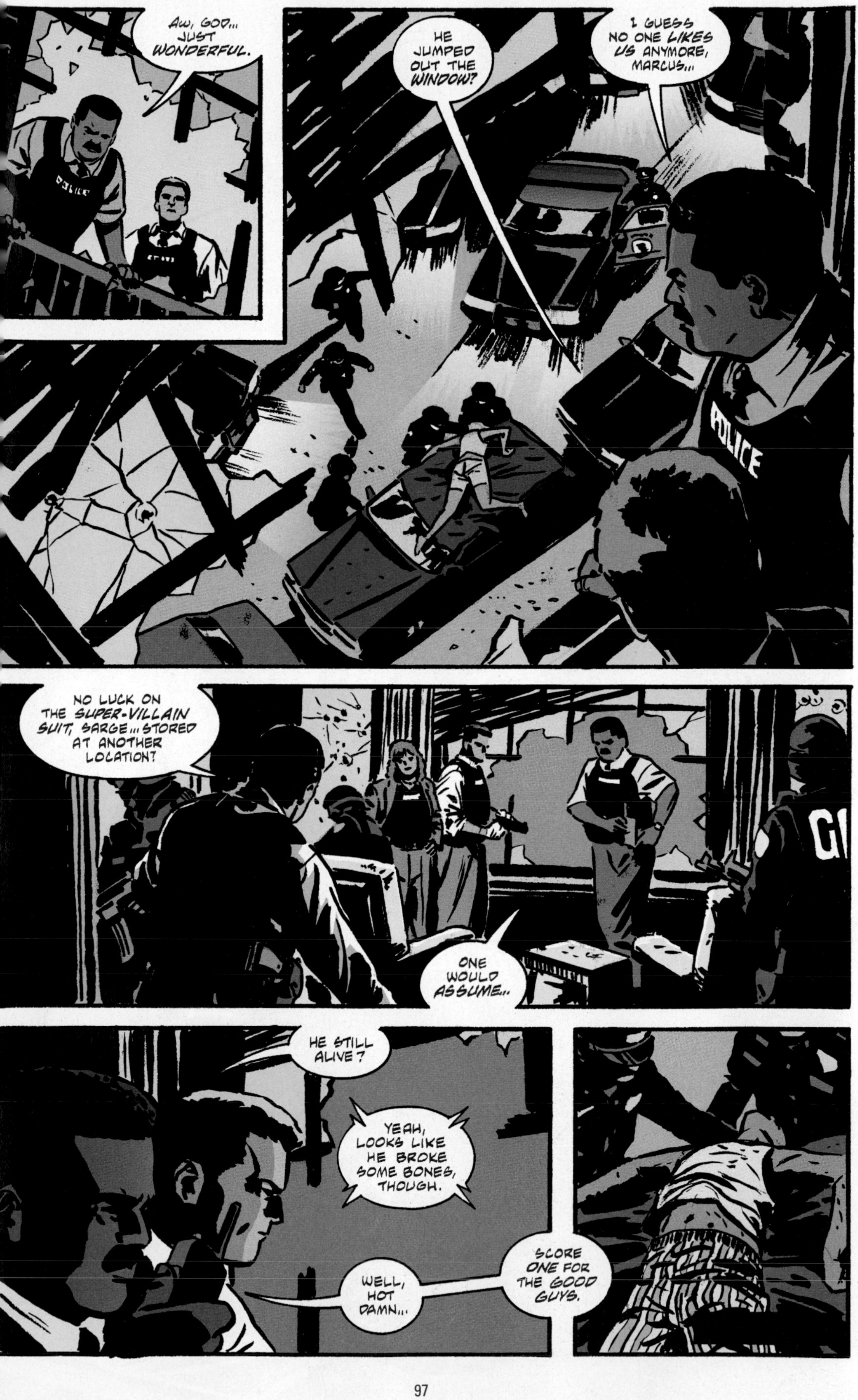
AW, GOD... JUST WONDERFUL.
HE JUMPED OUT THE WINDOW?
I GUESS NO ONE LIKES US ANYMORE, MARCUS...
NO LUCK ON THE SUPER-VILLAIN SUIT, SARGE... STORED AT ANOTHER LOCATION?
ONE WOULD ASSUME...
HE STILL ALIVE?
YEAH, LOOKS LIKE HE BROKE SOME BONES, THOUGH.
WELL, HOT DAMN...
SCORE ONE FOR THE GOOD GUYS.

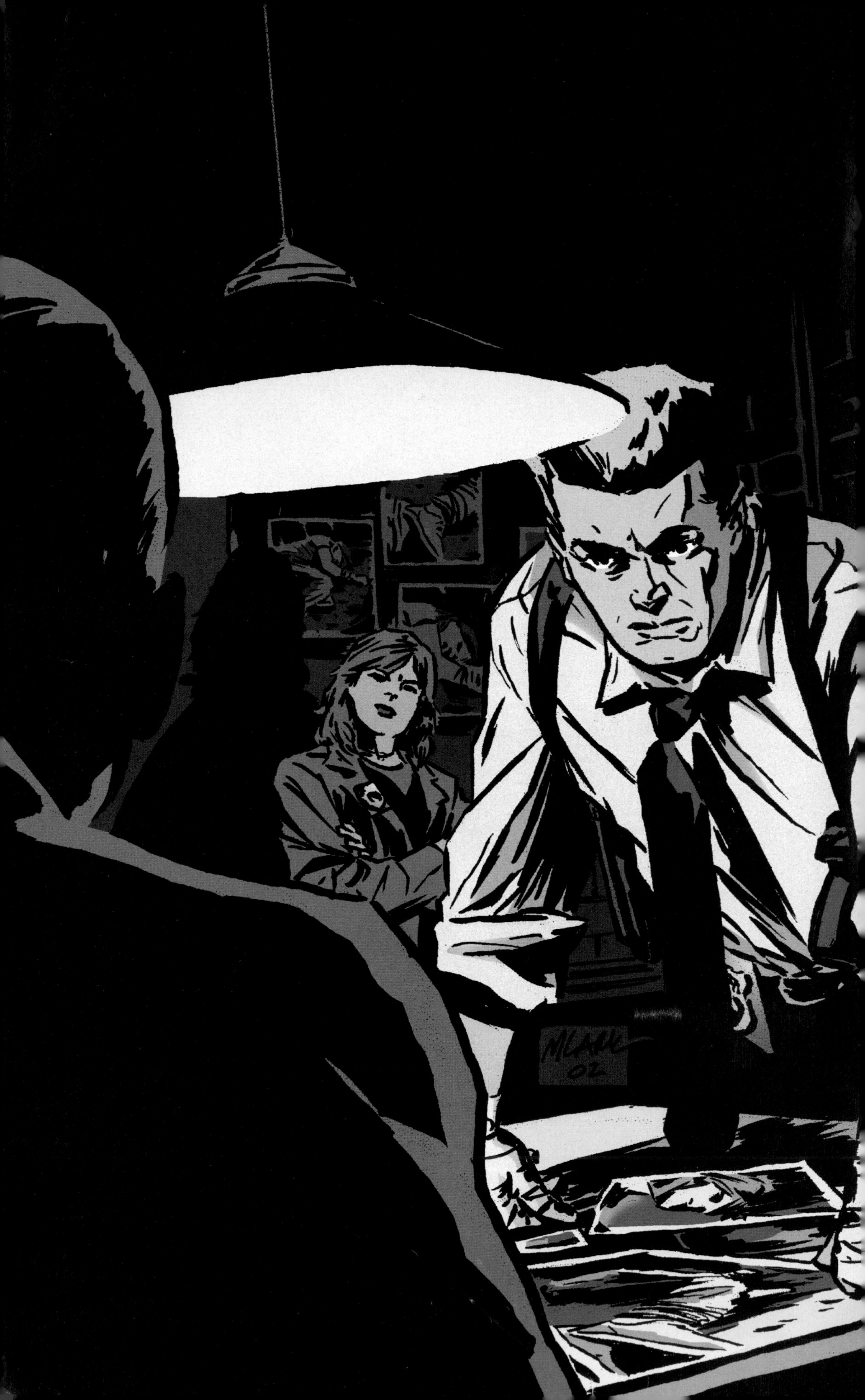

JUNE 27th, 6:45 p.m....

NO, I WAS NEVER A FULL-FLEDGED FED. JUST A CADET.

OKAY, BUT STILL WHY GIVE IT UP?

GOT TO KNOW A FEW AGENTS. GOT WARNED ABOUT THE BOREDOM LEVEL.

OH, C'MON, ROMY... WORSE THAN BEING A COP?

WAY.

FOR EVERY TIME THEY COME WALKING ALL OVER OUR CASES YANKING JURISDICTION, THEY'VE GOT LIKE *TWO THOUSAND* PIECES OF PAPER THEY HAVE TO FILE BEFOREHAND.

HELL, I CAN BARELY GET MY REPORTS IN ON TIME AS IT IS...

YEAH, ME TOO...

AND IF I WANTED TO SPEND MY DAYS TYPING, I'D'VE JOINED THE I.R.S.

EXCEPT THOSE SCHMUCKS CAN'T CARRY.

$#@%, MARCUS, THEY DON'T *NEED* TO.

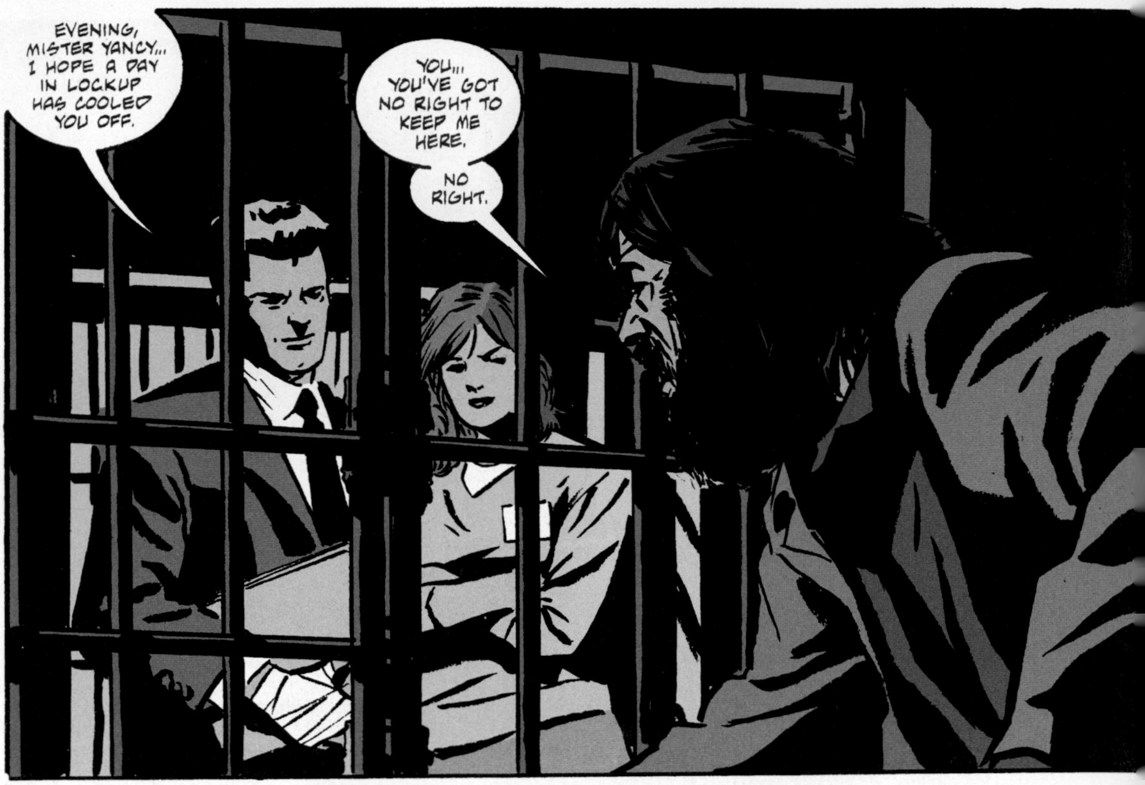
EVENING, MISTER YANCY... I HOPE A DAY IN LOCKUP HAS COOLED YOU OFF.
YOU... YOU'VE GOT NO RIGHT TO KEEP ME HERE.
NO RIGHT.

MOTIVE PART THREE

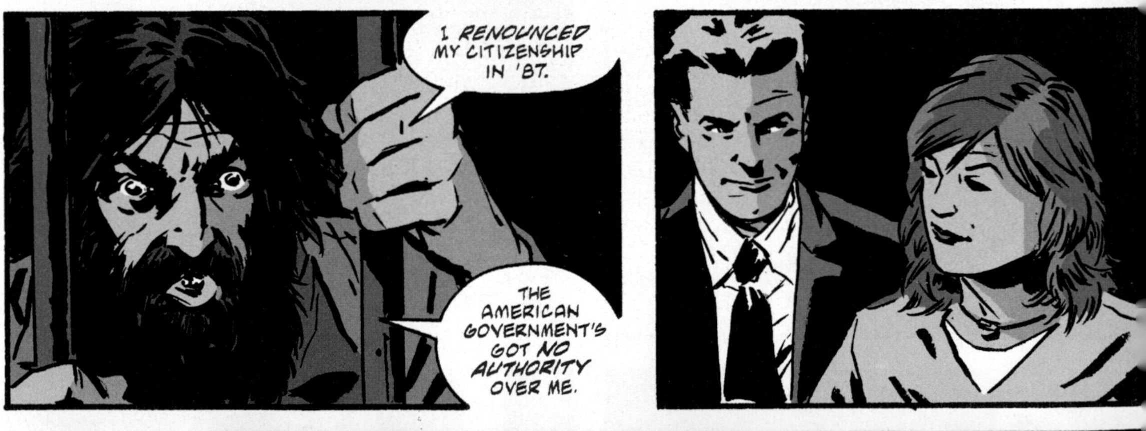
I RENOUNCED MY CITIZENSHIP IN '87.
THE AMERICAN GOVERNMENT'S GOT NO AUTHORITY OVER ME.

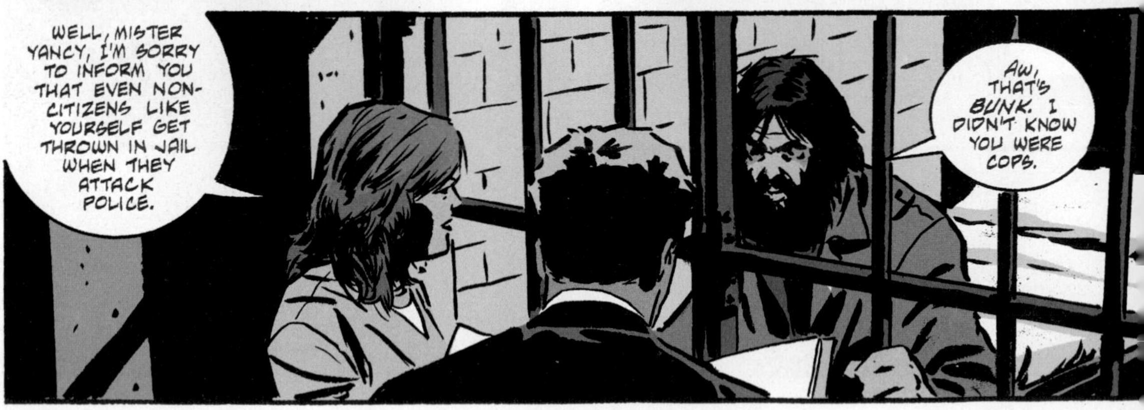
WELL, MISTER YANCY, I'M SORRY TO INFORM YOU THAT EVEN NON-CITIZENS LIKE YOURSELF GET THROWN IN JAIL WHEN THEY ATTACK POLICE.
AW, THAT'S BUNK. I DIDN'T KNOW YOU WERE COPS.

BLOOD-ALCOHOL LEVEL AS HIGH AS YOURS LAST NIGHT, I DON'T DOUBT IT.

SO, WHO *DID* YOU THINK WE WERE?

PEOPLE WHO WRECKED MY HOUSE LAST WEEK...

TRYIN' TO DRIVE ME OUT'VE MY *OWN* HOME.

LOCAL YUPPIES DON'T WANT YOU IN THEIR PARK, IS THAT IT?

SCREW WHAT *THEY* WANT.

I GREW UP THERE, THEY JUST SHOWED UP AFTER THE DEVELOPERS RUINED EVERY-THING...

IS THAT WHY YOU KILLED BONNIE LEWIS?

TO GET BACK AT THEM?

WHAT'RE YOU *TALKING* ABOUT?

YOU KNOW, THAT GIRL WHO USED TO BRING YOU FOOD.

HER BRAINS GOT *BASHED* IN LAST THURSDAY NIGHT.

FOUND ONE OF HER LIBRARY BOOKS BURIED IN THE REMAINS OF YOUR HOME.

HEY. HEY... SHE *LENT* ME THAT BOOK.

REALLY?

YEAH, SHE BORROWED BOOKS FOR ME ALL THE *TIME.*

SHE WASN'T LIKE THE REST OF THEM... SHE UNDERSTOOD MY *CAUSE...*

YOU GUYS WERE JUST *PALS,* HUNH?

YEAH, SHE'D BRING ME BOOKS AND FOOD AND STUFF ON HER WAY THROUGH THE PARK. TELL ME ABOUT THE *HYPOCRITES* SHE WORKED FOR.

SHE HATED THOSE *CARPETBAGGING MOTHERS* AS MUCH AS I *DID.*

WHAT ABOUT THE NIGHT OF THE 15th THAT LAST THURSDAY... *DID* YOU SEE HER THAT NIGHT?

NO...

SHE WAS *SUPPOSED* TO PICK UP THAT BOOK ON HER WAY HOME.

BUT SHE NEVER SHOWED UP. I WAITED FOR HER, TOO.

THEN THE NEXT DAY SOME SON OF A BS%*@ SETS MY *HOUSE* ON FIRE...

I *SHOULD* BE THE ONE FILING THE COMPLAINT HERE...

BUT I *SWEAR...* I'D NEVER'VE HURT *BONNIE...*

SHE WAS MY ONLY ALLY.

SO, WHERE DOES THAT LEAVE US?

I DON'T *KNOW*, LIEUTENANT.

SAYS HE'LL TAKE A *POLYGRAPH* IF WE WANT, BUT I'M GUESSIN' HE'LL PASS IT.

STILL HOLDING HIM JUST IN CASE?

YEAH, UNTIL WE DECIDE WHAT TO DO ABOUT THE *ASSAULT* CHARGE.

THIS *SUCKS*, DETECTIVES.

IT *DOES*.

BUT I JUST DON'T SEE THIS GUY BEING ABLE TO DO THE WHOLE BOGUS EMAIL RANSOM FAX, EITHER.

HE'S JUST SOME KOOK THINKS THE GOVERNMENT'S SCREWING HIM IN THE EAR.

WHAT'S WITH ALL THE LONG FACES?

SOMEBODY *DIE*?

AND THE LOCAL COMEDIANS RETURN...

...I HOPE YOU'VE GOT SOME SUNSHINE FOR ME THIS EVENING, SERGEANT.

WE'VE GOT A *STORY*. NOT SURE HOW IT STACKS UP, THOUGH...

SO, THIS FIREBUG SKEL BREAKS *BOTH* ARMS AND A LEG IN HIS LITTLE SWAN DIVE. GOT HIM ALL TRUSSED UP AND UNDER GUARD AT SAINT LUKE'S...

"...BUT HE'S STILL PRETTY COHERENT SO WE GO DOWN TO QUESTION HIM..."

"...AND HE'S ALL HARD-LUCK STORIES..."

--SERIOUS, MAN... JUST LOOK AT ME.

THAT FREAKIN' SUIT RUINED MY LIFE... I ALMOST *DIED.*

AND WHEN WOULD THIS'VE BEEN?

ALMOST TWO YEARS AGO.

MOB DOC SAVED MY HIDE, BUT HE COULDN'T DO ANYTHING ABOUT THE SCARRING...

I COULDN'T EXACTLY WALTZ INTO THE E.R. THOUGH, SO WHO WAS I TO COMPLAIN?

WE'RE CERTAINLY IN AGREEMENT YOU'RE AN *UGLY* PIECE OF WORK, JOEY...

"...BUT HOW DOES THAT PROVE YOU'RE NOT OUR PERP ON THESE *ARSON ROBBERIES?*

I DON'T EVEN *HAVE* A FIREBUG SUIT ANYMORE. I SOLD MY BACKUP *ONLINE* A YEAR AGO.

YOU CAN DO THAT?

JUST SELL YOUR *SUPER-VILLAIN JUNK* ON G-BAY OR SOME-PLACE?

SEEMS LIKE THAT WOULD BE SOME KIND OF A FELONY.

IT'S AN UNDERGROUND AUCTION HOUSE, STARTED OUT OF KEYSTONE CITY.

AND LISTEN, MY MERCH WAS CLEARLY ADVERTISED FOR COLLECTORS ONLY.

LET ME GET THIS STRAIGHT... YOU SOLD YOUR TOTALLY ILLEGAL FLYING ARSON SUIT, BUT IT'S OKAY 'CAUSE YOU SAID IT WAS FOR COLLECTORS ONLY?

YEAH, SOLD IT AS MEMORABILIA.

I FOUGHT BATMAN IN THAT SUIT ONCE...

PEOPLE PAY GOOD MONEY FOR THAT.

FOUGHT BATMAN. YEAH, FOR LIKE THREE SECONDS.

MORE'N YOU.

I DON'T NEED TO FIGHT BATMAN, JERK!

I GET TO FIGHT MORONS WITH FREEZE RAYS AND FEAR GAS ALL YEAR LONG.

HEY-- UKK!

ALL RIGHT, NATE... EASE OFF.

THAT'S POLICE BRUTALITY!

SHUT UP, JOEY, AND LISTEN TO YOUR CHOICES...

YOU CAN EITHER DO HARD TIME FOR SELLING AN ILLEGAL, DANGEROUS WEAPON, OR YOU CAN GIVE UP THE GUY WHO BOUGHT THE SUIT...

PICK ONE.

I DON'T KNOW HIS NAME.

IT WAS A BLIND AUCTION.

GUESS WE CAN'T HELP YOU THEN...

WAIT! WAIT!

I CAN IDENTIFY HIM!

I MET THE GUY ONCE, JUST TO SHOW HIM HOW EVERYTHING *WORKED*...

TO SHOW HIM HOW THE *MEMORABILIA* WORKED?

"... ANYWAY, HE SWEARS ON HIS MOTHER'S GRAVE-- AND SHE'S STILL ALIVE, I *CHECKED*-- THAT THE GUY WHO BOUGHT THE STUPID SUIT IS SOME RICH WHITE GUY."

SO, IT LOOKS LIKE WE'VE GOT SOME NEW *WANNABE* OUT THERE MAKING GOOD.

YOU GOING TO SIT HIM DOWN WITH AN ARTIST?

YEAH, THEY'RE WHEELING HIM IN LATER ON, I THINK.

GOT A GUY COMING BY TO DO A COMP...

WELL, I'M GLAD TO SEE *BOTH* OUR BIGGEST INVESTIGATIONS ARE GETTING NOWHERE.

I CAN HARDLY *WAIT* TO TELL THE COMMISSIONER...

I DIDN'T KNOW BETTER I'D THINK THE PROBE JUST MADE A FUNNY.

ON SON

TON | FIELDS | DR

NZO | O16 LEWIS | OO
ADY | | O2
CAS | | 167
TH | | 178

MARCUS...?

WHAT?

IS THIS SUPPOSED TO BE SOME KIND OF SÉANCE OR SOMETHING?

BONNIE LEWIS'S *SPIRIT* TALKING TO YOU?

IF IT WAS, I'M SURE IT WOULD BE NOTHING BUT COMPLAINTS.

JOB I'VE BEEN DOING ON THIS...

GIVE YOURSELF A BREAK.

A LOT'S *HAPPENED* SINCE THIS CASE STARTED...

I JUST, I CAN'T HELP THINKING THAT CHARLIE WOULD SEE SOMETHING WE'RE NOT...

IF HE WERE HERE.

CHARLIE FIELDS WAS A GREAT POLICE, MARCUS, BUT EVEN HE COULDN'T MAKE CONNECTIONS WHERE NONE EXIST.

ALL OUR LEADS ON THIS HAVE BEEN NON-STARTERS. IT'S NOT OUR FAULT.

NO, WE'RE MISSING SOMETHING, I KNOW IT.

WHAT?

LOOK-- SOMEONE KILLS BONNIE LEWIS, THEN THEY STASH HER BODY HERE, RIGHT?

I'M WITH YOU SO FAR...

BUT THEN THEY SENT A RANSOM NOTE TO THROW HER FOLKS AND US OFF-TRACK.

I MEAN, IF SHE'D JUST DISAPPEARED, WE'D BE AT LEAST PARTIALLY LOOKING FOR A RANDOM KILLER. BUT THE NOTE MAKES IT OUT TO BE SOMEONE WHO KNEW HER.

OTHERWISE, WHY WORRY ABOUT KEEPING US FROM THINKING SHE'S DEAD?

GIVE THEM TIME TO MAKE SURE ALL THE EVIDENCE IS CLEANED UP.

ESTABLISH A SOLID ALIBI.

RIGHT, AND NOT ONLY DOES EVERYONE HAVE AN ALIBI, BUT AS FAR AS I CAN TELL...

...THERE'S ABSOLUTELY NO MOTIVE FOR THIS MURDER.

BUT THE PROBLEM WITH THE MOTIVELESS CRIME IS THAT THERE'S ALWAYS A MOTIVE...

WE JUST CAN'T SEE IT.

'CAUSE NO ONE KILLS SOMEONE WITH NO REASON.

I MEAN, IT MAY BE BECAUSE THEY WANTED THEIR *SHOES,* OR THEY JUST HAPPENED TO WALK BY WHEN THE PERP SNAPPED...

BUT THERE'S ALWAYS SOME-THING.

WE'RE JUST MISSING THE SOMETHING.

SO, THAT'S WHY WE'RE BACK TO SQUARE ONE, *huh?*

I GUESS... IT'S WHAT CHARLIE ALWAYS DID...

WELL, YOU KNOW, TECHNICALLY, THIS IS SQUARE *TWO,* NOT ONE.

WHAT?

SHE WAS KILLED SOMEWHERE THEN DUMPED HERE. THAT SOMEWHERE IS SQUARE ONE.

...SOMEWHERE BETWEEN THE COMBS APARTMENT AND THE PARK...

AW, GOD...

WHAT?

YOU'RE A GENIUS...

THIS IS DETECTIVE 12 TO *CENTRAL...* COME IN.

THIS IS CENTRAL.

I NEED TO SPEAK TO SERGEANT DAVIES ASAP...

HEY, MISTER COMBS. THANKS FOR COMING DOWN ON SUCH SHORT NOTICE.

WELL, I HOPE THIS ISN'T GOING TO TAKE LONG, I HAVE AN EARLY MEETING TOMORROW...

JUST NEED YOU TO I.D. OUR PERP, AND I'LL BE OUT OF YOUR HAIR FOR GOOD, HOPEFULLY.

ANYTHING TO HELP, THEN, I SUPPOSE.

JUST RIGHT THROUGH HERE, SIR...

WELL?

HOW'D YOU FIND HIM?

OH, YOU KNOW... MOST POLICE WORK IS JUST BLIND LUCK, JOEY...

SO WHAT DOES THE D.A. THINK? THAT GOOD ENOUGH FOR A WARRANT, AT LEAST?

CALLING THE JUDGE RIGHT NOW...

OKAY, MISTER COMBS, IS ANY OF THESE MEN THE ONE WHO'S BEEN LOITERING IN THE PARK DOWN THE BLOCK FROM YOUR HOME?

YES, NUMBER FOUR.

YOU'RE CERTAIN?

ABSOLUTELY. HE'S BEEN BEGGING CHANGE FROM ME FOR YEARS...

...IS HE THE ONE WHO KILLED BONNIE?

I CAN'T REALLY COMMENT ON THAT, OFFICIALLY...

...BUT JUST BETWEEN YOU AND ME SIR, HE'S GOING DOWN.

ALL RIGHT, MISTER COMBS. I GUESS THAT DOES IT. THANKS FOR YOUR--

ACTUALLY, IF IT'S NOT A PROBLEM, I'D LIKE TO GO OVER ONE MORE THING ABOUT YOUR STATEMENT...?

WELL... HOW LONG IS THIS GOING TO TAKE?

JUST LIKE, TWENTY MINUTES AT THE MOST...

"...I JUST WANT TO MAKE SURE THERE'S NOTHING WE MISSED, IN CASE OF A TRIAL."

WAIT. WAIT A SECOND. MY HUSBAND ISN'T EVEN HERE.

I NEED TO CALL--

YOUR HUSBAND IS TALKING TO THE POLICE RIGHT NOW, MRS. COMBS. HE'S GOING TO BE A WHILE...

BUT-- WHAT ARE YOU LOOKING FOR?

IT'S ON THE WARRANT, MA'AM...

SORRY ABOUT THAT, MISTER COMBS. HAD A POSSIBLE *DEVELOPMENT* ON ANOTHER CASE...

I CAN HARDLY SEE HOW THAT'S ANY REASON TO KEEP ME WAITING NEARLY AN HOUR.

I TOLD YOU ALREADY THAT I--

LISTEN, WE'RE REALLY *SORRY*, HONESTLY.

WE'VE JUST HAD THIS *FIREFLY* GUY UP OUR BUTTS ALL WEEK.

I THOUGHT IT WAS THE FIRE*BUG*.

WASN'T IT?

IS THAT *RIGHT*, ROMY? FIREFLY OR BUG?

I THINK IT *IS* BUG, ACTUALLY.

ANYWAY, THAT'S NEITHER HERE NOR THERE--

ONE WACKO COSTUMED FREAK IS AS GOOD AS *ANOTHER*, RIGHT?

I SUPPOSE SO.

OKAY, LET ME SEE IF I'VE GOT THIS STRAIGHT--

YOUR WIFE AND YOU CAME HOME AROUND 9:00 P.M. THAT THURSDAY, AND BONNIE LEFT SHORTLY AFTER THAT?

THIS IS WHAT YOU WANTED TO GO OVER?

HOW MUCH DID YOU PAY HER THAT NIGHT?

EXCUSE ME?

HOW MUCH DID YOU PAY BONNIE FOR BABY-SITTING THAT NIGHT?

WHY?

IT'S JUST A DETAIL WE NEVER GOT STRAIGHT, THAT'S ALL.

SHE DIDN'T APPEAR TO HAVE BEEN ROBBED, BUT WE DIDN'T FIND ANY MONEY ON HER, SO...

WELL, I CAN'T THINK OFF THE TOP OF MY--

BEEP BEEP

ALARM

WEIRD MESSAGE FOR A BEEPER...

YES, IT MUST BE A MISTAKE... I GET PAGED A LOT BY ACCIDENT.

SHOULD LOOK INTO THAT.

HEY, MARCUS... YOU TAKE A QUICK CALL?

SURE...

113

HEY MARCUS, GOOD CALL ON THE YUPPIE SCUM...

IT WAS THERE?

YEAH, SOME KIND OF SECRET PANEL IN THE BACK OF HIS CLOSET. ALMOST MISSED IT.

FIND ANYTHING CONCLUSIVE YET?

GOT RESIDUE ON ONE OF HIS ANTIGRAV TANKS.

C.S.U.'S DOING A P.C.R. AS WE SPEAK.

--YOUR WIFE SAID YOU BOTH WALKED HER DOWN TO THE DOOR?

BUT WOULDN'T ONE OF YOU STAY WITH YOUR SON?

HE'S NOT AN INFANT.

OH, I'M SURE, IT'S JUST--

SORRY ABOUT THAT. EVERYTHING SEEMS TO BE WRAPPING UP, I GUESS.

WHAT DO YOU MEAN?

WELL, I HAD MOST OF IT FIGURED OUT, SIR...

I JUST DIDN'T KNOW HOW YOU KNEW BONNIE'D BEEN SNOOPING AROUND IN YOUR CLOSET.

WHAT ARE YOU TALKING ABOUT?

114

IT SEEMS BONNIE LIKED TO DIG THROUGH 'ER CUSTOMER'S STUFF. A REAL NOSEY LITTLE KID.

BUT YOU KNOW THAT, DON'T YOU? 'CAUSE SHE DISCOVERED YOUR SECRET.

I DON'T KNOW WHAT YOU'RE TALKING ABOUT, AND I WANT TO LEAVE NOW.

THAT BEEPER MESSAGE OF YOURS THAT JUST WENT OFF? THAT WAS BECAUSE ONE OF OUR DETECTIVES JUST POPPED THE SECRET DOOR OUT OF YOUR CLOSET, TOO.

SET OFF A SILENT ALARM WHICH GOES RIGHT TO YOUR PAGER.

SMART PLAN, REALLY.

IT'S SORT OF PATHETIC, THOUGH, TOO, ISN'T IT?

THE PEOPLE WHO DIED SO YOU COULD PROTECT YOUR SECRET IDENTITY?

I MEAN WE'VE GOT BONNIE LEWIS, WHOSE HEAD YOU BASHED IN WITH ONE OF YOUR ANTI-GRAV TANKS-- ACCORDING TO C.S.U. AT LEAST...

...AND THEN THERE'S MY PARTNER CHARLIE FIELDS, WHO DIED FOLLOWING UP A LEAD ON YOUR BOGUS KIDNAPPING.

THAT-- THAT WASN'T MY FAULT.

I DIDN'T... NO--

YOU TRICKED ME!

YOU DIDN'T READ ME MY RIGHTS! AND YOU TRICKED ME!

SCREW YOUR RIGHTS.

WE'VE GOT YOUR WIFE TALKIN' A MILE A MINUTE, RIGHT NOW. WE'VE GOT THE FIREBUG SUIT, AND WE'VE GOT BONNIE'S BLOOD ON YOUR TANK.

YOU CAN'T—YOU—

I CAN'T TELL YOU HOW MUCH I WAS HOPING YOU'D TRY THAT...

"I MUST SAY... THE NIGHT HAS BEEN KIND TO US, DETECTIVES...

"... THIS WAS DAMN FINE WORK FOR ALL OF YOU.

PROBSON
ATTON FIELDS DRIVER
ALONZO
DENNS
LUCA
MUR

016 LEWIS
009 LEVITZ
023 CARLIN
167 KAHN
178 LUTES
222 JOHNS

WA
SCH
IDEL
CAST
BON
BEN
DEN
STE

"THE COMMISSIONER'LL BE VERY PLEASED."

I'M OKAY WITH PLEASED, BUT I'LL BE HAPPIER IF THERE'S A BONUS, TOO.

DON'T GET YOUR HOPES UP, SERGEANT...

BUT I WILL SIGN OFF ON YOU ALL TAKING AN EARLY NIGHT TO CELEBRATE...

I GUESS THAT'LL HAVE TO DO... TINO'S, EVERYONE?

SOUNDS GOOD TO ME, WHERE'D DRIVER DISAPPEAR TO...?

"...IT'S HIS BIG NIGHT."

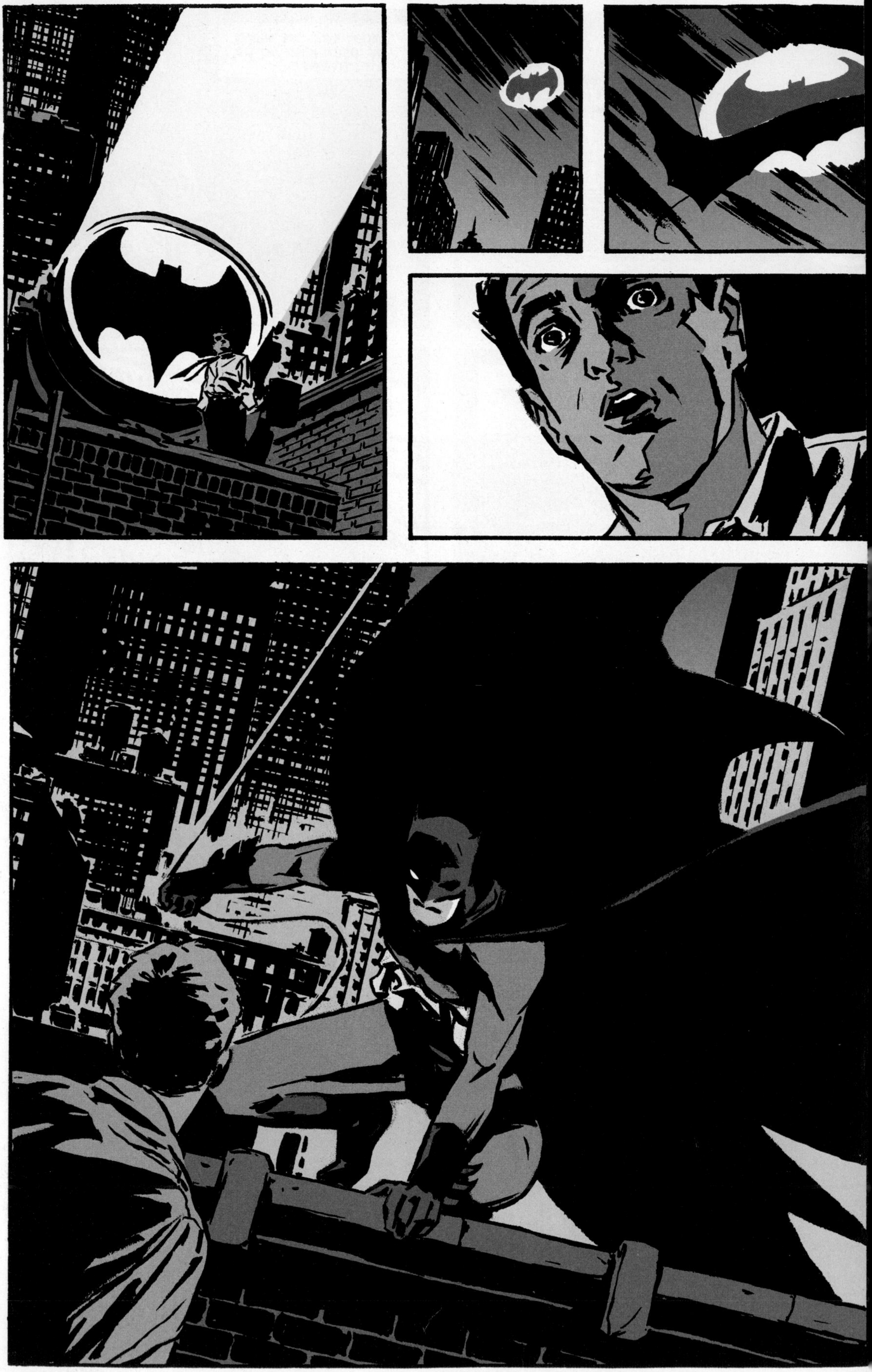

'ETECTIVE
DRIVER?

WHAT IS IT?

I JUST WANT YOU TO KNOW THAT *WE* TOOK DOWN THAT *FIREBUG* FREAK TONIGHT.

AND WE DID IT *ALONE*, WITHOUT YOUR HELP.

GOOD.

THANK YOU.

THAT'S *ALL* YOU'VE GOT TO SAY? A GOOD COP *DIED* BECAUSE OF THESE FREAKIN' NUTJOBS THAT JUST CRAWL OUT OF THE WOODWORK IN THIS GODFORSAKEN TOWN...

...AND THAT'S ALL YOU'VE GOT TO SAY?

NO, IT'S *NOT*...

DON'T USE THAT SIGNAL AGAIN UNLESS IT'S AN EMERGENCY.

I'M SORRY ABOUT DETECTIVE FIELDS, BUT I'VE GOT *WORK* TO DO.

KLIK

ARE YOU INSANE...?

119

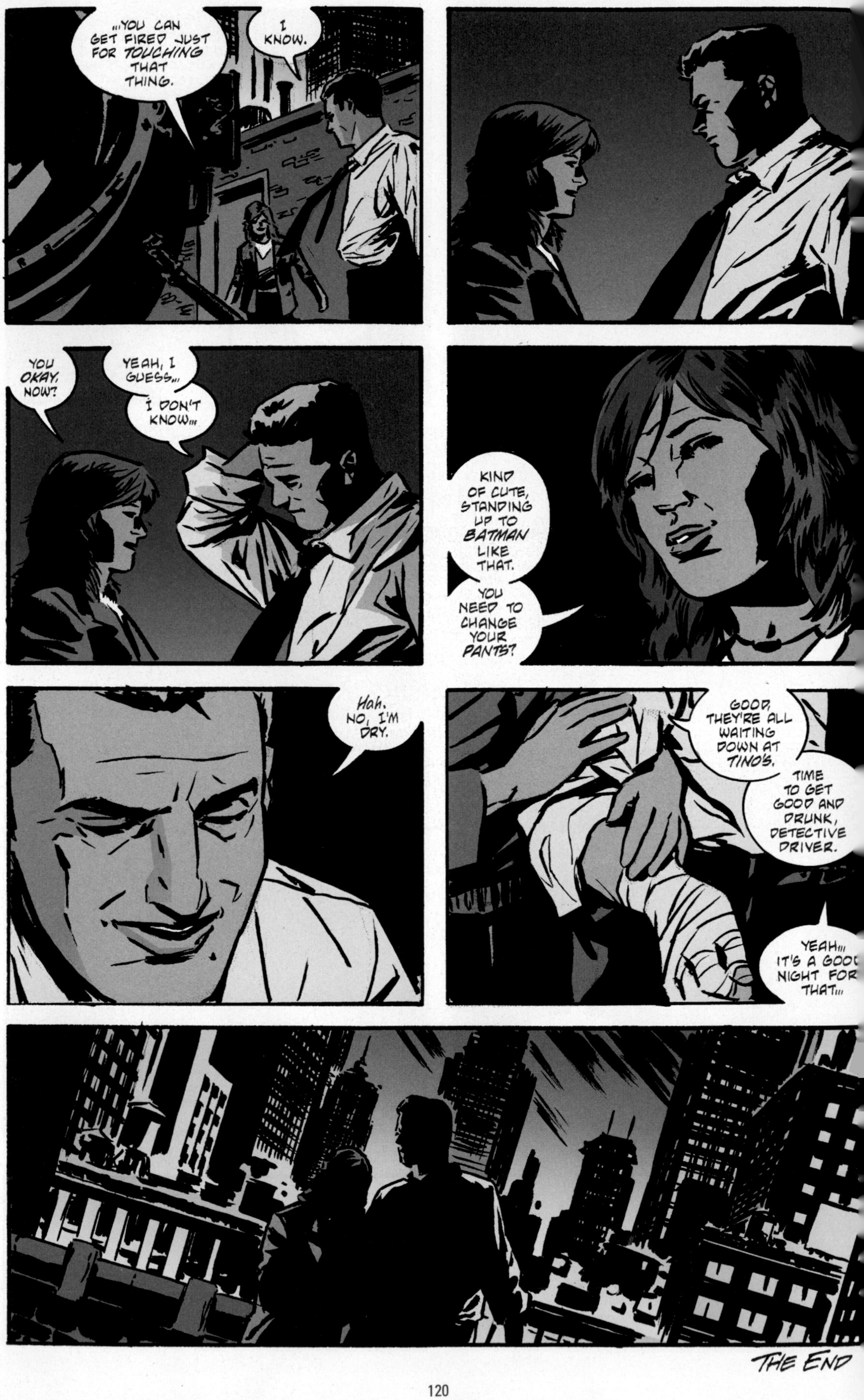
...YOU CAN GET FIRED JUST FOR TOUCHING THAT THING.
I KNOW.
YOU OKAY, NOW?
YEAH, I GUESS...
I DON'T KNOW...
KIND OF CUTE, STANDING UP TO BATMAN LIKE THAT.
YOU NEED TO CHANGE YOUR PANTS?
Hah. NO, I'M DRY.
GOOD, THEY'RE ALL WAITING DOWN AT TINO'S.
TIME TO GET GOOD AND DRUNK, DETECTIVE DRIVER.
YEAH... IT'S A GOO NIGHT FOR THAT...
THE END

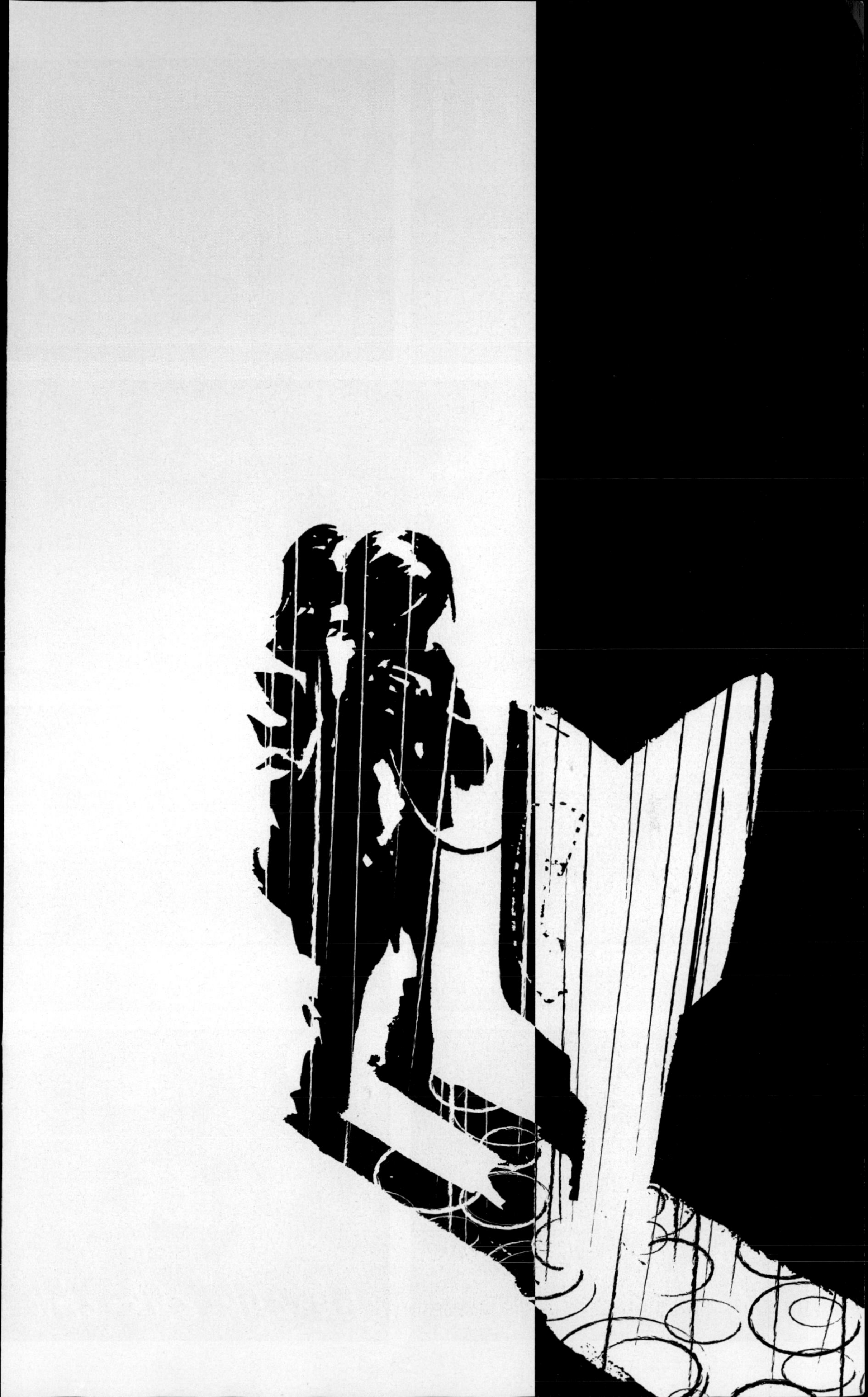

YEAH, *THAT'S* IT...

..."*THAT'S* WHAT WE'RE LOOKING FOR..."

chk-chk chk-chk

‹MORNING, RENEE!›

‹MORNING, MISTER HERRERA.›

‹YOU HAVE A GOOD DAY...›

‹YOU, TOO, RENEE.›

‹HEEL, LEO!›

RENEE MONTOYA?

WHO'S ASKING?

DETECTIVE SECOND GRADE RENEE MONTOYA?

YES, NOW WHO'S ASKING?

RENEE MONTOYA...

...YOU HAVE BEEN SERVED.

HAVE A NICE DAY.

Half a Life
Part One

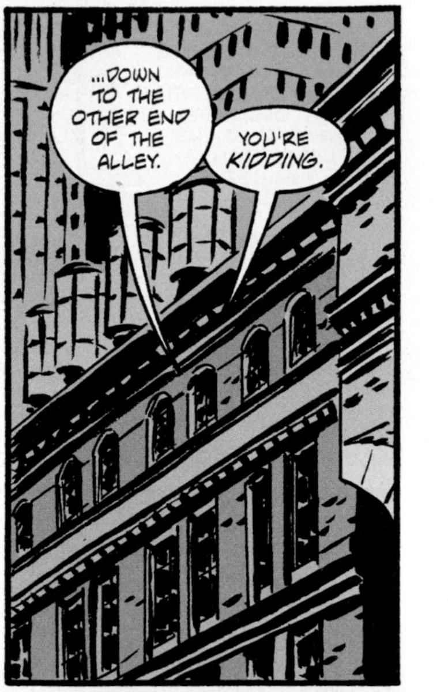
...DOWN TO THE OTHER END OF THE ALLEY.
YOU'RE KIDDING.

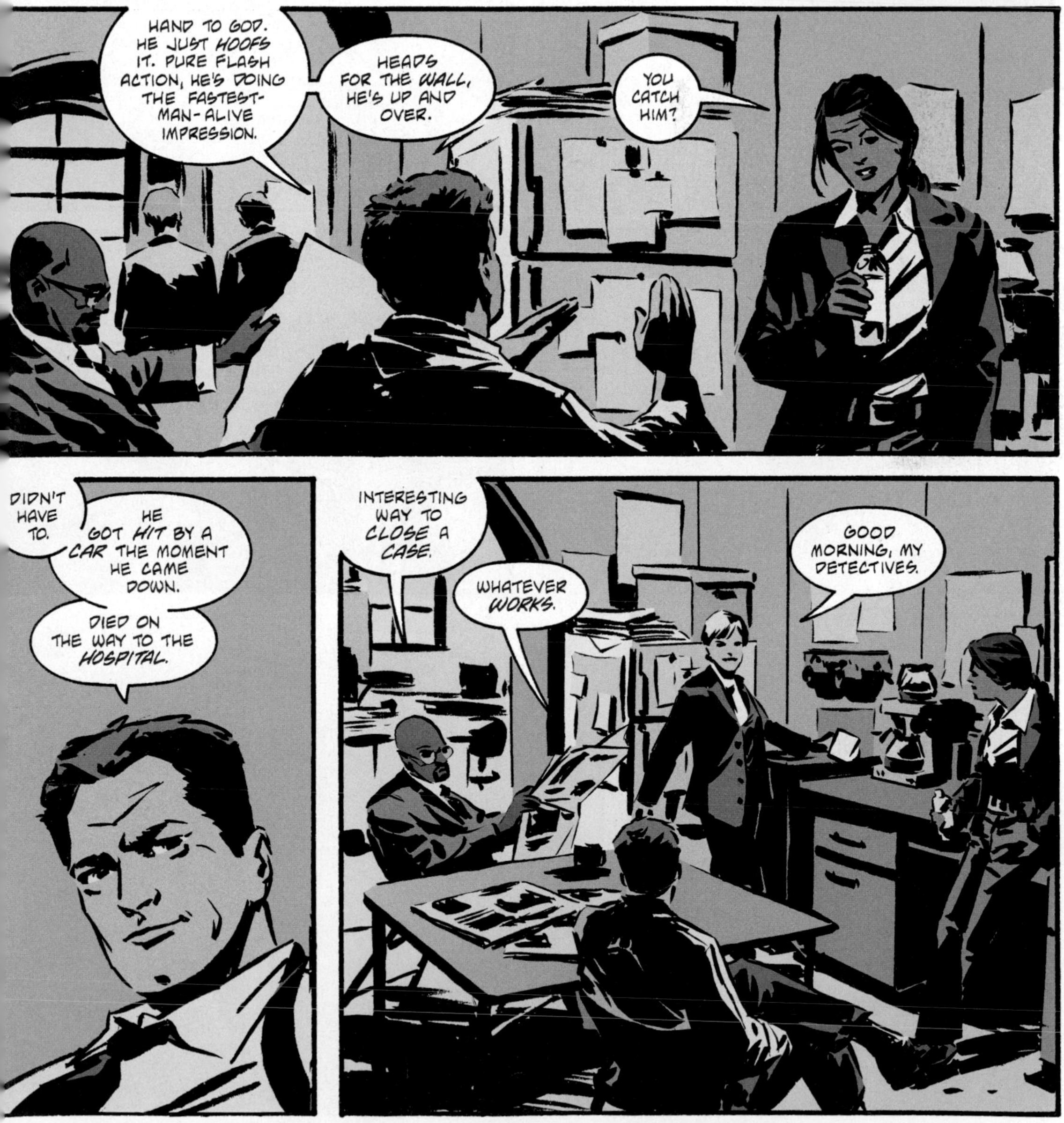
HAND TO GOD. HE JUST HOOFS IT. PURE FLASH ACTION, HE'S DOING THE FASTEST-MAN-ALIVE IMPRESSION.
HEADS FOR THE WALL, HE'S UP AND OVER.
YOU CATCH HIM?
DIDN'T HAVE TO.
HE GOT HIT BY A CAR THE MOMENT HE CAME DOWN.
DIED ON THE WAY TO THE HOSPITAL.
INTERESTING WAY TO CLOSE A CASE.
WHATEVER WORKS.
GOOD MORNING, MY DETECTIVES.

AND TO *YOU,* DETECTIVE DRIVER, WHO IS *NOT* ONE OF *MY* DETECTIVES, BUT BELONGS INSTEAD TO THE LIEUTENANT CALLED PROBSON.

GONNA BE A *BEAUTIFUL* DAY, TODAY.

A *BEAUTIFUL* DAY.

SOME-BODY HAD A GOOD NIGHT.

TOBY'S UP FROM METROPOLIS FOR THE WEEK.

THAT WOULD *EXPLAIN* IT.

RIGHT. I'M *OUTTA* HERE...

...MY *SHIFT* ENDED AN *HOUR* AGO. YOU KIDS STAY *SAFE.*

THANKS. WHATEVER.

WHAT'S YOUR PROBLEM WITH DRIVER?

HE *ANNOYS* ME.

WE *ALL* ANNOY YOU.

THIS IS *TRUE.*

126

I GOT *SERVED* WHILE JOGGING THIS *MORNING.*

TOLD YOU *EXERCISE* WAS *BAD* FOR YOU.

MARTY *LIPARI* IS *SUING* ME FOR *DAMAGES* TO THE TUNE OF *TEN MILLION DOLLARS.*

THAT LITTLE PUNK *WALKED* ON THE *EASLEY* RAPE, NOW HE'S *SUING* YOU?

HE *FORGET* THE PART WHERE HE TRIED TO STICK A *KNIFE* IN YOU--

EXCUSE ME--

--I'M *TALKING* HERE-- WHEN WE MADE THE *ARREST?* SOMEBODY NEEDS TO PUT A *BULLET* IN THAT GUY.

I SAID *EXCUSE* ME.

GOD, LOWE, *NOT AGAIN.*

I'M HERE TO TALK TO DETECTIVE ALLEN, *NOT* YOU, *MONTOYA.*

WE'VE BEEN WORKING THIS *CASE* DOWNSTAIRS IN *ROBBERY,* DETECTIVE, AND IT TURNS OUT--

NO YOU *DON'T,* LIKE HELL YOU *DON'T!*

IT'S A BURGLARY--

I KNOW WHAT IT IS! IT'S SOME THEFT THAT YOU CAN'T CLOSE, THAT'S WHAT IT IS!

SOME JUNK CASE YOU'VE HAD OPEN FOR SIX MONTHS, AND NOW SUDDENLY THIS INFORMANT'S COME FORWARD! AND HE'S SWEARING UP AND DOWN, "HEY! IT'S CATWOMAN DONE THE CRIME," RIGHT?

AM I RIGHT, OFFICER LOWE?

YOU AND YOUR BOUGHT-AND-PAID-FOR BUDDIES DOWN IN ROBBERY CAN'T BE BOTHERED TO DO YOUR JOBS?

NOW YOU'RE TRYING TO STICK ME -- A TRUE POLICE-- WITH SOME MADE UP KITTY-CAT CASE?

AM I RIGHT?

ON THE NOSE, JACKASS!

YOU SON OF A--

CRISPUS, NO!

C'MON, LET'S SEE WHAT YOU'VE GOT, YOU ARROGANT SNOT!

CALM DOWN!

M.C.U. SNOBS, ALL OF YOU. THINKING YOU'RE SO MUCH MORE THAN THE REST OF THIS DEPARTMENT.

ALL RIGHT, THAT'S ENOUGH.

HIDING UP HERE, HIDING BEHIND THE *BAT!*

YOU GUYS MAKE ME *PUKE!*

GET OUT.

CAPTAIN, I--

THIS IS THE *THIRD DEAD CASE* YOU'VE DROPPED ON *MY* DETECTIVES THIS *MONTH,* OFFICER LOWE...

IT'S A A *FREAK,* IT'S A *MAJOR--*

ARE YOU *PRESUMING* TO TELL ME HOW TO RUN MY *UNIT,* OFFICER?

OR IS THERE SOMETHING *ELSE* YOU WANT TO *SAY?*

NO, MA'AM, CAPTAIN.

THEN WHY ARE YOU *STILL* IN MY *SQUAD ROOM?*

THERE ARE *CASES* IN *RED,* BOYS AND GIRLS.

THEY WON'T TURN TO *BLACK* WITH YOU ALL STANDING AROUND.

YOU ALL RIGHT, PARTNER?

JUST *BACK OFF,* RENEE.

I'LL *TAKE IT,* CRIS.

HELL WITH *THAT.* IT'S *MINE.*

I'M GONNA *CLOSE* IT.

JUST FOR THE *SATISFACTION* OF WIPING THAT *SMIRK* OFF LOWE'S *FACE.*

...BUT THAT WAS *MONTHS* AGO!

WHERE DID YOU SAY YOU WERE FROM?

MAJOR CRIMES.

BUT IT'S A *ROBBERY.*

WE'RE INVESTIGATING IT NOW, MISS LAVELLE.

CAN YOU TELL ME WHAT WAS STOLEN?

AGAIN, YOU MEAN? FINE. THERE WERE *ELEVEN* PIECES.

SIX *NIGHT-GOWNS*, ITALIAN *SILK*...

...THREE SETS OF IMPORTED *GERMAN* UNDERGARMENTS, TWO *CORSETS* WITH BONE STAYS, THOSE WERE FROM ENGLAND...

...AND A *ONE-OF-A-KIND MERRY WIDOW*, IT WAS *HANDMADE.*

ABOUT HOW MUCH IS ALL OF THIS WORTH?

A LITTLE *OVER* TEN THOUSAND *DOLLARS.*

FOR UNDER-WEAR?

WHAT DO YOU *DO* WITH IT? HANG IT ON THE *WALL*?

NOT UNDERWEAR, DETECTIVE. *LINGERIE.*

HOW MANY PEOPLE WORK HERE WITH YOU, MISS LAVELLE?

JUST MYSELF AND MY PARTNER, CORY MARRA.

CAN WE TALK TO HER?

SHE'S IN SWITZERLAND RIGHT NOW, ON A *BUYING* TRIP, BUT IF YOU LIKE I CAN HAVE HER *CALL* AS SOON AS SHE'S BACK.

IF YOU COULD.

ANYONE *ELSE?* ANYONE YOU LET *GO?*

NO, IT'S ALWAYS BEEN JUST THE *TWO* OF US. CORY'S *BROTHER,* PAUL HELPED OUT WHEN WE *OPENED,* BUT THAT'S IT.

PAUL MARRA?

THAT'S RIGHT.

WHEN'D YOU OPEN, MISS LAVELLE?

ABOUT A MONTH BEFORE THE ROBBERY. FOUR, FIVE MONTHS AGO.

ALL RIGHT, THANKS...

...HERE'S MY *CARD.* IF CORY CAN *CALL* US WHEN SHE GETS BACK?

I WILL. THANKS FOR YOUR TIME.

NOTHING ON CORY MARRA...

...BUT HER BROTHER PAUL MARRA WAS POPPED DOWN IN TRICORNER LAST YEAR DURING A SWEEP.

PICKED HIM UP TRYING TO SOLICIT A PROSTITUTE.

THANKS, STACY.

NO PROB.

ANYTHING?

PAUL MARRA WAS PICKED UP LAST YEAR TRYING TO GET SOME.

LET'S GO TALK TO HIM.

WE COULD ASK HIM TO COME HERE.

PUT THE FEAR OF GOD IN HIM.

YOU THINK HE'LL VOLUNTEER TO COME ON OVER?

I THINK I CAN PERSUADE HIM.

CAN I HELP YOU?

YES, I THINK, I MEAN, I HOPE SO...

...I'M LOOKING FOR DETECTIVE MONTOYA. NO, WAIT, WHAT I MEAN IS THAT DETECTIVE MONTOYA ASKED ME TO STOP BY.

Uh-huh.

MY NAME'S PAUL MARRA, SHE CALLED ME--

RIGHT, WELL IF YOU'LL--

MISTER MARRA? I'M RENEE MONTOYA...

...THANKS SO MUCH FOR COMING DOWN ON SUCH SHORT NOTICE.

THANKS, STACY, I'VE GOT IT.

MISTER MARRA--CAN I CALL YOU PAUL?

Uh, SURE, YOU--

LISTEN, PAUL, WHY DON'T WE TALK IN HERE...

...WHERE WE CAN HAVE SOME PRIVACY.

UM... BUT WHERE ARE YOU GOING?

JUST MAKE YOURSELF COMFORTABLE, I'LL BE RIGHT WITH YOU.

HE'S A JUNKIE.

OH, YEAH?

PUT MONEY ON IT.

SO MAYBE THAT *ARREST* FOR *SOLICITING*...

YEAH. PUSHERS AND HOOKERS *DO* TEND TO *SHARE* THE SAME *CORNERS*.

CAN YOU *FINISH* HIM OFF? I'VE GOT A *DINNER* DATE.

WHAT WAS *THAT*? DID YOU SAY *DATE*?

WHO'S THE *LUCKY* GUY?

YOUR *DEDUCTION* IS *FLAWED*, DETECTIVE...

...IT'S WITH MY *PARENTS*.

I WILL *HAPPILY* BLOW IT OFF IF YOU WANT ME TO STICK AROUND.

Nah. GO AHEAD.

I'LL HAVE THIS GUY WRITING UP HIS *CONFESSION* IN FIVE MINUTES.

PAUL! NO, DON'T GET UP, MY NAME'S *DETECTIVE* ALLEN.

RENEE HAD TO RUN DOWN TO THE *LAB* TO CHECK ON SOME *FINGER-PRINTS*.

SO, PAUL-- YOU DON'T *MIND* IF I CALL YOU PAUL, *huh*?--SO, PAUL, HOW LONG YOU BEEN A *JUNKIE*...?

<REALLY, MOM, I'M *FULL*. IT WAS *DELICIOUS*, BUT I'VE HAD ENOUGH.>

<RENEE! YOU *BARELY* ATE!>

<LEAVE HER BE, LOUISA.>

<SHE'S WATCHING HER *WEIGHT*, WE SHOULDN'T *TEMPT* HER.>

<IS THAT WHAT YOU'RE DOING, RENEE? TRYING TO *CATCH* SOMEONE'S *EYE*?>

<NO, MOM, I'M *FULL*, THAT'S ALL.>

<PITY.>

<HERNANDO, *STOP* IT.>

<HE HAS *VISIONS* OF *GRANDCHILDREN* DANCING IN HIS HEAD.>

<AND YOU *DON'T*?>

<ISN'T *BENNY* SEEING SOME- ONE?>

<YOUR *BROTHER* IS SEEING SEVERAL YOUNG LADIES, FROM WHAT WE *UNDER- STAND*.>

<I WANTED HIM TO TALK TO FATHER RAMON, BUT OF COURSE, HE *REFUSED*.>

<HE'S A *BOY*. AND HE'S *YOUNG*, HE'LL *SETTLE DOWN* SOON ENOUGH.>

<BUT *YOU*, RENEE, YOU'RE *NOT* GETTING ANY *YOUNGER*.>

<YOU'LL BE AN *OLD MAID* AT THIS RATE...>

HELL
WITH
IT...

HEY,
IT'S
ME...

...NO, I
KNOW IT'S
BEEN A
WHILE...

...YEAH
WELL NOT
THAT GOOD,
ACTUALLY...

...I WAS
KINDA HOPING
I COULD COME
OVER...

RENEE.

AHHH!!!

YOU MAKE IT A *HABIT* TO SNEAK UP ON PEOPLE, INSPECTOR ESPERANZA? OR IS THAT JUST *SOMETHING* YOU PICK UP IN INTERNAL AFFAIRS?

YEAH, WE LEARN IT THE FIRST WEEK ON THE *JOB.*

THIS IS MY *PARTNER,* MATT CONWAY.

MAYBE WE CAN TALK INSIDE?

I DON'T HAVE A LOT OF *TIME*. I'M SUPPOSED TO BE IN AT *EIGHT*.

WE'LL MAKE IT *QUICK*.

LONG NIGHT?

LONG ENOUGH.

MIND TELLING US WHERE YOU *WERE*?

MIND TELLING ME *WHY* IT MATTERS?

TAKE IT *EASY*, RENEE...

...WE'RE ALL *FRIENDS*.

SURE, YOU I.A.D. GUYS ARE EVERYONE'S *PAL*.

I'M SURE *HARVEY BULLOCK* THOUGHT SO--

--THE DAY HE TURNED IN HIS *BADGE*.

BULLOCK WAS *ROTTEN* AS THE DAY IS LONG. HE GOT WHAT WAS *COMING* TO HIM.

WHAT DO YOU *WANT*?

YOU EVER HEAR OF A PRIVATE EYE NAME OF *BRIAN SELKER*?

SHOULD I HAVE?

HE WAS HIRED BY *MARTY LIPARI* TO LOOK INTO YOU.

WE HEAR THAT LIPARI IS *SUING* YOU.

ALSO THAT HE GOT A *WALK* ON THE *EASLEY* RAPE.

SOME- ONE IN EVIDENCE CONTROL *LOST* THE KNIFE.

MUST HAVE MADE YOU PRETTY *ANGRY.* FIRST HE TRIES TO *GUT* YOU WHEN YOU BRING HIM *IN,* THEN HE GOES *FREE.*

IT *HAPPENS.*

BUT *STILL,* YOU AND YOUR PARTNER SPEND ALL THIS *TIME* BUILDING A *CASE,* AND THE LITTLE PUKE *WALKS* BECAUSE SOME- ONE DOWNTOWN TOOK A *BRIBE.*

AND *NOW* HE'S GOT A P.I. *POKING* AROUND IN YOUR *BUSINESS,* AND HE'S AFTER *DAMAGES.*

LIKE I SAID. IT HAPPENS. IT'S *GOTHAM.*

YOU GOING TO TELL ME WHAT THIS IS ABOUT, OR DO WE PLAY *TWENTY* QUESTIONS?

SELKER'S DEAD AND WE CAN'T FIND *LIPARI.*

AND YOU'RE HERE AT SIX IN THE MORNING BECAUSE YOU THINK I *CARE?*

IT'S A *MURDER,* DETECTIVE.

YOU HAD DAMN WELL BETTER *CARE.*

140

SELKER'S *BODY* WAS DISCOVERED AT HIS *OFFICE*.

HE HAD A COPY OF HIS *CONTRACT* WITH *LIPARI* ON FILE DOCUMENTING THAT HE WAS INVESTIGATING YOU.

...BUT *NONE* OF THE RESULTS OF THE *INVESTIGATION*.

WHAT DOES THAT *MEAN*?

IT MEANS *NOTHING* WAS THERE, DETECTIVE. NO *NOTES*, NO *REPORTS*, NO ITEMIZED BILLS FOR *EXPENSES*, NADA.

WHICH LEADS US TO CONCLUDE THEY WERE *REMOVED*.

YOU THINK *LIPARI* DID IT?

THAT'S WHAT IT LOOKS LIKE.

AND THAT'S WHY WE'RE *HERE*, RENEE.

IT LOOKS LIKE LIPARI'S GOT A REAL *JONES* ON FOR YOU, DETECTIVE.

ONE HE MAYBE WANTS TO *FEED* WITH *VIOLENCE*.

FOR THE LOVE OF... *ANOTHER* WOMAN IN JEOPARDY STORY.

WE'RE JUST SAYING TO BE *EXTRA* CAREFUL.

NO MORE STAYING OUT *ALL* NIGHT.

WE FIND OUT ANYTHING *MORE* WE'LL BE IN TOUCH.

HAVE A *GOOD* DAY, RENEE.

YOU OWE ME MONEY, *PARTNER...*

...PAY UP!

THERE WAS NO *ACTUAL* BET, CRIS!

THERE SHOULD HAVE BEEN! *THREE* MINUTES, MARRA WAS BAWLING LIKE A *BABY*.

HE *STOLE* THE CLOTHES FOR RESALE TO SUPPORT HIS *HABIT*.

HIS *SISTER* KNEW?

HE CLAIMS SHE DIDN'T. NOT THAT IT MATTERS.

HEY, ALLEN. YOU'VE GOT A VERY PHOTOGENIC PARTNER, YOU KNOW THAT?

SHUT UP, NATE.

NO, WAIT. I'VE GOT TO *KNOW*, MONTOYA...

...IS THIS *JUST* AN *EXPERIMENTAL* PHASE OR ARE YOU THE *REAL* THING?

WHERE'D IT COME FROM?

SOMEONE ON *SECOND SHIFT* PUT IT UP. THEY SAY IT CAME BY *MESSENGER*--

--LAST NIGHT...

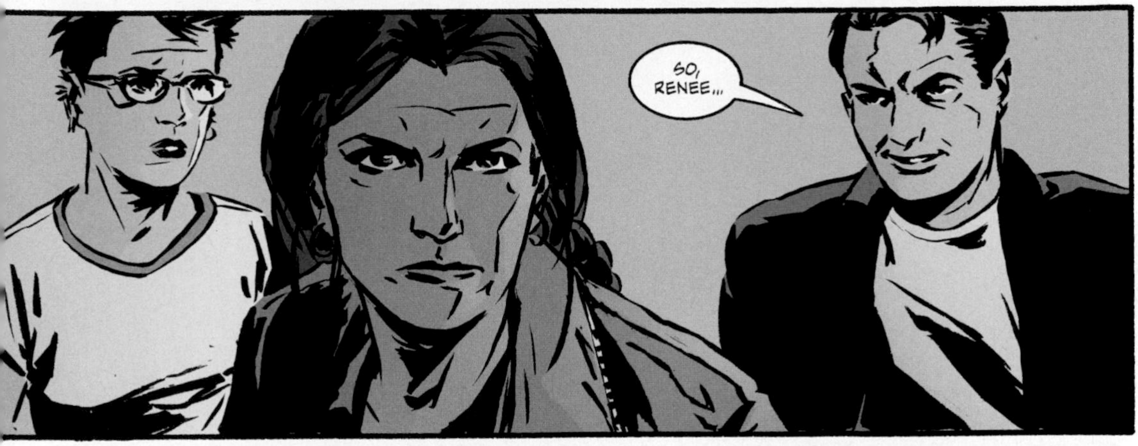
SO, RENEE...

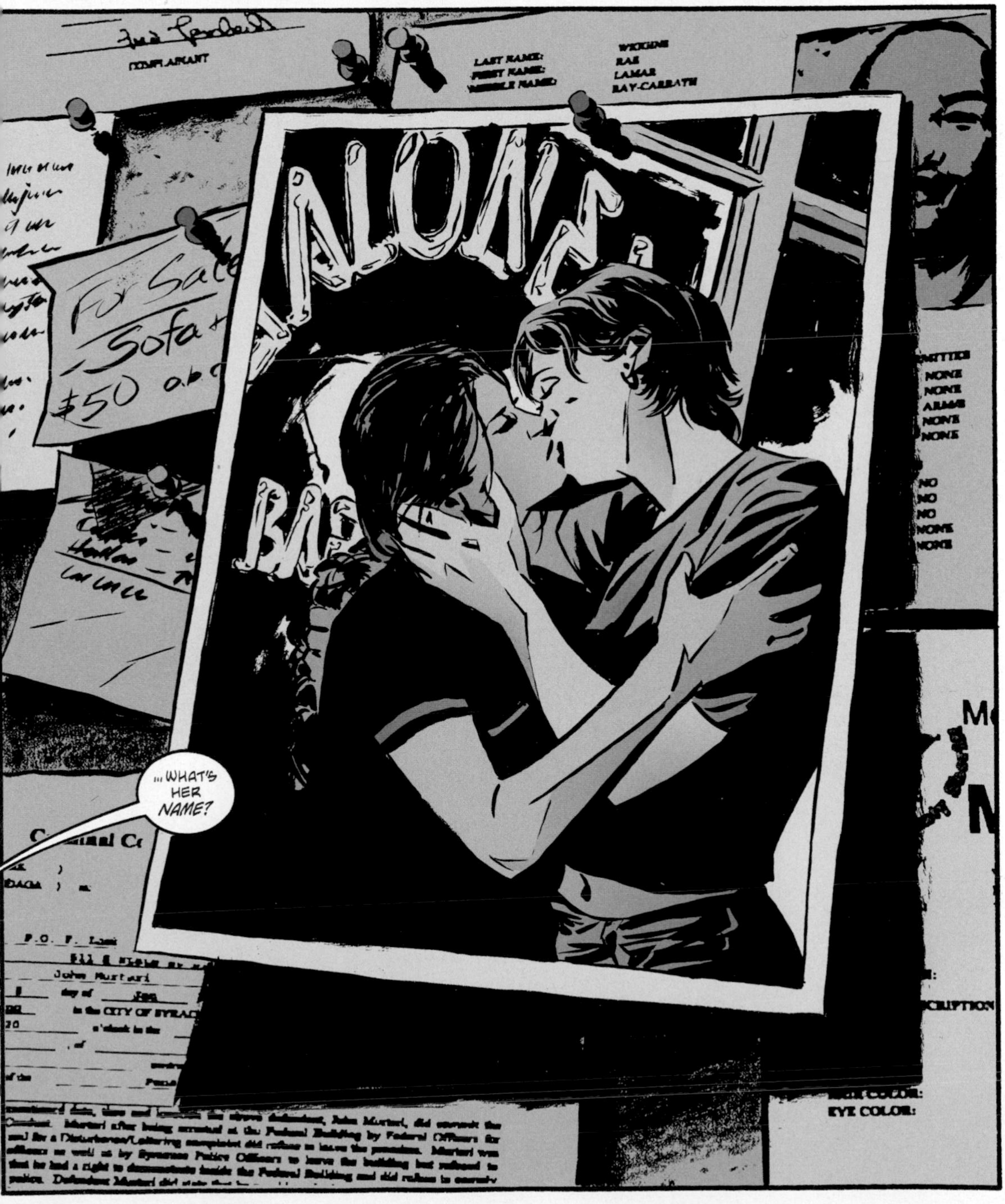
...WHAT'S HER NAME?

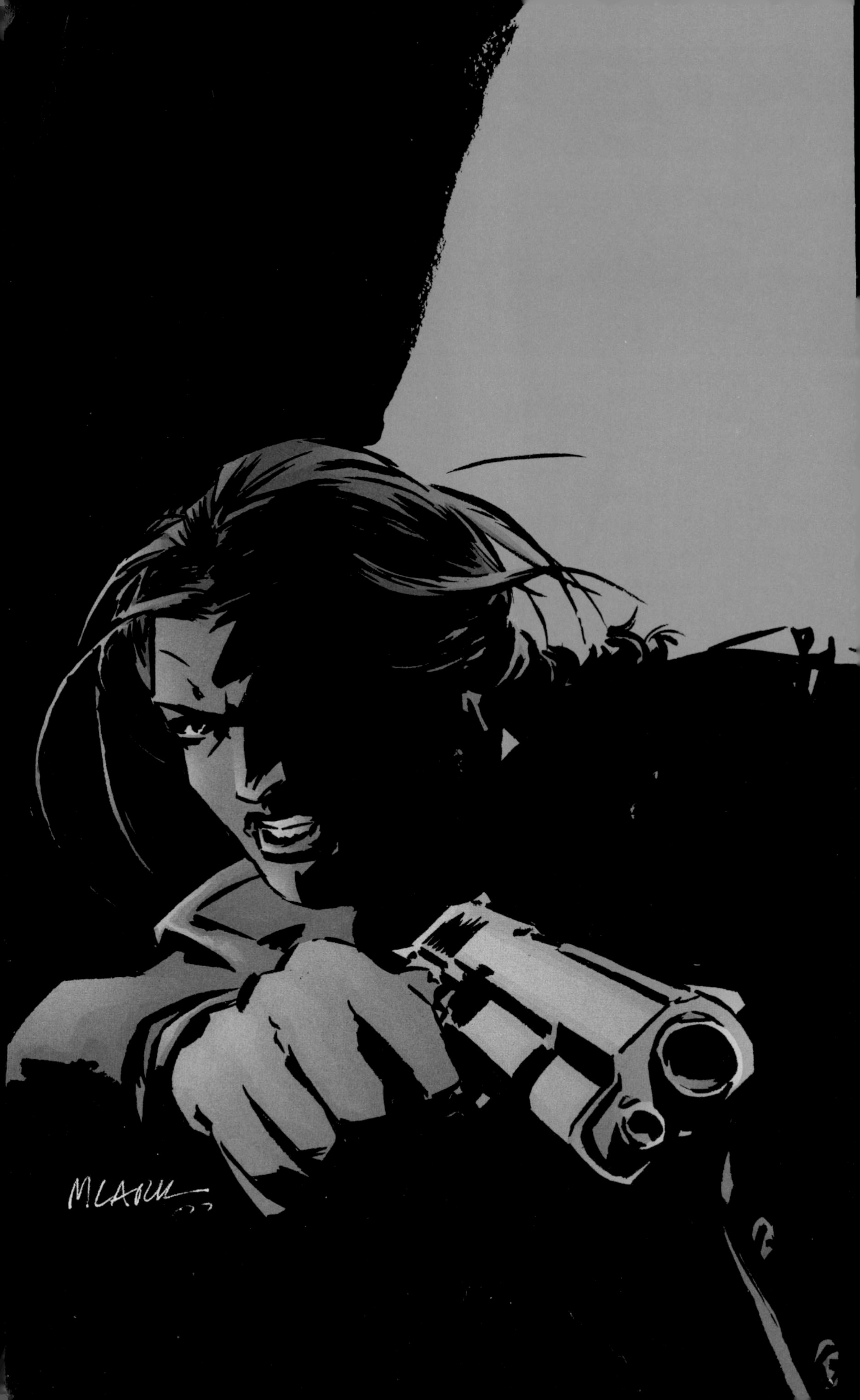

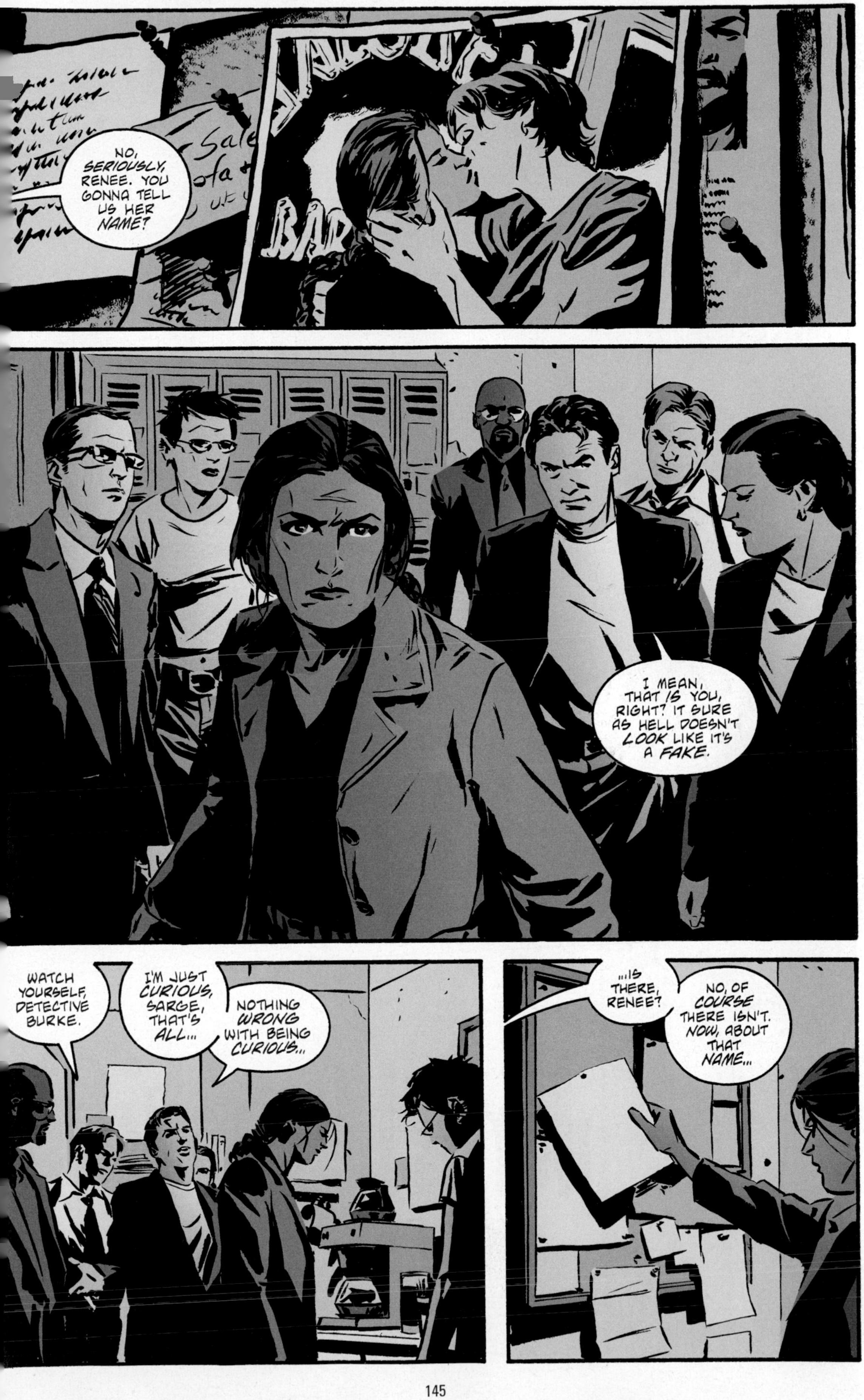
NO, SERIOUSLY, RENEE. YOU GONNA TELL US HER NAME?
I MEAN, THAT IS YOU, RIGHT? IT SURE AS HELL DOESN'T LOOK LIKE IT'S A FAKE.
WATCH YOURSELF, DETECTIVE BURKE.
I'M JUST CURIOUS, SARGE, THAT'S ALL...
NOTHING WRONG WITH BEING CURIOUS...
...IS THERE, RENEE?
NO, OF COURSE THERE ISN'T. NOW, ABOUT THAT NAME...

"... I'M THINKING SOMETHING LIKE *MAX* OR *SAM*, ALONG *THOSE* LINES, OR IS THAT *TOO* BUTCH?"

TOMMY, PUT A *SOCK* IN IT.

MAYBE SOMETHING MORE *FEMME?* OH, I *KNOW,* I'VE GOT IT--

DARIA.

DARIA. *Huh.*

half a life
Part Two

WHAT FILE IS THAT?

CRIS? WHAT *FILE* IS THAT?

LIPARI'S.

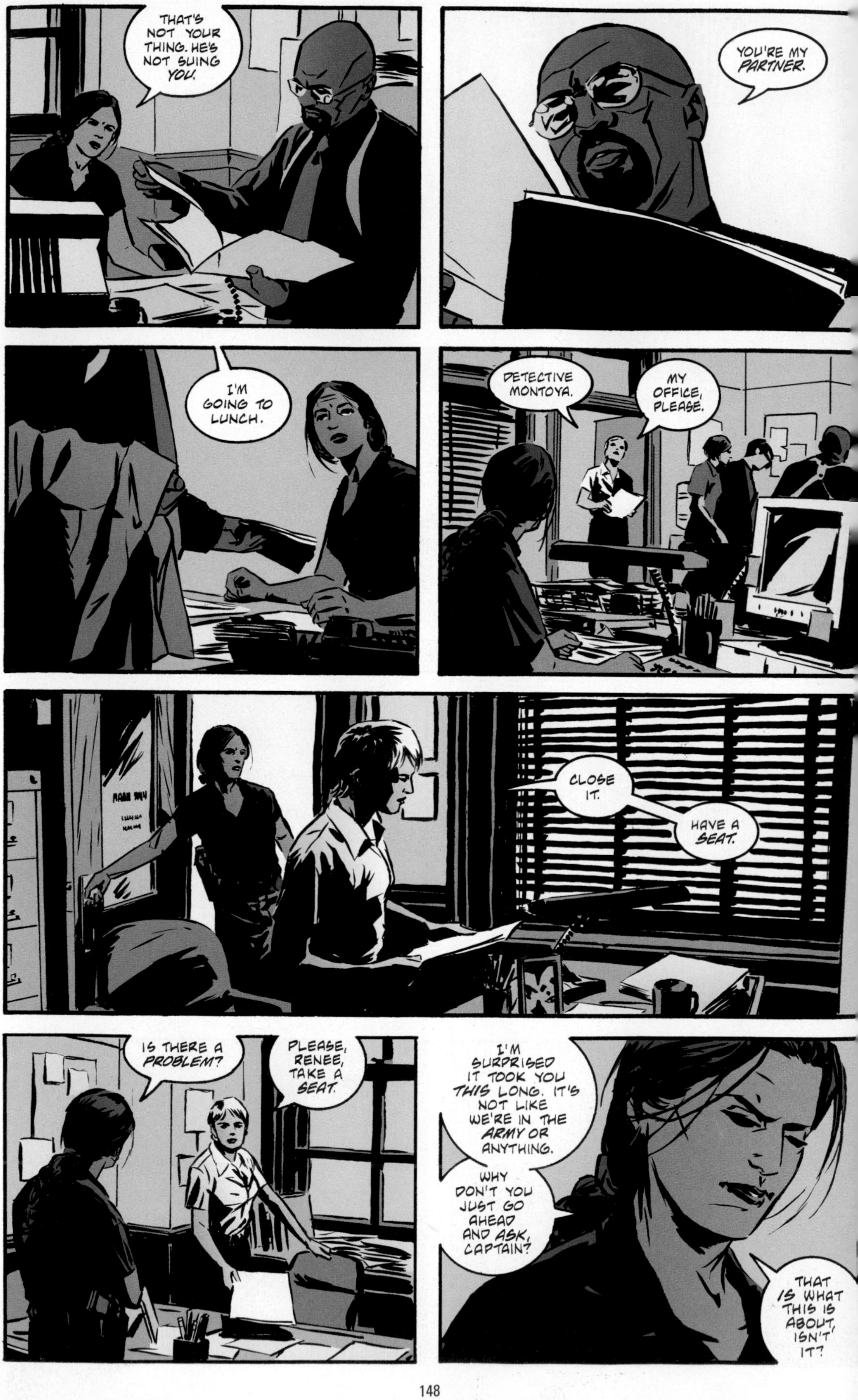
THAT'S NOT YOUR THING. HE'S NOT SUING *YOU*.
YOU'RE MY *PARTNER*.
I'M GOING TO LUNCH.
DETECTIVE MONTOYA.
MY OFFICE, PLEASE.
CLOSE IT.
HAVE A *SEAT*.
IS THERE A *PROBLEM*?
PLEASE, RENEE, TAKE A *SEAT*.
I'M SURPRISED IT TOOK YOU *THIS* LONG. IT'S NOT LIKE WE'RE IN THE *ARMY* OR ANYTHING.
WHY DON'T YOU JUST GO AHEAD AND *ASK*, CAPTAIN?
THAT *IS* WHAT THIS IS ABOUT, ISN'T IT?

I GOT A CALL FROM AN ESPERANZA IN I.A.D. THIS MORNING.

YOU KNOW THIS GUY?

HE'S THE ONE WHO NAILED BULLOCK.

HE'S STAND-UP, AS FAR AS THAT GOES.

ESPERANZA SAYS HE AND HIS PARTNER TALKED TO YOU THIS MORNING ABOUT THE MURDER OF A P.I. NAMED SELKER.

THAT'S RIGHT, YEAH. PARTNER'S NAME IS CONWAY.

WHY IS I.A.D. TALKING TO YOU ABOUT SELKER'S MURDER?

THEY TOLD ME IT LOOKED LIKE MARTY LIPARI HIRED SELKER TO LOOK INTO ME, THAT MAYBE LIPARI KILLED SELKER.

THEY WERE TELLING ME TO BE CAREFUL, THAT LIPARI MIGHT COME AFTER ME. HE MIGHT BE VIOLENT.

LIPARI RAPES ELEANOR EAGELY, TRIES TO STAB ME WHEN CRIS AND I COLLAR HIM, AND I.A.D. THINKS HE MIGHT BE VIOLENT.

I TOLD THEM THANKS FOR THE WARNING.

THAT WASH WITH YOU? I.A.D. LOOKING INTO SELKER'S MURDER, THEY COME TO WARN YOU ABOUT LIPARI?

THAT DOESN'T WASH WITH ME, YOU SEE WHAT I'M SAYING?

YOU THINK I.A.D.'S LOOKING AT ME?

I'D NEVER EVEN HEARD OF SELKER UNTIL THIS MORNING.

THAT PICTURE ON THE BULLETIN BOARD WAS TAKEN BY SOMEONE.

COULD SELKER HAVE SNAPPED IT WHILE HE WAS FOLLOWING YOU?

I DON'T HAVE TO ANSWER THAT.

YOU ONLY GET TO DO THIS *ONCE*, DETECTIVE.

TRUST ME, YOU WANT TO GET IT *RIGHT*.

I DON'T THINK I *ASKED* FOR YOUR *ADVICE*, CAPTAIN.

MAYBE YOU WANT TO *RETHINK* THAT.

I'VE BEEN WHERE YOU ARE, RENEE, I'VE BEEN THERE AND IT'S NO FUN, AND IT'S *WORSE* WHEN YOU'RE IN IT *ALONE*.

YOU'VE *BEEN* WHERE I AM? ARE YOU *SURE*?

BECAUSE SOMEHOW I *DON'T* THINK YOU *HAVE*. I JUST HAVE A *HARD* TIME PICTURING THAT.

I HAVE A HARD TIME PICTURING YOU AS A *LATINA*, FOR INSTANCE.

I HAVE A HARD TIME PICTURING YOUR PARENTS AS IMMIGRANTS FROM THE *D.R.* WHO GO TO MASS *EVERY* SUNDAY.

AND I DON'T REALLY SEE YOU HAVING TO EXPLAIN *EVERY* TIME YOU SEE THEM WHY THEY *DON'T* HAVE GRAND-CHILDREN YET.

OR WHY IT IS THAT YOU'RE GOING TO *HELL* WHEN YOU *DIE*.

THIS *ISN'T* METROPOLIS, CAPTAIN, AND *NOT* JUST BECAUSE OUR GUY WORKS AT *NIGHT*. THIS *ISN'T* THE CITY OF TOMORROW, IT'S NOT *SAN FRANCISCO*, IT'S NOT *NEW YORK*.

IT'S GOTHAM, AND IF YOU WANT TO SEE WHAT THAT MEANS, JUST CHECK OUT YOUR *SQUAD ROOM*.

SO YOU'LL *FORGIVE* ME IF I ASK YOU TO KEEP YOUR *ADVICE* TO *YOURSELF*.

YOU THROUGH?

YES.

GOOD. THEN I'LL SAY *MY PIECE* AND THAT'LL BE IT.

IT'S A *ONE-WAY DOOR*, DETECTIVE. ONCE THE CLOSET IS OPEN, IT DOESN'T *SHUT AGAIN*.

WHAT YOU DO NEXT, YOU GET TO LIVE WITH IT FOR THE *REST* OF YOUR *LIFE*.

ESPERANZA OR CONWAY TALKS TO YOU AGAIN, I WANT TO KNOW ABOUT IT, AND *NOT BECAUSE THEY* TOLD ME. IS THAT *UNDER-STOOD?*

YES, MA'AM.

GOOD. NOW GET BACK TO WORK.

...HEAR THAT *SAWYER'S* COLLECTING A WHOLE *SET* OF THEM--

--SPEAK OF THE *DEVIL*, IT'S THE *LATEST* ADDITION.

HOW YOU *DOING*, DETECTIVE MONTOYA? HAVE GOOD DAY UP IN THE M.C.U.?

LOWE.

OH, HEY, I DIDN'T MEAN TO *STOP* YOU OR ANYTHING.

YOU'RE *PROBABLY* IN A HURRY TO GET HOME TO YOUR LITTLE *LADY* OR WHATEVER YOU CALL HER, *huh?*

THE *NIGHT TIME* IS THE *RIGHT* TIME FOR *LOVE* AND ALL *THAT*, RIGHT?

THAT'S WHAT YOUR *MOTHER* TELLS ME.

DYKE.

WHO IS IT?

OPEN THE DOOR AND FIND OUT, COPPER.

HEY, BIG
SISTER.

HEY, LITTLE
BROTHER.

THIS *IS*
A SURPRISE.
COME ON
IN.

YOU
ALONE?

YEAH.
I WAS ABOUT
TO MAKE SOME
DINNER IF
YOU WANT
TO *JOIN*
ME?

Ah, NO
THANKS. MOM
AND POP
ALREADY
FED ME.

THEY
HAD ME FOR
DINNER LAST
NIGHT.

YOU MEAN THEY
HAD YOU *OVER* FOR
DINNER LAST
NIGHT.

NO, I
GOT THE
LECTURES,
TOO.

THEY'RE
PARENTS. IT'S
PART OF THEIR
JOB.

I ACTUALLY
WASN'T SUPPOSED
TO SEE THEM UNTIL
SUNDAY, BUT MOM
CALLED ME AT THE
STATION, ASKED
ME TO COME
OVER.

SHE'D
GOTTEN
THIS IN
THE
MAIL.

SHE
WAS PRETTY
WORKED-UP,
YOU CAN
GUESS.

DID
YOU KNOW
ABOUT
THIS?

YEAH, 'VE EN IT.

SHE'D ALREADY TOLD *POP* WHEN I GOT THERE. HE WAS BOUNCING OFF THE *WALLS.*

I GOT THEM *CALMED* DOWN...

...TOLD THEM IT WAS A *FAKE,* DONE WITH *COMPUTER.* TOLD THEM THAT IT WAS PROBABLY SOMEONE'S IDEA OF A *JOKE.*

MAYBE SOMEONE YOU *ARRESTED* OR SOMETHING, YOU KNOW, TRYING TO GET *BACK* AT YOU, TRYING TO *EMBARRASS* YOU.

ALL THE *FREAKS* YOU DEAL WITH IN YOUR JOB, IT WASN'T *THAT* HARD TO *CONVINCE* THEM.

ESPECIALLY SINCE THEY DIDN'T WANT TO BELIEVE IT IN THE *FIRST* PLACE.

THAT *HELPED,* YEAH.

I *COVERED* FOR YOU, BUT YOU HAVE TO *TALK* TO THEM. LET THEM KNOW THEY'VE GOT NOTHING TO *WORRY* ABOUT.

SO THEY CAN FEEL *BETTER* ABOUT THEM- SELVES?

YOU WANT TO TELL THEM YOU'RE GAY? YOU REMEMBER HOW *FREAKED* I WAS WHEN I FOUND *OUT* AND YOU WANT TO TELL THEM THEIR DAUGHTER'S A *LESBIAN?*

MOM WAS *CRYING* WHEN SHE CALLED ME, RENEE! WHEN SHE WASN'T ASKING ME WHAT SHE DID *WRONG,* SHE WAS *PRAYING* FOR YOUR SOUL.

POP JUST *SAT* THERE, HOLDING THAT DAMN *PICTURE,* HIS HAND *SHAKING!*

155

YOU TELL THEM YOU'RE GAY, ALL IT'LL DO IS *HURT* THEM.

WHY WOULD YOU WANT TO *DO* THAT?

‹MAYBE IT'S NOT ABOUT *THEM*.›

‹AND NOT *EVERYTHING* IS ABOUT *YOU!*›

‹TAKE ANOTHER LOOK AT THAT *PICTURE,* BENNY, *THEN* TELL ME WHO THIS IS *ABOUT!*›

‹YOU MADE YOUR *CHOICE,* RENEE, MADE A *DECISION,* AND IF THAT'S WHAT WORKS FOR *YOU,* GREAT--›

‹-- BUT THERE'S *NO REASON* MOM AND POP HAVE TO *SUFFER* FOR IT!›

‹MAYBE IT *WASN'T* A *CHOICE,* BEN!›

‹MAYBE, JUST *MAYBE,* I NEVER HAD A *SAY* IN THE *MATTER!*›

‹AND *MAYBE* I'M *GLAD.*›

‹MAYBE, BUT *NEITHER* DID *THEY.*›

‹*NONE* OF US *DID.*›

DAMMIT.

DAMMIT
TO HELL.

HEY,
IT'S
ME...

YOU SURE THIS IS *PRIVATE* ENOUGH?

THIS *TABLE* IS ALMOST *WELL-LIT*, RENEE. SOMEONE MIGHT *SEE* US TOGETHER.

THEY MIGHT THINK WE'RE *LOVERS* OR *SOMETHING*.

THAT'S *REALLY* FUNNY, DEE. THAT'S *JUST WHAT* I WAS HOPING I'D GET FROM YOU.

IT'S A *STEP* UP FROM MEETING BEHIND *CLOSED* DOORS.

I SUPPOSE I SHOULDN'T *COMPLAIN*.

I GOT OUTED AT WORK TODAY.

WHAT?

I GOT OUTED--

I HEARD YOU, OUTED HOW?

SEE FOR YOURSELF.

THERE WAS ONE HANGING ON THE BULLETIN BOARD IN THE SQUADROOM THIS MORNING.

THAT COPY WAS SENT TO MY PARENTS.

YOUR PARENTS SAW THIS?

YES. MY LITTLE BROTHER--WHO INCIDENTALLY HAS KNOWN I'M QUEER SINCE HE WAS FIFTEEN AND AFTER TEN YEARS STILL CAN'T DEAL WITH IT-- COVERED FOR ME.

HE TOLD THEM IT WAS PROBABLY SOMEONE'S IDEA OF A JOKE.

AT LEAST YOU CAN TELL THEM I KNOW HOW TO COOK.

IT'S NOT FUNNY, DEE.

NO. I KNOW IT ISN'T.

YOU GOING TO TELL THEM?

MY PARENTS? LOOKS LIKE IF I *DON'T* MARTY LIPARI *WILL.*

MARTY LIPARI'S THE GUY WHO *TOOK* THE *PICTURE?*

MARTY LIPARI'S THE GUY WHO *PAID* SOME *P.I.* TO TAKE THE PICTURE.

MARTY LIPARI DOESN'T LIKE ME *VERY* MUCH.

YOU WANT TO GET OUT OF *HERE?*

DESPERATELY.

MAY I WALK YOU *HOME?*

I'D *LIKE* THAT.

WHAT ARE YOU GOING TO DO?

YOU MEAN ABOUT THE *PHOTO?*

I MEAN ABOUT *ALL* OF IT.

I DON'T KNOW IF IT IS MARTY LIPARI WHO'S *DOING* THIS. AND I GO AFTER HIM, ALL I DO IS GIVE HIM *MORE* AMMUNITION FOR HIS CIVIL SUIT.

THAT JUST GETS ME *AND* THE DEPARTMENT IN MORE TROUBLE, AND RIGHT NOW I NEED ALL THE *FRIENDS* IN THE G.C.P.D. I CAN *GET.*

BUT IT'S AN INVASION OF *PRIVACY.* YOU CAN GET HIM FOR SLANDER OR LIBEL, WHICHEVER IT IS.

THE PHOTOS ARE TECHNICALLY *PRINT,* SO IT'D BE *LIBEL.*

THING IS, I.A.D. WAS WAITING FOR ME THIS MORNING, WHEN I GOT HOME FROM *YOUR* PLACE. THEY TOLD ME THE P.I.--SELKER-- HAD BEEN *MURDERED.*

THEY SAID THEY'D COME BY TO *WARN* ME THAT LIPARI MIGHT BE *VIOLENT.*

YOU DON'T SOUND *CONVINCED.*

I THINK THEY'D SEEN THE *PHOTO* ALREADY, AND THAT THEY WERE CHECKING ME FOR THE *CRIME,* THAT'S WHAT I THINK.

I THINK THEY WERE LOOKING AT ME AS A *SUSPECT.*

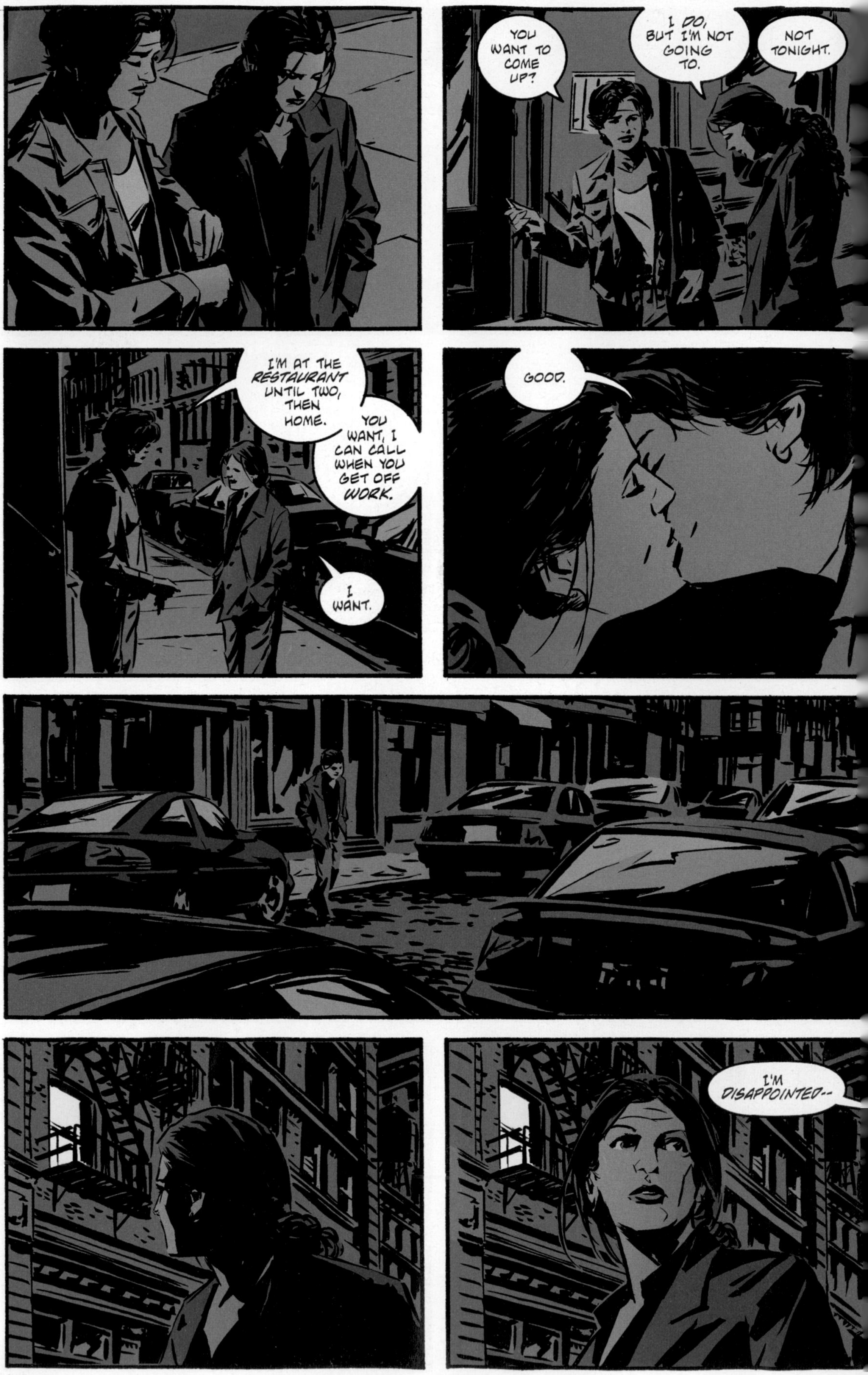
YOU WANT TO COME UP?
I DO, BUT I'M NOT GOING TO.
NOT TONIGHT.
I'M AT THE RESTAURANT UNTIL TWO, THEN HOME.
YOU WANT, I CAN CALL WHEN YOU GET OFF WORK.
I WANT.
GOOD.
I'M DISAPPOINTED--

--I WAS HOPING FOR SOMETHING WITH A LITTLE MORE *HEAT.* A LITTLE MORE WHAT THE *BOYS* LIKE, YOU KNOW?

THAT WAS *HARDLY* WORTH THE VIDEOTAPE, MONTOYA. YOU WEARING A *CHASTITY BELT* OR WHAT?

I MEAN, IS THAT *ANY* WAY TO SAY *GOODNIGHT* TO YOUR *LOVER?*

NOW *SMILE* FOR THE *CAMERA.*

GET *OUT* OF HERE, LIPARI.

AW, YOU *REMEMBER* MY *NAME.*

OF *COURSE,* YOU DAMN WELL *SHOULD,* CONSIDERING WHAT YOU DID TO *ME.*

DON'T DO ANYTHING *HASTY,* DETECTIVE.

YOU'D *HATE* FOR ME TO GET ANY *MORE* OF YOUR *DEVIANT* BEHAVIOR ON FILM...

...ESPECIALLY WITH YOUR *GIRLFRIEND* WATCHING.

●REC

WOULDN'T WANT HER FINDING OUT *EXACTLY* HOW *ROUGH* YOU CAN *PLAY,* DO YOU?

MAYBE I SHOULD *TALK* TO HER, huh? I MIGHT BE ABLE TO *STRAIGHTEN* HER *OUT.*

AFTER ALL, YOU *KNOW* MY *REPUTATION* WITH THE *LADIES--*

HEY, SHOULDN'T HAVE DONE THAT...

NNGG

HUH

YOU COME AFTER *ME,* THAT'S ONE THING, MARTY--

--YOU GO AFTER *HER,* I SWEAR TO GOD YOU WON'T BE ABLE TO *DIE* ENOUGH.

SWEAR TO GOD.

DON'T *EVER* COME BACK HERE *AGAIN!*

RENEE!

RENEE, WHAT--

JUST GO BACK INSIDE, DEE.

BUT *WHAT* WAS--

JUST GO BACK INSIDE AND DON'T *WORRY* ABOUT IT, DARIA.

IT'S *OKAY...*

...HE WON'T BE *BOTHERING* YOU *AGAIN.*

THINK YOU CAN DO THAT TO ME, DON'T KNOW WHO YOU'RE MESSING WITH

THINK TEN MILLION SUE YOU FOR FIFTY MILLION GET A DOCTOR TAKE SOME PICTURES OF ME.

--OH GOD NO--

BLAMM BLAMM BLAMM BLAMM BLAMM BLAMM

BLAMM

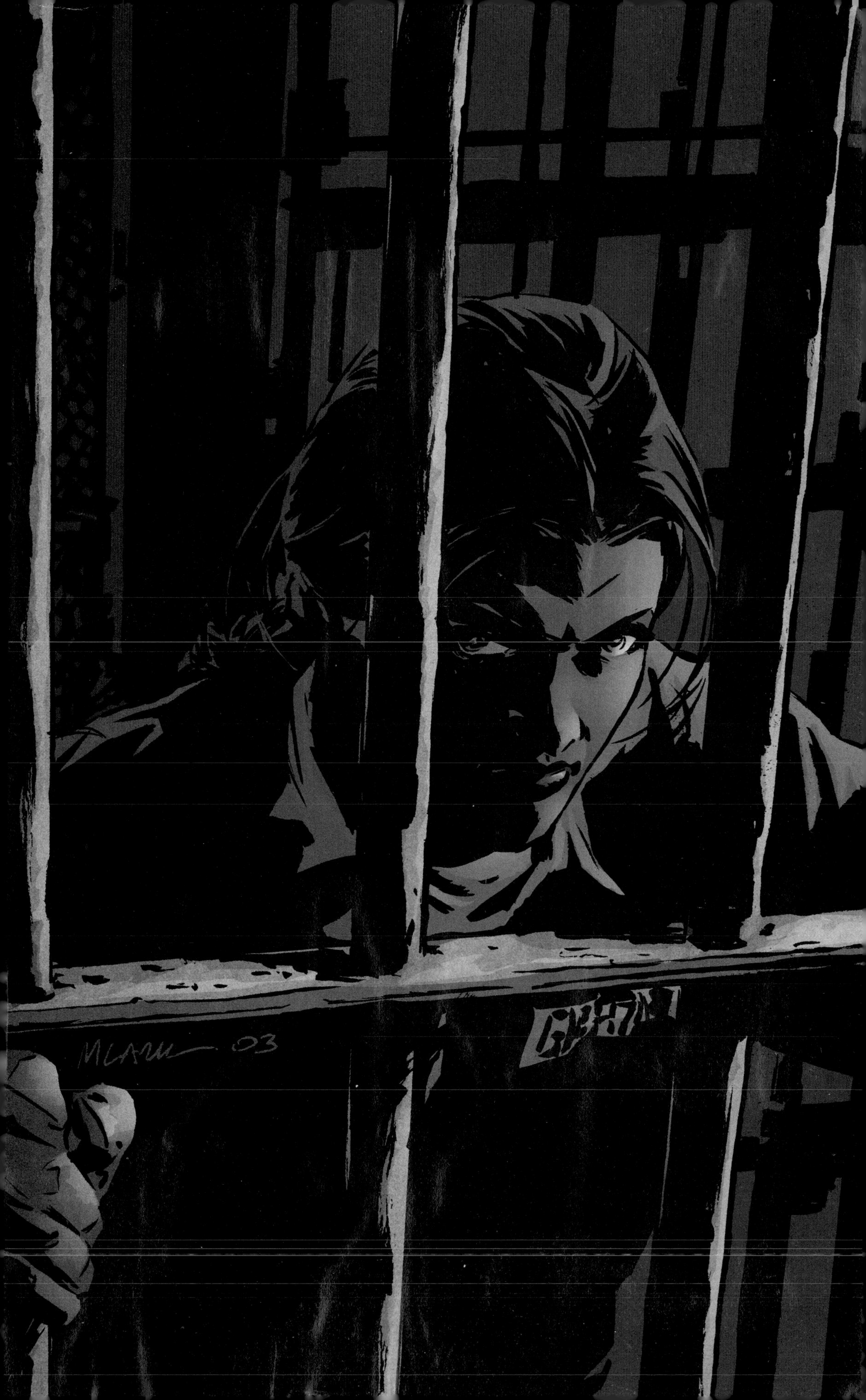

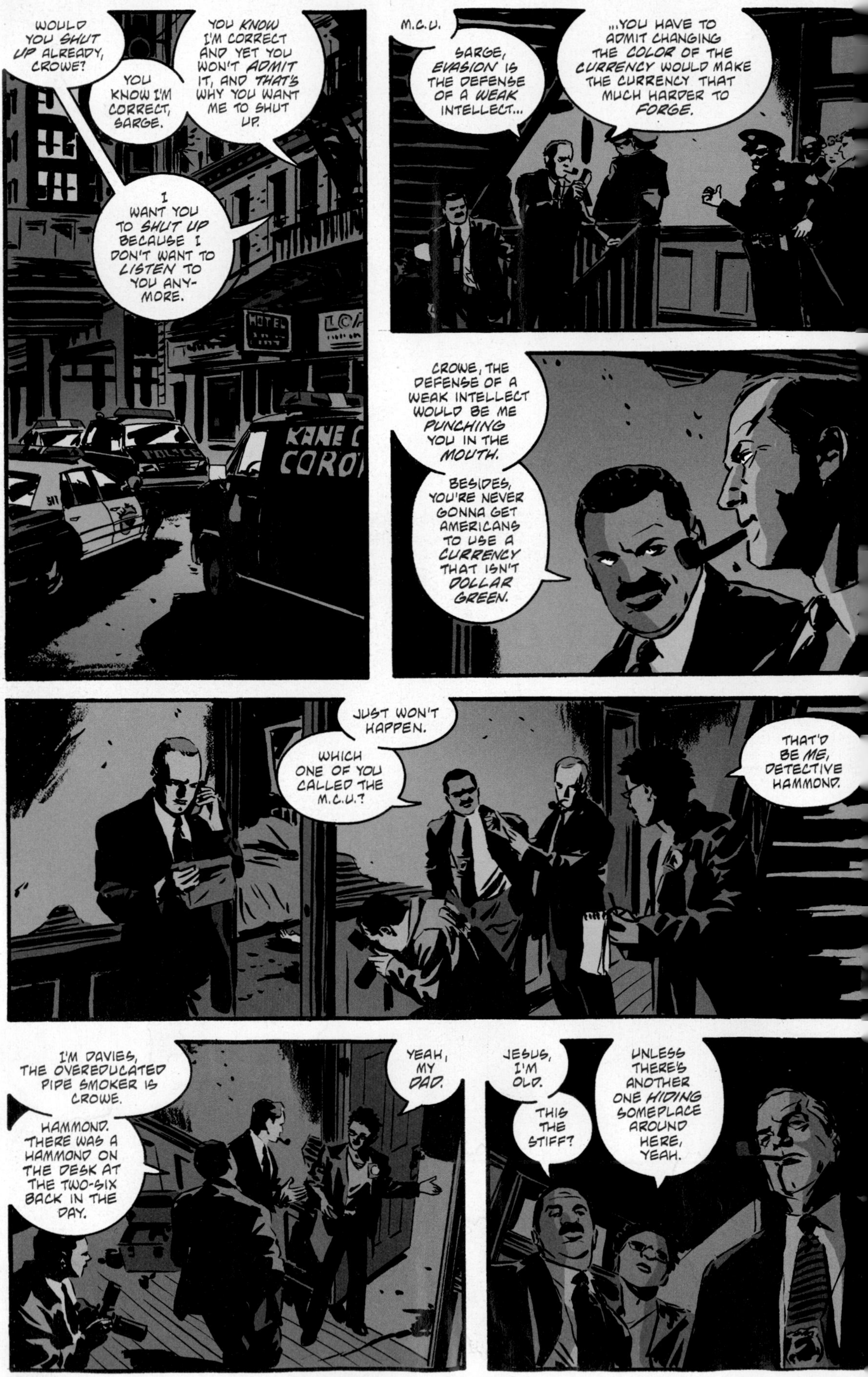

WOULD YOU SHUT UP ALREADY, CROWE?
YOU KNOW I'M CORRECT, SARGE.
YOU KNOW I'M CORRECT AND YET YOU WON'T ADMIT IT, AND THAT'S WHY YOU WANT ME TO SHUT UP.
I WANT YOU TO SHUT UP BECAUSE I DON'T WANT TO LISTEN TO YOU ANYMORE.
HOTEL
KANE C
CORO
M.C.U.
SARGE, EVASION IS THE DEFENSE OF A WEAK INTELLECT...
...YOU HAVE TO ADMIT CHANGING THE COLOR OF THE CURRENCY WOULD MAKE THE CURRENCY THAT MUCH HARDER TO FORGE.
CROWE, THE DEFENSE OF A WEAK INTELLECT WOULD BE ME PUNCHING YOU IN THE MOUTH.
BESIDES, YOU'RE NEVER GONNA GET AMERICANS TO USE A CURRENCY THAT ISN'T DOLLAR GREEN.
JUST WON'T HAPPEN.
WHICH ONE OF YOU CALLED THE M.C.U.?
THAT'D BE ME, DETECTIVE HAMMOND.
I'M DAVIES, THE OVEREDUCATED PIPE SMOKER IS CROWE.
HAMMOND. THERE WAS A HAMMOND ON THE DESK AT THE TWO-SIX BACK IN THE DAY.
YEAH, MY DAD.
JESUS, I'M OLD.
THIS THE STIFF?
UNLESS THERE'S ANOTHER ONE HIDING SOMEPLACE AROUND HERE, YEAH.

WELL TOAST MY NUTS AND CALL ME HAPPY.

THAT MAN LOOKS LIKE MARTY LIPARI, DOWN A COUPLE *PINTS*.

HIS I.D. *AGREES* WITH YOU. THE LIPARI PART, *NOT* THE BIT ABOUT THE PINTS.

HIT WHEN HE ENTERED THE ROOM?

HOW IT LOOKS. THE LIGHTS WERE *OFF* WHEN THE FIRST *UNIFORM* FOUND HIM, BUT OF COURSE THE *DUMB ASS* SWITCHED THEM ON.

SO HE COULD LOOK FOR CLUES.

HOW VERY CLEVER OF HIM. AT LEAST HE DIDN'T *STEP* IN THE *POWDER*.

TECHS RAN A POCKET TEST?

YEAH, IT'S *SMACK*. FIGURE A *KILO* IN THE PACKAGE, ABOUT *HALF* THAT MISSING.

OKAY, GIVE IT TO THE TECHS, MAKE SURE IT MATCHES UP.

NO ARGUMENT THAT IT'S A *HOMICIDE*, DETECTIVE HAMMOND, BUT THAT DOESN'T EARN YOU THE M.C.U.

YEAH....

"...SEE, I THINK THAT WAS A *MISTAKE*. THIS SHOULD *PROBABLY* GO TO *I.A.D.*

THAT WAS THE *MURDER WEAPON* IN THE BAG?

LAB'LL HAVE TO *RUN* IT.

BUT YOUR *PARTNER*, HE WAS CHECKING THE *REG*, RIGHT?

YEAH.

SO WHO *OWNS* THE GUN?

HAMMOND, YOU CALLED *US*, REMEMBER?

I CALLED YOU GUYS BECAUSE I'D HEARD THAT *LIPARI* WAS GIVING YOUR *NEWEST DYKE* SOME LEGAL GRIEF.

THOUGHT MAYBE YOU SHOULD KNOW SOMEONE HAD *POPPED* HIM.

DYKE IS A *PEJORATIVE*, DETECTIVE. I'D *REFRAIN* FROM USING IT TO DESCRIBE A FELLOW OFFICER.

THAT *FELLOW OFFICER* IS ALSO THE *REGISTERED OWNER* OF THE WEAPON MY PARTNER'S NOW SENDING TO THE LAB.

SO I THINK I'M GONNA SHUT UP, NOW, AND LEAVE THE *REST* OF MY FINDINGS FOR *I.A.D.*

THANKS FOR *RESPONDING* TO THE CALL.

half a life
Part Three

...LEADING TO CONTINUED TENSIONS IN THE REGION. THE WHITE HOUSE HAS CONFIRMED A SPECIAL ENVOY IS EN ROUTE TO ITARI, BUT DOUBTS FURTHER NEGOTIATIONS WILL ACHIEVE ANY MEANINGFUL GAINS.

LOCAL NEWS IS NEXT.

THIS IS GARY BARTON WITH G.P.B.S., GOOD MORNING, IT'S SEVEN O'CLOCK.

AT A FUND-RAISING DINNER LAST NIGHT, MAYOR DICKERSON ANNOUNCED PLANS TO COMBINE GOTHAM'S FIRE AND EMERGENCY MEDICAL RESPONSE DIVISIONS INTO A SINGLE DEPARTMENT...

...A CHANGE HE CLAIMS WILL BOLSTER EMERGENCY RESPONSE TIMES WHILE ELIMINATING BUREAUCRACY.

PROTESTS CONTINUE TODAY IN CATHEDRAL SQUARE, DEMANDING THE IMMEDIATE RESIGNATION OF CARDINAL WAVERLY AMID GROWING ALLEGATIONS OF SEXUAL MISCONDUCT.

TRAFFIC, AND THERE ARE BACKUPS ON THE VINCENZO AND KANE BRIDGES HEADING IN BOTH DIRECTIONS, LEADING TO DELAYS OF OVER HALF AN HOUR.

GOTHAM POWER AND LIGHT IS CONTINUING REPAIR WORK ON M.L.K. FROM 76th TO 94th STREETS...

...THE USE OF ALTERNATE ROUTES IS ADVISED...

IN THE WEATHER FOR TODAY, LOW SIXTIES AND OVERCAST THIS MORNING, BUT LOOK FOR CLEARING IN THE AFTERNOON--

CLK

AND, OF COURSE, MY *BACKUP* IS GONE, TOO.

LIPARI, YOU BASTARD.

STACY? IT'S RENEE. CHRIS IN YET?

...WHAT ABOUT Del ARRAZIO? OR THE CAPTAIN?

NOK NOK NOK

HOLD ON A MINUTE.

WHO IS IT?

IT'S *ESPERANZA* RENEE. YOU GOTTA LET ME IN.

WE'VE GOT A WARRANT...

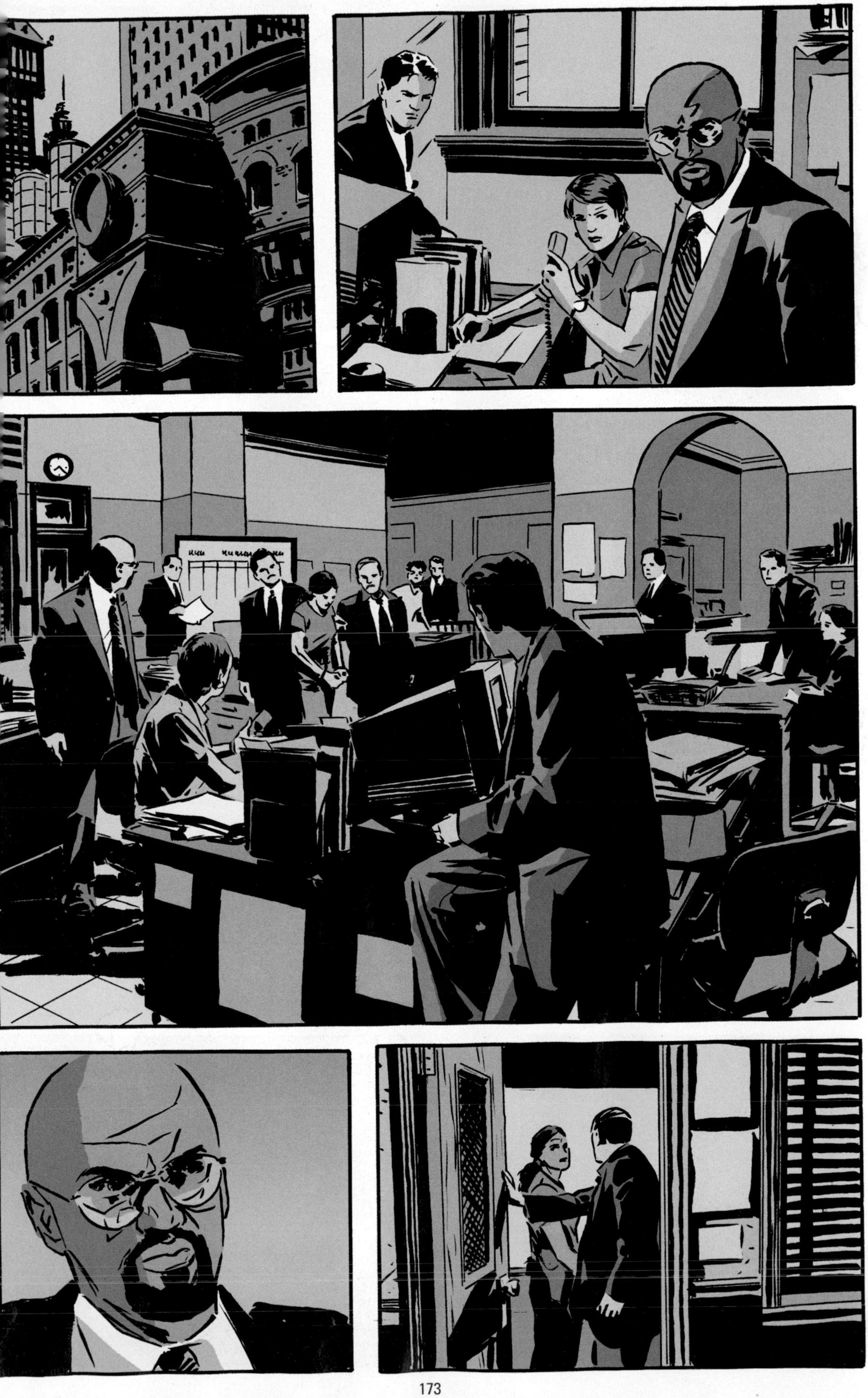

ESPERANZA!

YOU BETTER HAVE A *DAMN* GOOD REASON FOR MAKING *MY* PARTNER *PERP-WALK* THROUGH THIS SQUADROOM!

WELL, I'VE GOT AN *ANTE* OF *POSSESSION* WITH *INTENT*.

THINK THAT'LL GET ME INTO THE *GAME*, SMART GUY?

THAT'S *CRAP*. THAT'S *CRAP* AND YOU *KNOW* IT.

SHE'S A *RIGHTEOUS* COP, YOU *KNOW* THAT.

RIGHTEOUS. RIIIGHT...

...THAT'S WHAT *EVERYONE* SAID ABOUT *BULLOCK*, TOO, ISN'T IT?

PRICK.

174

YOU MADE YOUR POINT, CONWAY.

YOU GONNA TAKE THESE *OFF* NOW?

NOT LIKE YOU'RE GONNA BE *GOING* ANYWHERE, IS IT?

THE SMACK'S *NOT* MINE. I DON'T KNOW *HOW* IT GOT IN MY APARTMENT.

WHERE WERE YOU LAST NIGHT, RENEE? SAY AROUND *ONE* IN THE MORNING?

INSPECTOR, *LISTEN* TO ME.

I OPENED MY GUN SAFE THIS MORNING TO GET MY *DUTY WEAPON*, THERE'S A *BAG* OF *HEROIN* IN THERE AND MY *BACKUP* IS MISSING.

OH, IT'S *MISSING*, IS IT?

YES, *MISSING*. MORE PRECISELY, *STOLEN*.

THIS HAPPEN TO YOU A *LOT?* PEOPLE *STEALING* YOUR *BACKUP* WEAPON?

IT WAS *STOLEN* LAST NIGHT, BY THE SAME S.O.B. WHO PLANTED THE *SMACK* IN MY HOME.

MARTY LIPARI.

LIPARI. YOU'VE BEEN HAVING SOME *TROUBLE* WITH HIM.

WHAT IS THAT? YOU KNOW WHAT LIPARI'S BEEN *DOING,* HELL, YOU AND MANNY *WARNED* ME ABOUT HIM, ABOUT WHAT HE'D HIRED THAT P.I.-- WHAT'S HIS NAME, SELKER?--TO DO!

BALLISTICS CHECKED?

YEAH, WE *RUSHED* IT. IT'S HER *GUN* KILLED LIPARI, CAPTAIN.

PRINTS?

I *WISH.* IT WAS CLEAN.

SO, YOU DIDN'T *ANSWER* ME, RENEE...

JUST THE WAY IT'D BE CLEAN IF A *COP* WAS USING IT AS A *DROP* GUN.

...WHERE WERE, YOU LAST NIGHT?

HOME. MY *BROTHER* CAME BY. HE LEFT, I WENT OUT, MET A *FRIEND.*

OKAY, YOU KNOW HOW THIS PLAYS. LET'S HAVE THE FRIEND'S *NAME.*

HERNANDEZ, DARIA HERNANDEZ.

SHE'S THE *PASTRY* CHEF AT XENON.

DON'T EVEN *THINK* ABOUT IT, CRIS.

YOU DON'T *KNOW WHAT* I WAS THINKING, SERGEANT DEL ARRAZIO.

YOU GO IN TO TALK TO HER AND I.A.D. FINDS OUT, YOU'LL BE *EATING* THEIR QUESTIONS FOR A *MONTH*.

THEY THINK SHE'S *WRONG*, THEY'RE SURE AS HELL GONNA LOOK AT HER *PARTNER*.

HOW THE *HELL* DID THIS HAPPEN? LIPARI PHONE IN A *TIP*, SAY RENEE WAS *HOLDING*?

THEY DON'T WANT HER FOR *POSSESSION*, CRIS.

THEY'RE *FITTING* HER FOR *MURDER*.

MARTY LIPARI TOOK THE *EXPRESS* TO HIS *MAKER* SOMETIME DURING THE *WEE* HOURS THIS MORNING.

177

G.C.P.D. WE'RE LOOKING FOR DARIA HERNANDEZ.

KITCHEN'S THAT WAY.

BUT IF YOU'RE AFTER A *TASTE* OF THE *TIRAMISU*, DON'T BOTHER. SHE'LL CUT YOUR *HAND* OFF, MAN.

I'LL KEEP IT IN MIND.

SEAN, I NEED THE GANACHE FROM THE WALK-IN.

THE CHOCOLATE?

THE RASPBERRY.

BEGGING YOUR *PARDON.*

MY NAME'S CONWAY, THIS IS INSPECTOR ESPERANZA. WE'RE FROM THE G.C.P.D.

DARIA HERNANDEZ HERE?

THAT'D BE ME.

CAN I HELP YOU?

YOU KNOW A DETECTIVE NAMED RENEE MONTOYA?

YES, OF COURSE. WHAT IS THIS ABOUT?

WE WERE WONDERING IF YOU'D COME DOWN TO CENTRAL WITH US, ANSWER A FEW QUESTIONS.

IS RENEE ALL RIGHT? SHE ISN'T *HURT*, IS SHE?

OH MY GOD. *PLEASE* TELL ME SHE'S NOT HURT.

SHE'S *FINE*, MISS HERNANDEZ. WE JUST HAVE A FEW *QUESTIONS* TO ASK YOU.

ALL RIGHT... I THINK THAT'S... JUST GIVE ME A MOMENT.

SEAN? I NEED YOU TO FINISH THIS SHEET, THEN THE MOUSSE.

I SHOULD BE BACK SOON.

YEAH, IT WON'T TAKE LONG. WE PROMISE.

SORRY ABOUT THE WAIT.

THE POSSESSION IS *BOGUS*, CONWAY. WHY ARE YOU *STRINGING* ME ALONG LIKE THIS?

YOU HAVE MY APOLOGIES. YOU KNOW HOW IT IS. A THOUSAND *THINGS* TO TAKE CARE OF BEFORE WE CAN GET TO BUSINESS.

WOULD YOU STOP WITH THAT? I *KNOW* THIS GAME. I'VE PLAYED IT A *MILLION* TIMES.

IF YOU'VE GOT QUESTIONS, THEN GO AHEAD AND *ASK...*

...ME...

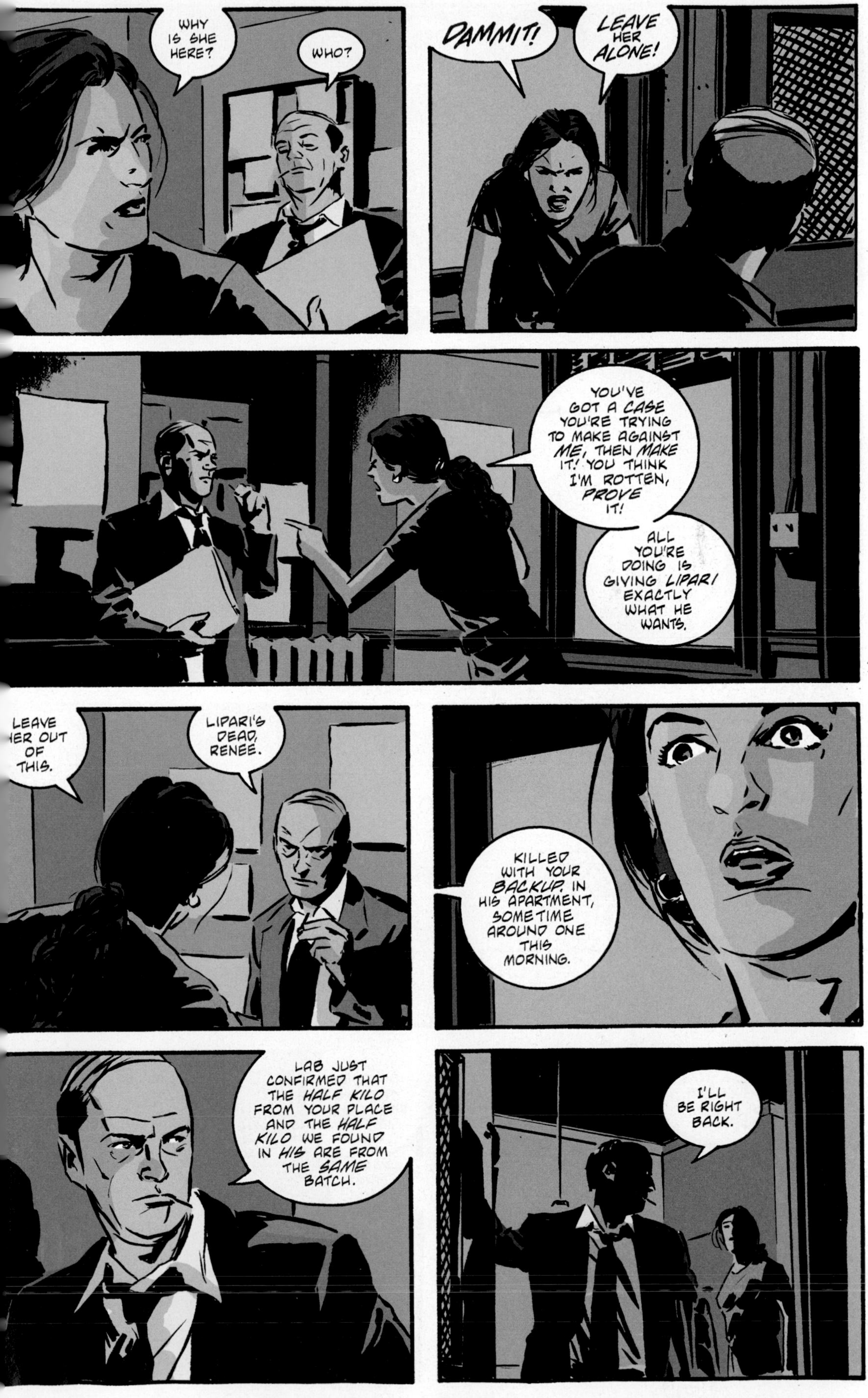
WHY IS SHE HERE?
WHO?
DAMMIT!
LEAVE HER ALONE!
YOU'VE GOT A CASE YOU'RE TRYING TO MAKE AGAINST ME, THEN MAKE IT! YOU THINK I'M ROTTEN, PROVE IT!
ALL YOU'RE DOING IS GIVING LIPARI EXACTLY WHAT HE WANTS.
LEAVE HER OUT OF THIS.
LIPARI'S DEAD, RENEE.
KILLED WITH YOUR BACKUP, IN HIS APARTMENT, SOMETIME AROUND ONE THIS MORNING.
LAB JUST CONFIRMED THAT THE HALF KILO FROM YOUR PLACE AND THE HALF KILO WE FOUND IN HIS ARE FROM THE SAME BATCH.
I'LL BE RIGHT BACK.

LIGHT AND SWEET, RIGHT?

YES, THANK YOU.

WHAT IS THIS *ABOUT*, INSPECTOR?

CALL ME MANNY, PLEASE.

YOU WERE WITH RENEE LAST NIGHT?

WHY?

WE'RE TRYING TO *ACCOUNT* FOR HER *MOVEMENTS*. YOU COULD BE A BIG HELP TO US, YOU JUST TOLD US WHAT YOU KNOW.

IS SHE IN TROUBLE?

YEAH, MISS HERNANDEZ. YOU *COULD* SAY THAT. YOU COULD EVEN SAY SHE'S IN A *LOT* OF *TROUBLE*.

SO YOU CAN *SEE* WHY WE'RE *HOPING* YOU CAN *HELP* US HERE.

IS IT THAT *MAN*, THE ONE WHO CAME *AFTER* HER?

LIPARI? IS THAT HIS NAME?

SHE [TOL]D YOU [A]BOUT [L]IPARI?

TOLD ME, AND THEN THE THING *LAST* NIGHT.

HE'S... HE'S A *VILE* MAN.

SOMETHING HAPPENED LAST NIGHT?

SHE WALKED ME HOME. WE MET FOR COFFEE AND RENEE WALKED ME HOME, AND LIPARI WAS OUTSIDE MY APARTMENT.

HE HAD A *CAMERA*...A VIDEO CAMERA, AND HE... HE MADE SOME *THREATS.*

HE *THREATENED* HER?

NOT RENEE. ME. I THINK. I DIDN'T HEAR ALL OF IT. BUT THEY... HE MUST HAVE *DONE* SOMETHING BECAUSE SHE *HIT* HIM.

IF YOU DIDN'T *HEAR,* HOW DO YOU KNOW HE THREATENED *YOU?*

NO, I HEARD *SOME* OF IT. I MEAN, THERE WAS *SHOUTING.* RENEE WAS SHOUTING AT HIM.

TELLING HIM TO STAY AWAY FROM ME OR SHE'D...

...OH MY GOD...

...HE'S *DEAD,* ISN'T HE?

STAY AWAY FROM YOU OR WHAT, MISS HERNANDEZ?

DID DETECTIVE MONTOYA *THREATEN* HIM?

I DON'T HAVE ANYTHING ELSE TO SAY TO YOU GENTLEMEN.

ALL RIGHT, RENEE...

...LET'S CUT TO THE CHASE.

YEAH. LET'S DO THAT.

MISS HERNANDEZ SAYS THAT LIPARI THREATENED HER LAST NIGHT, IN YOUR PRESENCE. SHE SAYS YOU *BEAT* LIPARI *DOWN*.

SHE SAYS YOU *THREATENED* HIS LIFE.

SO THIS IS WHAT *HAPPENED*, AND YOU CAN FILL IN THE BITS I GET *WRONG*, OKAY?

HERE'S LIPARI, HE RAPES ELENOR EASLEY, AND WHEN YOU BRING HIM IN, HE TRIED TO *CUT* YOU. THEN HE *SKATES* AT TRIAL.

THAT *SUCKS*, BUT YOU'RE A *GOTHAM* COP, YOU KNOW HOW IT WORKS. YOU CAN TAKE IT.

BUT THEN LIPARI DECIDES HE WANTS SOME *PAYBACK*, SO HE *SUES* YOU FOR SOME GARBAGE *BRUTALITY* RAP, AND MAYBE YOU CAN TAKE *THAT*, TOO.

BUT SOMEWHERE ALONG THE LINE, HE HIRES BRIAN SELKER TO LOOK INTO YOU, TO *DIG* SOME *DIRT*.

AND SELKER HITS IT *BIG*. TURNS OUT YOU HAVE A *SECRET*, ONE YOU'VE BEEN *HIDING* FOR YEARS.

TURNS OUT YOU'RE GAY.

AND NOW LIPARI KNOWS THE *NAME* OF THE WOMAN YOU'VE BEEN SEEING, KNOWS *WHERE* SHE LIVES.

HE'S GOT A WHOLE *NEW* AVENUE OF REVENGE.

SOMETHING HAPPENS WITH LIPARI AND SELKER, THEY FIGHT. SELKER'S NOT THE *BEST* CITIZEN, IT *COULD* HAPPEN. LIPARI *KILLS* SELKER.

AND THEN, LAST NIGHT, LIPARI THREATENS DARIA. HE'S A *RAPIST*... AND HE *THREATENS* HER.

AND YOU KIND OF *LOSE* IT, AND WHO COULD *BLAME* YOU, THE DAY YOU HAD? THIS PIECE OF *TRASH* THREATENED MY WIFE, I'D LOSE IT, *TOO.*

YOU GO TO HIS APARTMENT WITH YOUR *BACKUP*.. YOU'VE GOT HIS ADDRESS FROM THE EASLEY CASE-- AND YOU WAIT UNTIL HE WALKS IN THE *DOOR*...

...AND YOU *SHOOT* THE *BASTARD* SIX TIMES IN THE CHEST.

AS FOR THE *SMACK*, YOU WEREN'T THINKING STRAIGHT, YOU JUST GRABBED IT. MAYBE YOU COULD PLANT IT SOMEWHERE LATER, SOMETHING.

THING IS, WE'VE GOT THE *GUN*, AND YOU CAN'T *ALIBI* FOR THE TIME OF THE *MURDER.*

A.D.A. GERMAIN IS IN SAWYER'S OFFICE *NOW.* SHE'S READY TO *CHARGE.*

IT'S TIME TO COME *CLEAN,* RENEE.

YOU TAKE A *TEMPORARY* INSANITY PLEA, THE JURY'LL BUY IT. THE *STRAIN OF THE JOB,* OF YOUR *DOUBLE* LIFE, THE *THREAT* TO SOMEONE YOU *LOVE*...

...TELL US WHAT HAPPENED.

I DIDN'T DO IT, MANNY.

I SWEAR TO GOD, I DIDN'T DO THIS.

DETECTIVE RENEE MONTOYA, I'M PLACING YOU UNDER ARREST FOR THE MURDER OF MARTY LIPARI.

STAND UP, PLEASE.

YOU HAVE THE RIGHT TO REMAIN SILENT. YOU HAVE THE RIGHT TO AN ATTORNEY.

I KNOW MY RIGHTS.

I KNOW YOU DO.

IF YOU CANNOT AFFORD AN ATTORNEY, ON WILL BE PROVIDED FOR YOU...

WHAT ARE YOU DOING?

SHE'S BEING CHARGED.

NOW LET GO OF ME, DETECTIVE...

...I'VE GOT TO INFORM YOUR SHIFT COMMANDER THAT SHE'S JUST LOST ONE OF HER BEST COPS.

FIVE MINUTES, DETECTIVE.

YOU SHOULDN'T HAVE *LIED* TO ME, RENEE.

I *DIDN'T* LIE TO YOU. I *DIDN'T* DO IT.

I'M NOT TALKING ABOUT THAT.

MY LAST PARTNER WAS HARVEY *BULLOCK.*

HOW LONG DID YOU *THINK* I WOULD HAVE LASTED IF HE'D KNOWN I WAS *QUEER?*

I'M *NOT* HARVEY BULLOCK.

I KNOW. I SHOULD HAVE TRUSTED YOU.

THAT'S ALL I WANTED TO HEAR.

WHO'S SETTING YOU *UP*, PARTNER?

IT'S *DENT.*

IT'S *TWO-FACE.*

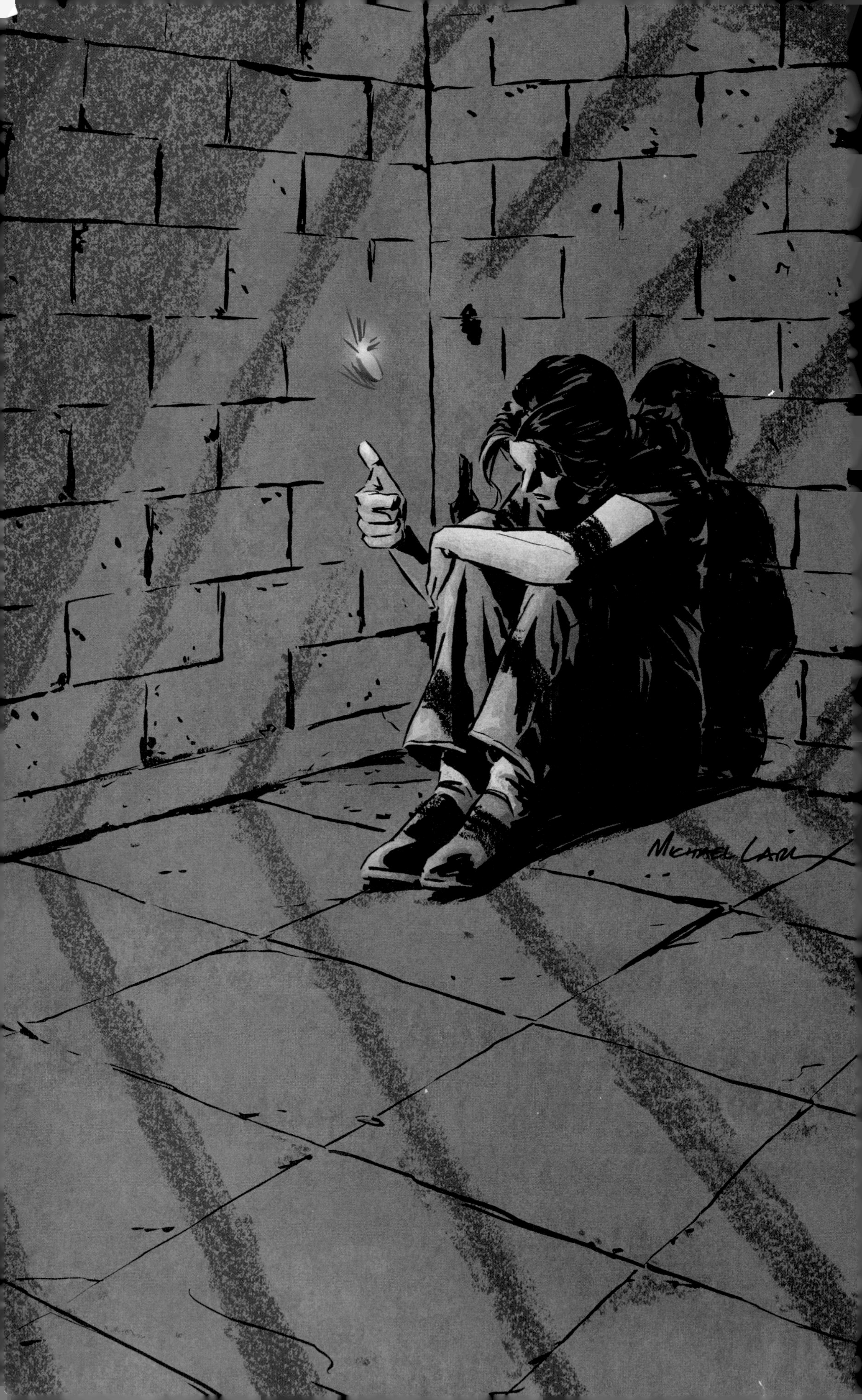

"...DOCKET NUMBER EIGHT-SEVEN-SEVEN-FOUR-FIVE-FOUR-SIX-TWO, THE *PEOPLE* OF GOTHAM VERSUS *RENEE MONTOYA*..."

halfalife
Part Four

"...THE CHARGE IS *MURDER* IN THE *FIRST DEGREE*.

MISTER BARKLEY?

YOUR HONOR, MISS MONTOYA IS A *MEMBER* OF THE G.C.P.D., AND AS SUCH CARRIES THE *TRUST* AND *RESPECT* OF THE COMMUNITY--

SHE'S BEEN IN MY COURT *BEFORE*, DANNY, I *KNOW* WHO SHE IS.

ENTER A *PLEA*.

WHERE'S COTTEN?

MISTER COTTEN IS *NO LONGER* REPRESENTING YOU, DETECTIVE. *I* AM.

RACHEL GREEN. PLEASED TO MEET YOU.

WAIT A GODDAMN MIN--

SOMEONE *NEEDS* TO ENTER A *PLEA* HERE, MS. GREEN.

APOLOGIES, YOUR HONOR. I'VE JUST TAKEN DETECTIVE MONTOYA'S *CASE.*

WONDERFUL FOR *HER,* AND I'M STILL WAITING FOR A *PLEA.*

NOT *GUILTY,* YOUR HONOR.

SO ENTERED--

YOUR HONOR, I'D LIKE TO TAKE THIS OPPORTUNITY TO REQUEST A *HEARING* ON *BAIL,* AND TO *INFORM* THE DISTRICT ATTORNEY THAT WE'LL BE MOVING TO *DISMISS* THE CHARGES AGAINST MY CLIENT FOR *LACK OF EVIDENCE.*

YOUR HONOR!

WE'VE GOT A *COP* CHARGED WITH *MURDER* HERE, NOT TO MENTION THE *OTHER* CHARGES PENDING FOR *POSSESSION* WITH *INTENT* AND--

MY CLIENT HAS A HISTORY OF *DISTINGUISHED* SERVICE TO *THIS CITY,* YOUR HONOR, AND THE D.A.'S *INSINUATION* THAT SHE IS A *FLIGHT RISK* IS--

ENOUGH.

BAIL HEARING WILL BE SET FOR THIS AFTERNOON...

...NEXT!

I'LL MEET YOU IN THE HOLDING CELLS. YOU CAN *FIRE* ME THEN, IF YOU WANT TO.

BUT I *DON'T* THINK YOU WANT TO, NOT SINCE BRUCE WAYNE IS *FOOTING* MY *BILL* AND WILLING TO POST YOUR BOND--

‹RENEE! RENEE--›

‹--WHAT THE *HELL* IS GOING ON?›

‹THIS IS A *MISTAKE*, RENEE! THIS *MUST* BE A *MISTAKE*--›

‹THAT GIRL...›

‹...THAT'S THE *GIRL* FROM THE *PICTURE*, ISN'T IT?›

I'M SO *SORRY*, DEE.

NICE JOB, INSPECTOR.

NOT *MY* FAULT SHE *KILLED* LIPARI, DETECTIVE ALLEN.

BEG YOUR PARDON.

SHE *DIDN'T* KILL LIPARI.

SHE'S *CLEAN,* AND YOU'RE *BUSTING* YOUR *ASS* TRYING TO MAKE HER *DIRTY.*

IF *WISHES* WERE *DIAMONDS,* ALLEN, YOU'D BE DeBEERS.

YOU'LL *EXCUSE* ME, I'VE GOT TO *MAKE* A CALL.

WAIT. WAIT!

YOU'RE DARIA?

YOU WERE IN THE M.C.U.?

I DON'T *HAVE* TO TALK TO YOU. HAVEN'T YOU BASTARDS USED ME *ENOUGH* TO *BURY* HER?

IT'S *NOT* LIKE THAT DARIA, *I'M* NOT LIKE THAT.

I'M *HER* PARTNER. MY NAME'S CRISPUS.

DETECTIVE ALLEN, YES... SHE'S TALKED ABOUT YOU.

NICE TO MEET YOU.

NICE TO MEET YOU, TOO.

LET ME *BUY* YOU A CUP OF *COFFEE,* DARIA...

HOW'D IT GO?

AT THE ARRAIGNMENT.

SHE PLEADED N.G. BRUCE WAYNE'S ATTORNEY, GREEN, SHOWED UP, SAID SHE WAS REPPING RENEE.

SORRY, DID YOU SAY BRUCE WAYNE?

YEAH. DON'T KNOW WHAT HIS INTEREST IS, BUT GREEN'S GOT TO BE A BETTER BET THAN THAT P.B.A. HUMP SHE WAS STUCK WITH.

WHEN'S THE BAIL HEARING?

GREEN'S HOPING FOR LATER TODAY...

...YEAH...

KEEP US INFORMED.

DETECTIVE ALLEN? THE CAPTAIN--

IN A MINUTE.

HEY, YOU!

UH, YEAH?

GET YOUR FEET THE HELL OFF THIS DESK!

SORRY... ...CAPTAIN TOLD ME TO TAKE A DESK, AND THIS ONE WAS FREE.

IS IT YOURS?

IT'S MY PARTNER'S.

NOW GET YOUR CARDBOARD COLLECTIBLES OFF IT, TOO.

DETECTIVE ALLEN...

...THIS IS DETECTIVE MacDONALD, SHE JUST CAME UP FROM MISSING PERSONS.

SHE'S RIDING WITH YOU FOR THE TIME BEING.

JOSEPHINE MacDONALD, BUT EVERYONE CALLS ME JOSIE.

CAPTAIN, THIS ISN'T COOL.

IT ISN'T? YOU NEED A PARTNER, MacDONALD NEEDS A VET.

WORKS FOR ME.

I'M WORKING SOMETHING RIGHT NOW, CAPTAIN, I CAN'T BABY-SIT THE ROOKIE.

SHE CAN'T BE OLDER THAN TWENTY-FIVE.

SHE'S TWENTY-SIX, AND I DON'T CARE WHAT YOU'RE WORKING, CRIS. SHE'S RIDING WITH YOU.

I'M *NOT* HERE BY *ACCIDENT*, DETECTIVE ALLEN.

THE COMMISSIONER PICKED *ME* FOR THE M.C.U., SAME WAY EVERYONE *ELSE* GETS HERE.

AIKINS, *NOT* GORDON.

GORDON DON'T WORK HERE *ANY-MORE.*

OK, LET'S GET THIS *STRAIGHT* RIGHT AT THE *START,* JOSIE.

YOU'RE *NOT* MY PARTNER.

I ALREADY *HAVE* A PARTNER, SHE'S *DOWN* AT THE CRIMINAL COURTS BUILDING, WAITING TO BE *SHIPPED* BACK TO THE SCHRECK.

MY PARTNER IS A GOOD POLICE, AND I'M NOT GOING TO SIT IDLE WHILE SHE'S *FRAMED* FOR CRIMES SHE DIDN'T DO.

THEN WHAT ARE *WE* STILL DOING STANDING AROUND HERE?

COME ON, MOVE IT!

TAKE YOUR SEATS AND KEEP YOUR MOUTHS CLOSED!

YOU WANT AN ESCORT, SWEET-HEART?

GO ON, TAKE A SEAT!

THAT'S ALL OF THEM?

THAT'S IT, MOVE 'EM OUT!

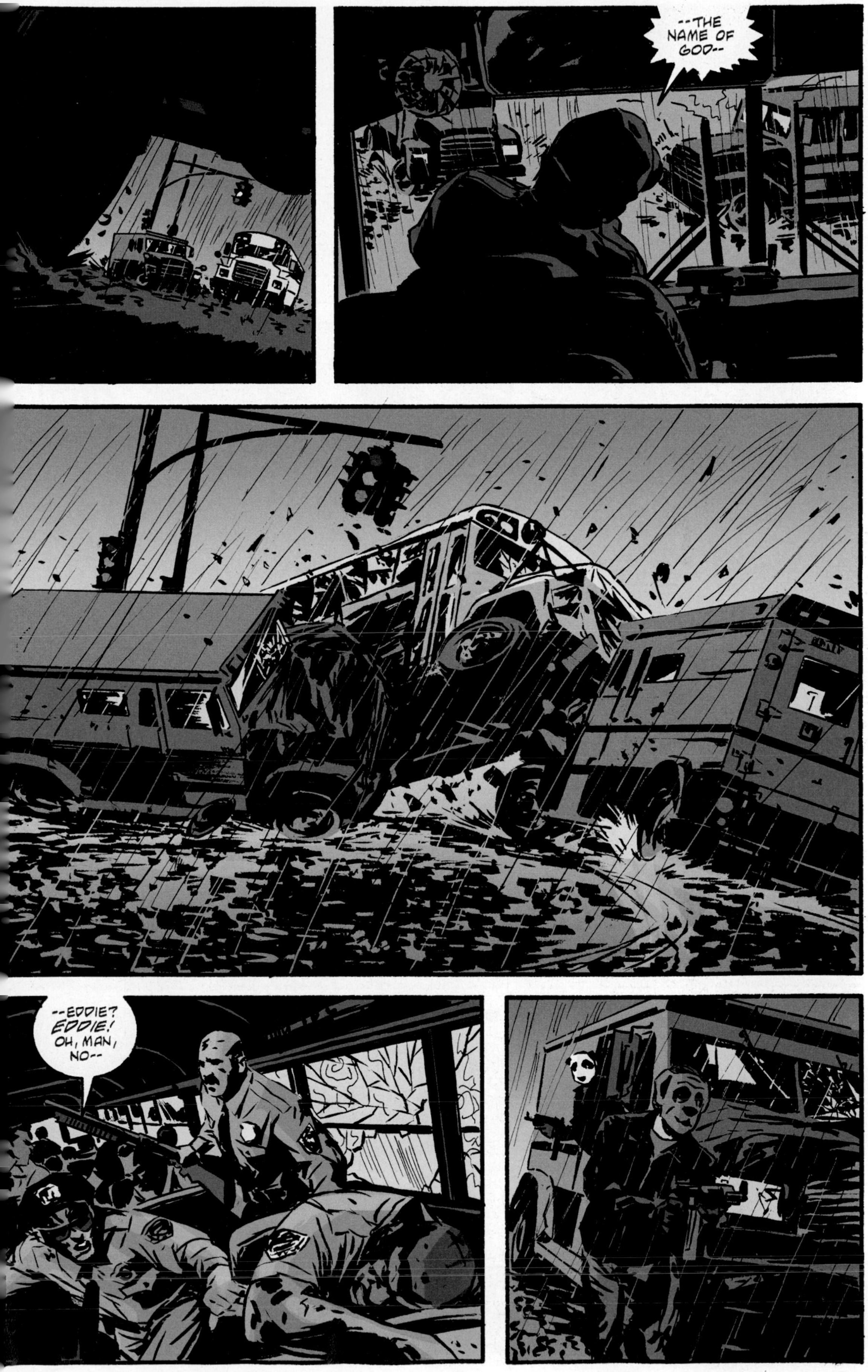
--THE NAME OF GOD--
--EDDIE? EDDIE! OH, MAN, NO--

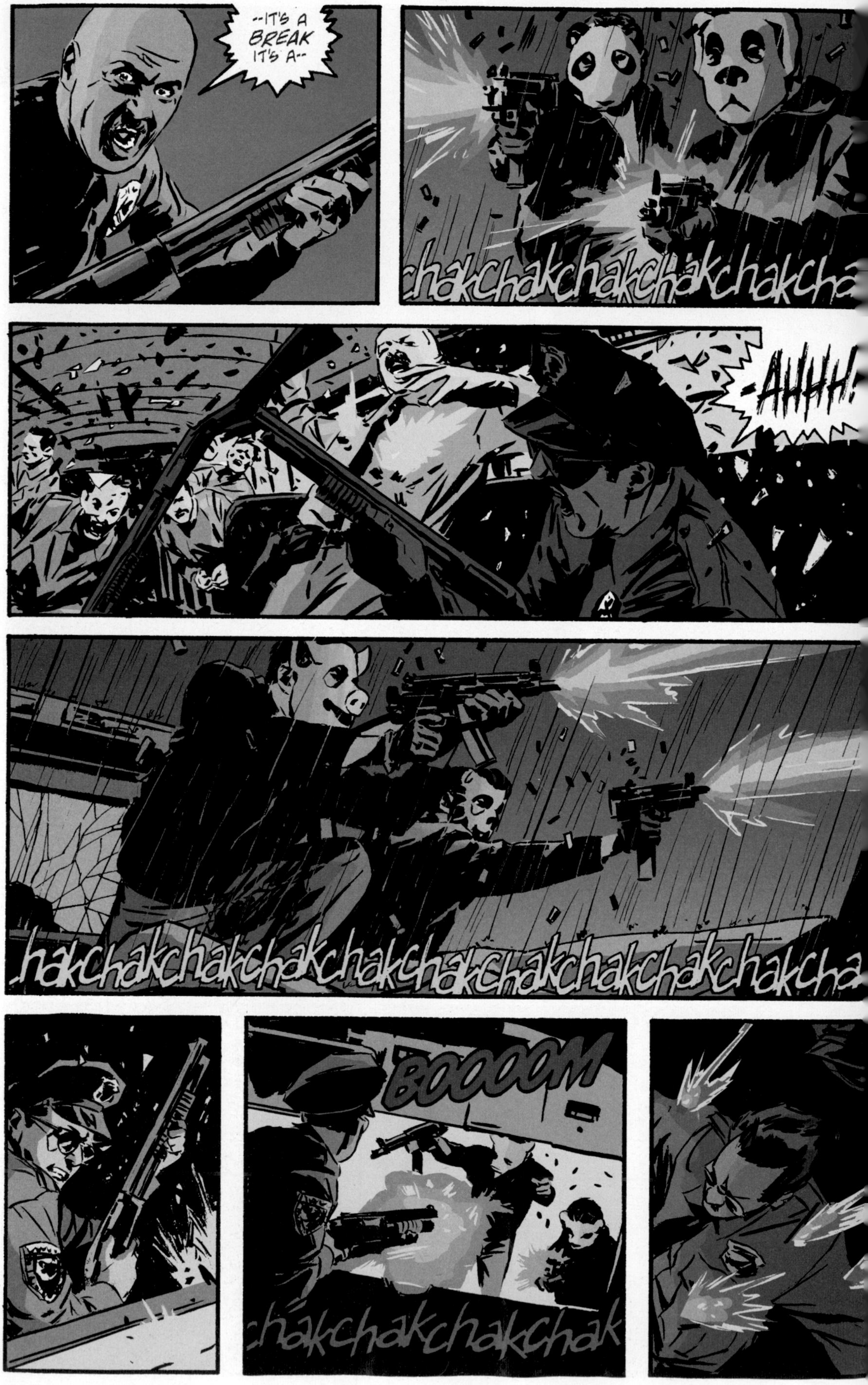
--IT'S A BREAK IT'S A--
chakchakchakchakchakcha
-AHHH!
chakchakchakchakchakchakchakchakchakcha
BOOOOM
chakchakchakchak

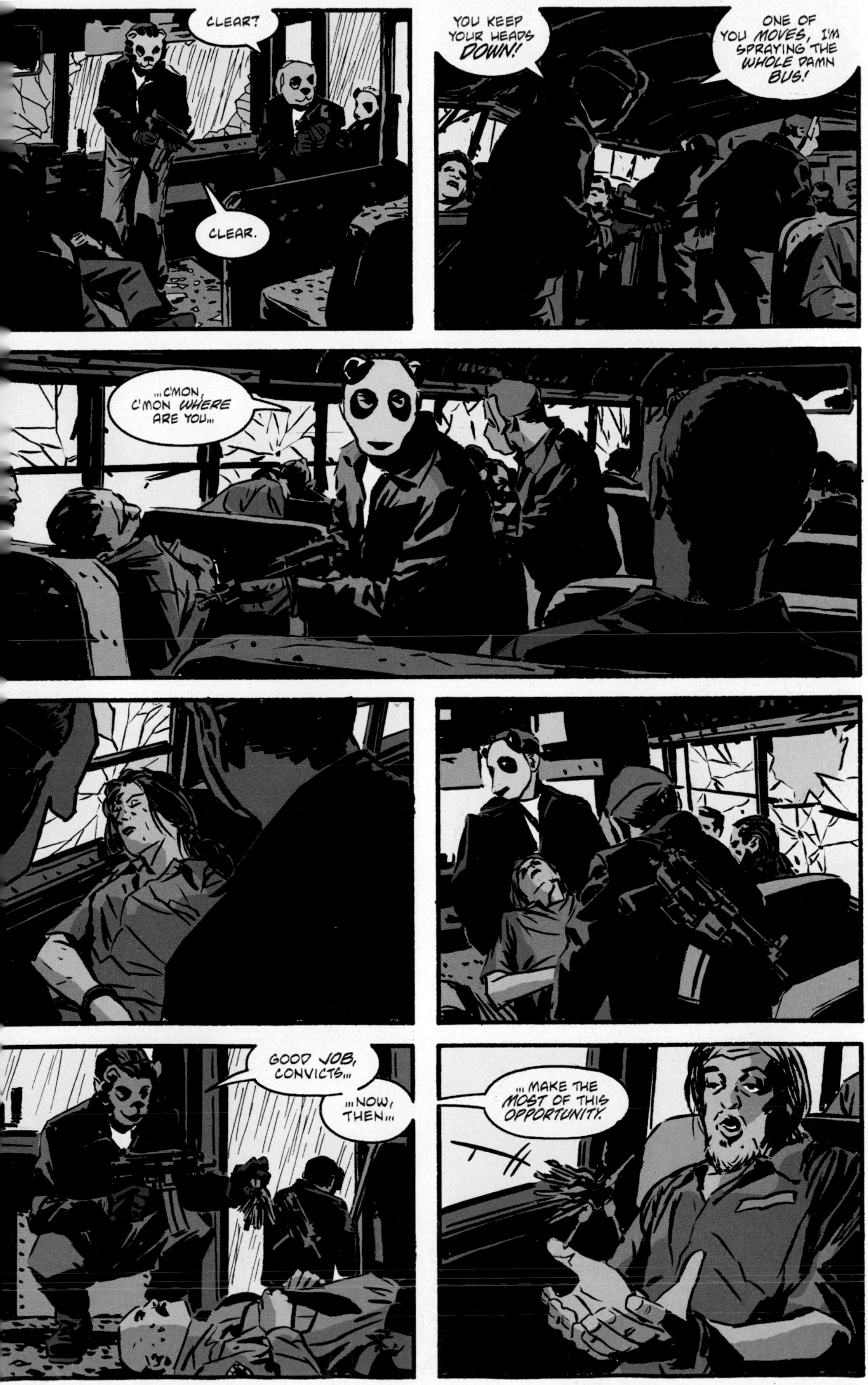
CLEAR?
CLEAR.
YOU KEEP YOUR HEADS DOWN!
ONE OF YOU MOVES, I'M SPRAYING THE WHOLE DAMN BUS!
...C'MON, C'MON WHERE ARE YOU...
GOOD JOB, CONVICTS...
...NOW, THEN...
...MAKE THE MOST OF THIS OPPORTUNITY.

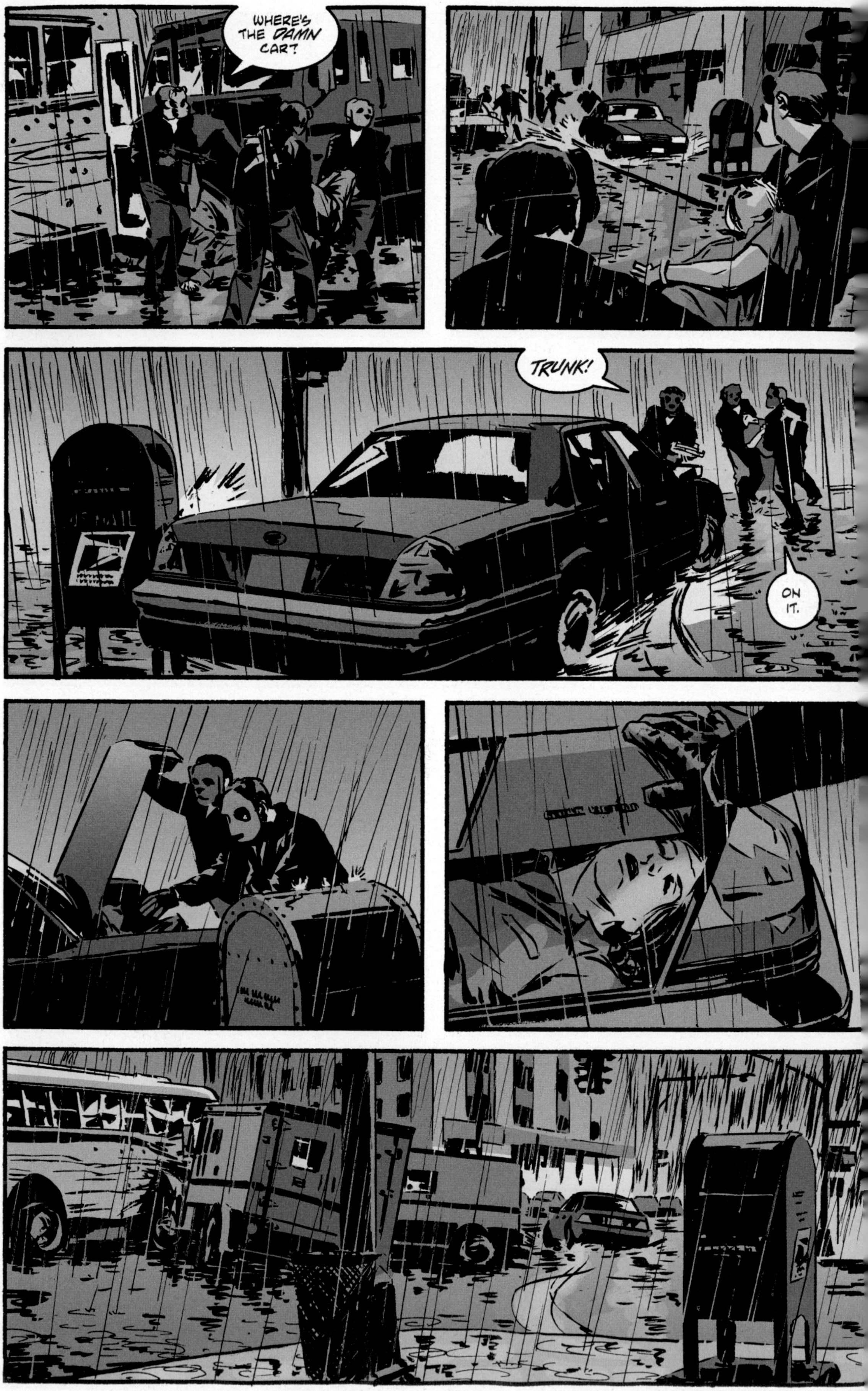
WHERE'S THE DAMN CAR?
TRUNK!
ON IT.

"...COUNT SOMETHING LIKE FORTY *ROUNDS* FIRED.

--*MANHUNT* GOING FOR THE ESCAPEES--

"GET A PICTURE OF THIS, SOMEONE, PLEASE?

--SOMETHING LIKE *FIFTEEN* OF THEM ON THE *LOOSE*, AT LEAST"

--CAPTAIN! CAPTAIN! JUST *ONE* QUESTION--

"...THE *WEAK* SECURITY SURROUNDING THIS TRANSFER...

--DOWN *BOTH* GUARDS AND THE *DRIVER* IN *COLD BLOOD*...

CAPTAIN!

WHAT THE *HELL* HAPPENED?

IT WAS A *COORDINATED* BUST OUT, CRIS...

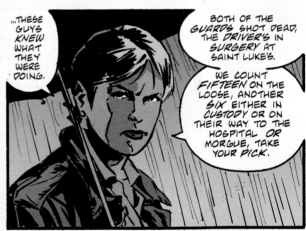

"...THESE GUYS *KNEW* WHAT THEY WERE DOING.

BOTH OF THE *GUARDS* SHOT DEAD, THE *DRIVER'S* IN *SURGERY* AT SAINT LUKE'S.

WE COUNT *FIFTEEN* ON THE LOOSE, ANOTHER *SIX* EITHER IN *CUSTODY* OR ON THEIR WAY TO THE HOSPITAL *OR* MORGUE, TAKE YOUR *PICK*.

IT WAS *HER BUS*, CRIS.

AND WE CAN'T *FIND* HER.

WHAT DO YOU *MEAN*?

WHAT IT SOUNDS LIKE. MONTOYA'S UNACCOUNTED FOR.

NOT AT THE HOSPITALS. NOT AT THE MORGUE.

WHICH MEANS SHE HOOFED IT WHEN SHE GOT THE CHANCE.

IT DOESN'T MEAN THAT, BARTLETT!

TAKE IT EASY--

SCREW EASY, VINCENT! YOUR PARTNER SHOULD KNOW BETTER THAN TO CRACK LIKE THAT!

MONTOYA WOULD NEVER HAVE RUN, MAN! IT WOULD JUST MAKE THINGS WORSE FOR HER!

SHE WAS THE TARGET

YOU'RE SAYING YOUR PARTNER WAS INTO SOMEONE WITH THIS MUCH MUSCLE, SOMEONE WHO WOULD PUT THIS TOGETHER TO SPRING HER?

WHAT ARE YOU NOT TELLING ME?

FORGET IT.

204

WHAT, YOU GOT A LETTER YOU NEED TO MAIL OR SOMETHING?

NO, IT LOOKS LIKE SOMETHING SCRAPED UP AGAINST THE BOX, THAT'S ALL.

MAYBE THE GETAWAY CAR?

YEAH, OR, MAYBE SOMEONE ELSE'S CAR AND IT HAPPENED LAST EASTER.

YOU SAW THIS FROM WAY OVER THERE?

HEY, MAN, PERFECT VISION, WHAT CAN I SAY.

SARGE! NEED A TECH AND A PHOTOGRAPHER OVER HERE! MacKENZIE FOUND SOMETHING!

MacDONALD.

COME HERE.

HEY, LET GO.

COME.

HERE.

C'MON, I JUST WANTED YOU TO GET MY *NAME* RIGHT.

SHUT UP, ROOKIE.

TWO-FACE DID THIS.

WHAT THE *HELL* ARE YOU TALKING ABOUT?

I'M SAYING *TWO-FACE* PUT THIS TOGETHER BUT I DON'T THINK HE DID IT *HIMSELF.*

PUT TOGETHER A *CREW* FOR IT, MOST LIKELY, GAVE THEM THE *PLAN,* BUT HE DIDN'T TOUCH IT HIMSELF.

ARE YOU JUST *MAKING* THIS UP, HAZING THE NEWBIE?

THERE'S BEEN *NO* MENTION, NO *SIGN* THAT TWO-FACE HAD *ANYTHING* TO DO--

YOU GONNA *ARGUE* WITH ME, OR YOU GONNA *BELIEVE* ME?

DON'T *ASK* ME HOW I *KNOW,* I JUST *KNOW,* OKAY, MacDONALD?

THIS WAS TWO-FACE AND ALL THE *ESCAPEES,* EVERYTHING ELSE, THAT'S JUST *SMOKE.*

HE DID THIS TO GRAB MONTOYA.

HELL IF I KNOW.

WHY?

BUT WE'VE GOT TO FIND HIM, AND WE'VE GOT TO DO IT *FAST.*

OKAY, I'M *NEW*, I'M THE FIRST TO *ADMIT* THAT.

BUT *WHY* IN THE WORLD WON'T YOU GO TO THE CAPTAIN WITH THIS?

I MEAN, IF MONTOYA ISN'T MAKING THIS UP--

SHE *ISN'T*.

--THEN WE'RE TALKING ABOUT ONE OF THE ORIGINAL GANGSTERS.

...WE'RE TALKING ABOUT A *PSYCHO* WHO REGULARLY GIVES THE BATMAN *MIGRAINES*.

SEEMS TO ME YOU'D WANT ALL THE HELP YOU CAN *GET*!

WHAT?

UNLESS YOU'RE AFTER *SOMETHING ELSE*.

YOU *HONESTLY* THINK I'M *GLORY-RIDING?* TWO-FACE GIVES ME *NIGHTMARES*, LITTLE ROOKIE.

IF I HAD ONE SHRED OF *PROOF* TO BACK MY PARTNER UP, I'D BE IN SAWYER'S OFFICE RIGHT *NOW*, SCREAMING FOR THEM TO *TURN ON THE DAMN SIGNAL*, I DON'T *CARE* IF IT'S DAYTIME.

BUT ALL I'VE GOT IS *HER* WORD, AND JUST BECAUSE IT'S *MORE* THAN GOOD ENOUGH FOR ME--

--HEY, YOU LISTENING TO ME, ROOKIE?

HEY, MacKENZIE!

MacDONALD.

SO YOU *DO* HEAR ME.

YOU *LOSE* SOMETHING?

I... ...I THOUGHT I SAW SOMETHING...

THERE YOU *ARE*, YOU LITTLE SON OF A--

WHAT'D YOU *FIND*?

IT GOT *SCRAPED*. WHEN IT *NICKED* THE MAILBOX.

GOT SCRAPED WHEN SOME HOTSHOT FROM VICE TOOK A CORNER TOO FAST--

NO. LOOK--

--IT'S FROM THE MAILBOX.

SON OF A BITCH.

STAY WITH THE CAR ROOKIE, DON'T LET ANYONE TOUCH IT!

WHERE ARE YOU GOING?

TO GET SAWYER AND SOME TECHS...

...AND TO FIND OUT THE NAME OF THE LAST DETECTIVE TO USE THAT CAR...

IF HE'S *WITH* HIM DON'T *HESITATE.*

NO WORRIES. DEALT WITH HIM BEFORE.

YOU'LL HAVE TO TELL ME ABOUT IT SOMETIME.

WE READY?

Q.R.T. SAYS GO.

ding-dong

WHAT--

NOT A **WORD** OUT OF YOU.

CLEAR!

CLEAR!

CLEAR!

THEY'RE **NOT** HERE.

NOBODY'S HERE.

WE **FOUND** THE CAR, INSPECTOR, THE CAR YOU **USED** TODAY. THAT WAS **SLOPPY**, THAT WAS **STUPID**, USING A **DEPARTMENT** VEHICLE.

WE FOUND **BLOOD** IN THE **TRUNK**, AND IF IT'S MY **PARTNER'S**, AND SHE **DIES**, I WILL **PERSONALLY** ASK TO ADMINISTER THE **LETHAL** INJECTION MYSELF.

IT'S **NOT** LIKE THAT, IT'S **NOT**--

THEN **TELL** ME WHAT IT **IS** LIKE! WHERE'S **TWO-FACE?**

WHERE'S MY PARTNER?

EASY, DETECTIVE!

I HAVE A **RIGHT** TO REMAIN SILENT.

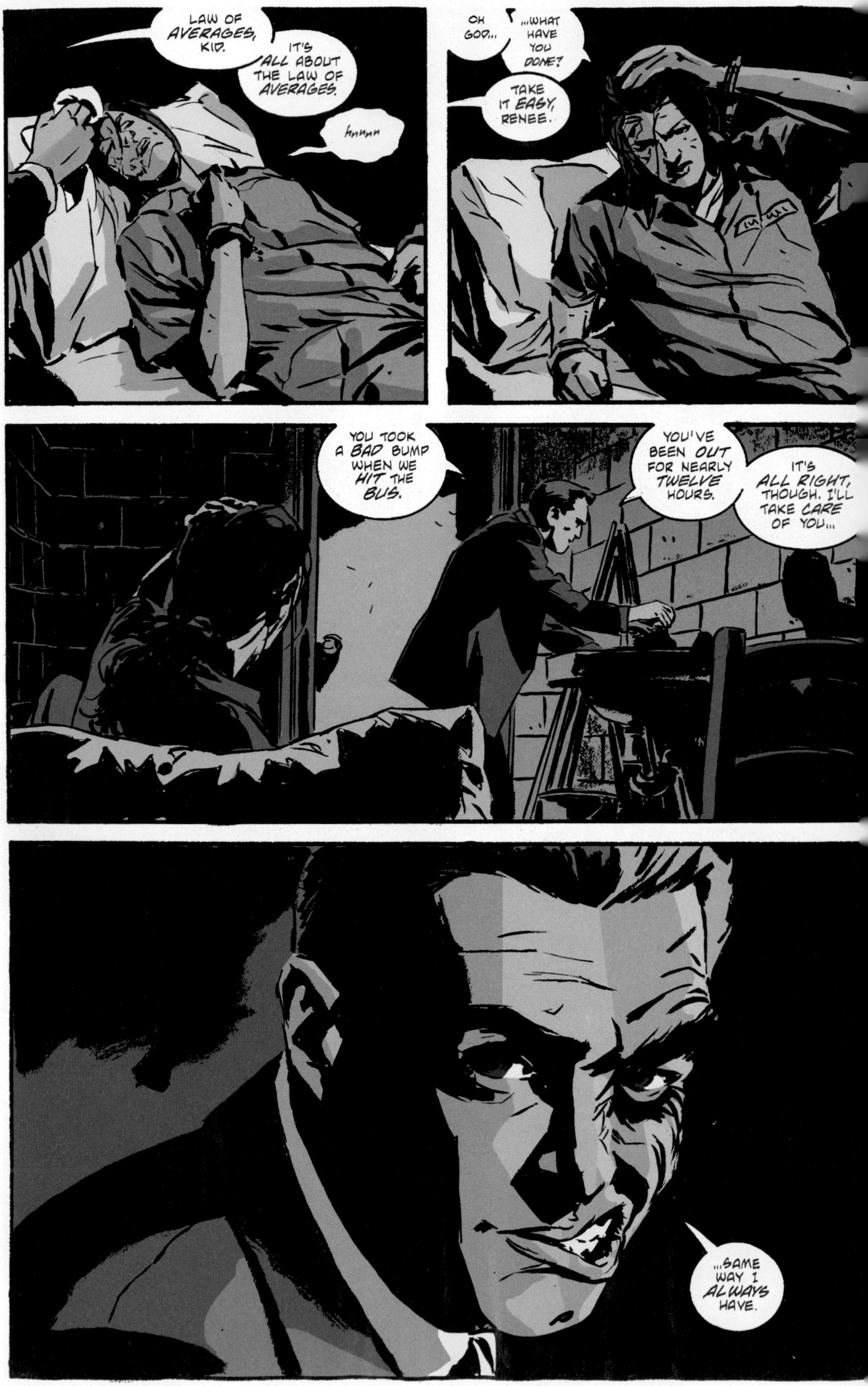
LAW OF AVERAGES, KID.
IT'S ALL ABOUT THE LAW OF AVERAGES.
hnnnn
OH GOD...
...WHAT HAVE YOU DONE?
TAKE IT EASY, RENEE.
YOU TOOK A BAD BUMP WHEN WE HIT THE BUS.
YOU'VE BEEN OUT FOR NEARLY TWELVE HOURS.
IT'S ALL RIGHT, THOUGH. I'LL TAKE CARE OF YOU...
...SAME WAY I ALWAYS HAVE.

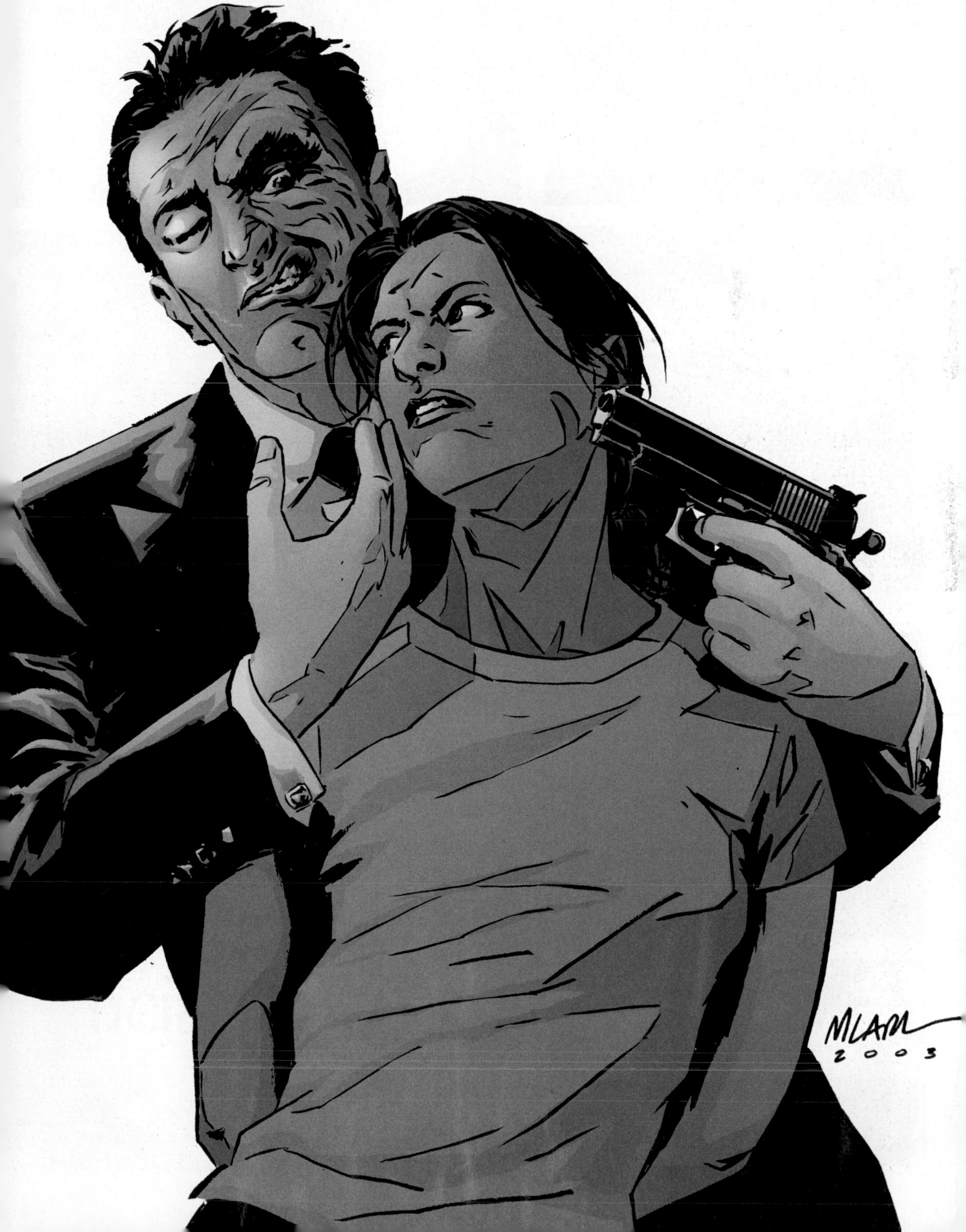
MLAM
2003

I'VE GOT YOU.

HOW'S YOUR HEAD?

WHAT DO *YOU* THINK, HARVEY?

IT *HURTS.*

I CAN GET YOU SOME ASPIRIN.

YOU CAN *LET* ME GO.

RENEE, THAT'S WHAT I *LOVE* ABOUT YOU.

YOU *NEVER* LOSE YOUR SENSE OF *HUMOR.*

COME ON.

C'MON, RENEE...

I WON'T BITE...

half a life
Conclusion

...NOT UNLESS YOU *WANT* ME *TO,* AT LEAST.

THERE'S *FOOD*, IF YOU'RE *HUNGRY*. YOU HAVEN'T EATEN *ALL DAY*, AT *LEAST*, AND *THAT'S* ASSUMING YOU CHOKED DOWN THAT *SWILL* THEY SERVE AT THE SCHRECK.

MAN. I *HATE* THAT FOOD, AND TRUST ME, I *KNOW* WHAT I'M TALKING ABOUT, I'VE HAD TO *EAT* IT OFTEN ENOUGH.

I HAD SOME *STEAKS* DONE, YOURS IS *RARE*, THE WAY YOU *LIKE* IT--

HARVEY...

...WHERE ARE WE?

STOP IT!

WH--

I SAID--

--STOP IT! NO ONE *LOOKS* AT HER *THAT* WAY--

--YOU DON'T *LOOK* AT *HER* THAT WAY I'LL *PAINT* THE WALL WITH YOUR *BRAINS* YOU *DIRTY* LITTLE--

HARVEY!

LEAVE HIM ALONE.

HE WAS LOOKING AT YOU--

I KNOW, IT'S ALL RIGHT.

THERE'S DINNER, STEAKS, LIKE I SAID, WITH NICE BAKED POTATO, CAESAR SALAD, A GOOD MERLOT...

...I EVEN HAD ONE OF THE CREW RUN OVER TO THAT RESTAURANT XENON, WHERE MISS HERNANDEZ WORKS...

...PICKED UP TWO TIRAMISU FOR DESSERT...

...RENEE?

...IF YOU DON'T LIKE STEAK, I CAN SEND OUT FOR SOMETHING ELSE...

...RENEE? SAY SOMETHING, PLEASE. ANYTHING.

YOU WANT ME TO...ALL RIGHT, HARVEY...

WHY HAVE YOU RUINED MY LIFE?

I DIDN'T.

HE DID.

IT'S HOW THE COIN CAME DOWN, RENEE...

WORTHLESS!

SIX **HOURS** HE SITS THERE AND **NOTHING!**

BLAH BLAH NOT MY FAULT BLAH BLAH MADE ME DO IT...

...BLAH BLAH **THREATENED** MY KID...

YOU'RE TALKING ABOUT **CONWAY?**

HEY, CROWE. TURN ON THE **LIGHT,** WOULD YOU?

YEAH, THAT I.A.D. **RAT BASTARD.**

DIDN'T **KNOW** HE HAD A KID.

HE'S **DIVORCED.** WIFE GOT CUSTODY OF THE **KID**--HE'S **EIGHT**--MOVED 'EM **BOTH** OUT OF GOTHAM TO SAN FRANCISCO.

SAN FRANCISCO! AND CONWAY'S **TERRIFIED** TWO-FACE IS GONNA **FLY** CROSS-COUNTRY TO MAKE GOOD ON THE **THREAT,** LIKE TWO-FACE **EVER** LEAVES GOTHAM.

WELL...WE **ARE** TALKING ABOUT TWO-FACE.

IF HE WAS **YOUR** KID, WOULD YOU WANT TO TAKE THE **CHANCE?**

OH, **SHUT** UP.

FACT IS, CONWAY DOESN'T HAVE THE **FIRST** IDEA WHERE TWO-FACE IS **HOLDING** RENEE.

THEY WERE IN COMMUNICATION WITH ONE ANOTHER?

YEAH. CONWAY GAVE US THE **NUMBER.**

STOLEN **CELL PHONE?**

OH, **VERY GOOD.** YOU MUST BE A **DETECTIVE.**

HE SAYS THEY HAD ONE **FACE-TO-FACE** MEETING, THOUGH.

THE **PRESIDENTIAL** SUITE AT SOME **HOTEL,** OR SO CONWAY THINKS. HE **CAN'T** BE SURE, OF COURSE, CUZ TWO-FACE'S GOONS **BLIND-FOLDED** HIM DURING TRANSIT...

...SO WE'RE CHECKING THE HOTELS, BUT WE ALL KNOW THAT'S A LONG SHOT.

YOU GOING TO TURN ON THAT DAMN LIGHT...

...CROWE?

MACKENZIE!

MACDONALD, AND STOP SHOUTING--

GRAB YOUR COAT, COME ON!

WHAT? ALL OF A SUDDEN YOU KNOW WHERE TWO-FACE IS HIDING?

NOT ME...

WOW.

...HIM.

DAMMIT, MOVE, ROOKIE! WE CAN'T LOSE HIM--

I'M COMING.

SUDDEN RUSH, MY DEAR DETECTIVE ALLEN? A LEAD SUDDENLY DROP IN YOUR LAP?

THE BATMAN'S GOT HIS IMPERSONATION OF YOU DOWN COLD, CROWE.

I'M SORRY, WHAT?

HE'S THE LEAD, DAMMIT--

--CAN'T TALK NOW, TELL THE CAPTAIN WE'LL RADIO WHEN WE HAVE SOMETHING--

--AND HAVE THEM MAKE SURE Q.R.T. IS ON STAND-BY!

YOU'RE NOT HUNGRY?

NO.

I DON'T SEEM TO HAVE MUCH OF AN APPETITE.

IF YOU DON'T EAT YOUR DINNER, YOU WON'T GET DESSERT.

YOU HIRED SELKER?

I HAD LIPARI HIRE SELKER. NEEDED TO FIND SOMETHING ON YOU, SOMETHING I COULD USE. FIGURED THERE'D BE AN AFFAIR OR SOMETHING IN YOUR PAST, SOMETHING YOU DIDN'T WANT OUT IN THE OPEN.

MAYBE A KID OR AN ABORTION.

SOMETHING YOU WERE HIDING.

BOY, DID YOU GET LUCKY.

BOY, DID I.

I SENT THE *PICTURES*, IF *THAT'S* WHAT YOU'RE ASKING.

HOW *ARE* YOUR *PARENTS*, BY THE WAY? I UNDERSTAND THAT BENNY'S BECOME A *FIREFIGHTER*.

WELL, MY *PARENTS* AREN'T *TOO* HAPPY RIGHT NOW, YOU KNOW.

TURNS OUT THEIR DAUGHTER'S GAY. TURNS OUT *THEIR* DAUGHTER'S ACCUSED OF *MURDER.*

THINGS LIKE *THAT.*

I *NOW.*

THEN WHY'D YOU *ASK?*

TO MAKE SURE *YOU* KNEW IT, TOO.

YOU KILL *SELKER?*

YEAH. I WANTED LIPARI TO DO *IT*, BUT HE'D HAVE SCREWED IT UP. IT HAD TO BE *CLEAN.*

AND *LIPARI?* YOU DID *LIPARI*, *TOO?*

OH, *YEAH. HAD* TO DO *THAT* ONE MYSELF.

HE SET HIMSELF UP *BEAUTIFULLY*, THOUGH, DIDN'T HE?

THAT *WHOLE* THING OUTSIDE MISS *HERNANDEZ'S APARTMENT*, THE *VIDEO CAMERA*, TALK ABOUT GIVING *YOU* A *MOTIVE.*

I HAVE TO *SAY*, RENEE, WHEN YOU GIVE A *BEAT-DOWN*, YOU DON'T *MESS* AROUND.

YOU WERE *WATCHING?*

LONG ENOUGH TO BE *SURE* EVERYTHING WENT THE WAY I WANTED. SOON AS YOU WENT AFTER LIPARI, I WENT TO *HIS* PLACE.

WITH MY *BACKUP.*

RIGHT. YOU WERE HAVING *COFFEE* WITH MISS *HERNANDEZ*, I WAS *CRACKING* INTO YOUR *GUN* SAFE.

SO WHEN LIPARI GOT BACK TO HIS APARTMENT, I WAS THERE. GUNNED HIM DOWN LIKE THE RAPIST BASTARD HE WAS.

DROPPING THE BACKUP AT THE *SCENE* WAS A MISTAKE. I THOUGHT IT WOULD *READ* AS OUT OF *CONTROL*, THAT YOU KILLED LIPARI IN A *RAGE*.

IN RETROSPECT, I SHOULD HAVE PUT IT *BACK* IN YOUR *SAFE* WHEN I PLANTED THE *SMACK*.

ANY *OTHER* QUESTIONS?

WHY'D YOU *SPRING* ME?

AH...YEAH, THAT *WASN'T* MY INITIAL PLAN. BUT AS SOON AS I REALIZED *WAYNE* HAD AN INTEREST, I KNEW YOU'D BE *OUT* ON *BAIL* BEFORE NIGHTFALL.

IF THAT *HAPPENED*, IT WAS JUST A MATTER OF *TIME* BEFORE THE *CASE* AGAINST YOU *COLLAPSED*.

I HAD TO *NAIL* THE *COFFIN* CLOSED ON YOU.

NOW YOU'RE A *FUGITIVE* ON TOP OF *EVERYTHING* ELSE.

KILLED THE *GUARDS*, TOO?

OF COURSE.

NO, FORGET IT.

I *WON'T* DO THIS, HARVEY. I WON'T *PLAY* AT THIS *ANYMORE!*

SIT DOWN, RENEE.

NO, DAMN YOU, HARVEY, ENOUGH'S ENOUGH!

AND I'M NOT GOING TO SIT HERE LIKE WE'RE ON SOME KIND OF PERVERTED DATE!

YOU'VE TORN MY LIFE APART! YOU'VE SHATTERED MY FAMILY, YOU'VE KILLED MY CAREER--

--YOU'VE MURDERED PEOPLE IN MY NAME!

I'VE GOT NOTHING LEFT!

THAT'S THE POINT.

THAT WAS ALWAYS THE POINT.

BUT YOU'RE WRONG.

YOU HAVE ME.

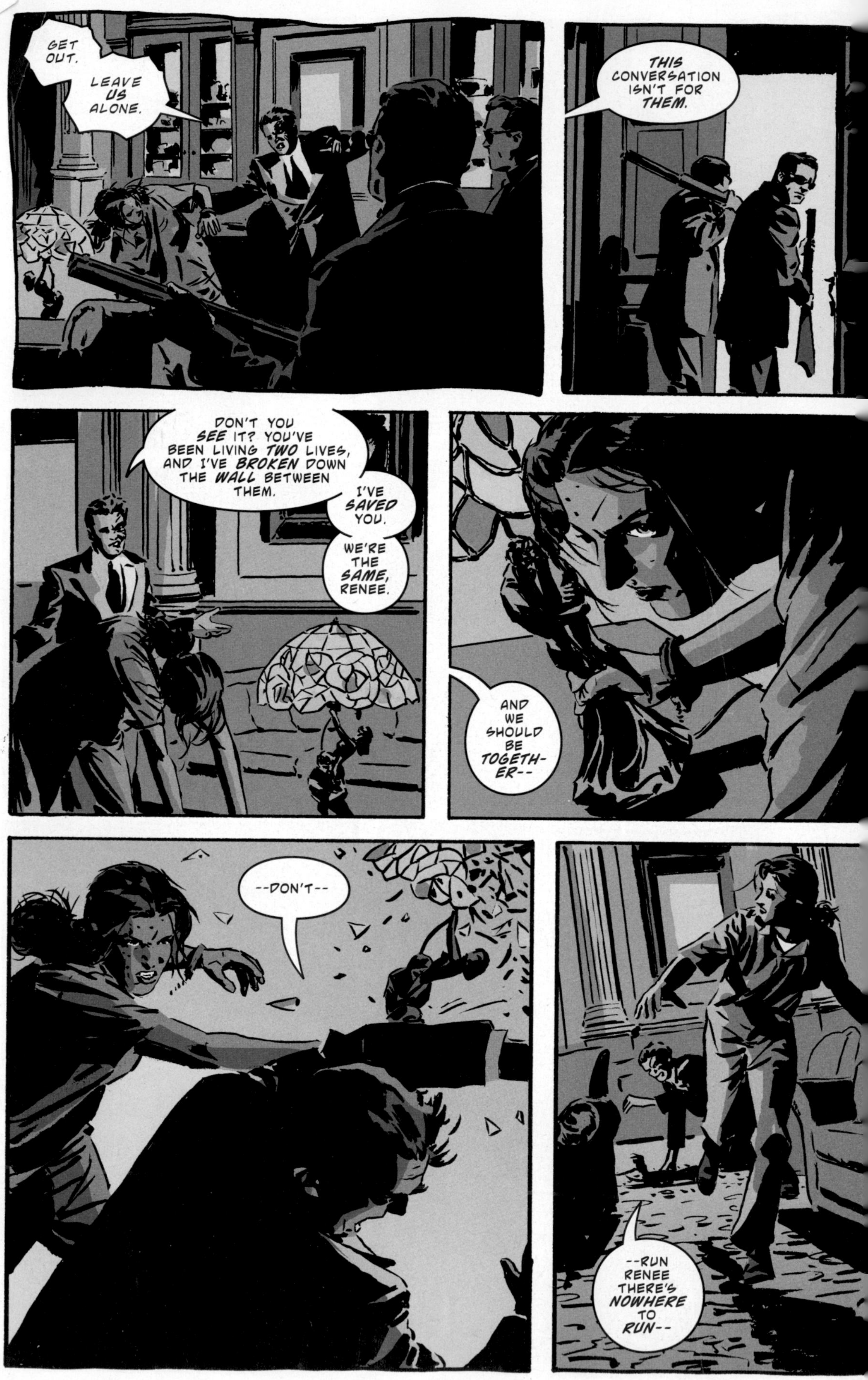
GET OUT.
LEAVE US ALONE.
THIS CONVERSATION ISN'T FOR THEM.
DON'T YOU SEE IT? YOU'VE BEEN LIVING TWO LIVES, AND I'VE BROKEN DOWN THE WALL BETWEEN THEM.
I'VE SAVED YOU.
WE'RE THE SAME, RENEE.
AND WE SHOULD BE TOGETH- ER--
--DON'T--
--RUN RENEE THERE'S NOWHERE TO RUN--

--IT'S *JUST US,* NOW--

--YOU AND ME--

--THE *WAY WE* BOTH KNOW IT *SHOULD* BE.

WE'RE UNDERGROUND.

YEAH, THIS PLACE GOT *PAVED* OVER AFTER THE *EARTH-QUAKE.*

FIXED IT *UP* PRETTY GOOD THOUGH, DIDN'T I?

IT'S *OURS,* OUR *PLACE.*

FOR YOU AND ME. WE CAN BE *TOGETHER* HERE.

YOU'RE THE *ONLY* PERSON WHO *NEVER* TREATED ME WITH *PITY.*

YOU'VE BEEN *KIND* TO ME. YOU VISITED ME AT *ARKHAM.*

IT'S *OBVIOUS* HOW I FEEL ABOUT *YOU,* RENEE.

AND I THOUGHT THAT, PERHAPS, YOU FELT THE *SAME.*

THAT YOU *LOVED* ME, TOO.

HARVEY, **YOU** OUTED **ME!**

I'M **GAY!** I'M A **DYKE,** A **LESBIAN,** I LIKE **GIRLS!**

DIDN'T YOU LOOK AT THE **PICTURE** BEFORE YOU STARTED SENDING IT AROUND?

YEAH, I KNOW ALL THAT.

RENEE, YOU HAVE **NOTHING** TO GO **BACK** TO. I MADE **CERTAIN** OF **THAT.** YOU'RE **STAYING** WITH **ME,** NOW.

AND I CAN MAKE YOU **WHOLE.**

NO.

I **DON'T** SEE WHAT **THAT** HAS TO DO WITH **US.**

I **DON'T** LOVE YOU. I'M **NEVER** GOING TO LOVE YOU.

AND IF YOU'VE **MISINTERPRETED** THE **KINDNESS** I'VE SHOWN YOU, I AM TRULY SORRY.

BUT YOU WILL **NEVER** GET WHAT YOU **WANT** FROM ME, HARVEY. NOT WILLINGLY, NOT **EVER...**

...AND YOU HAVE TO KNOW THAT I WILL DO **EVERYTHING** I CAN DO TO **ESCAPE** YOU.

NO, **WRONG** ANSWER--

--SHUT UP, JUST **SHUT** UP--

HARVEY--

--IT'S **HER,** ISN'T IT, THAT **BITCH** CHEF--

--NO HARVEY, SHE HAS *NOTHING* TO DO WITH THIS, THIS IS ABOUT US--

LIAR!

LIED TO US!

MISSED ONE, IS THAT IT?

AND IF *SHE'S* GONE, THEN WHAT, DETECTIVE? IF I TAKE *HER* FROM YOU, TOO? *THEN* WHAT?

HARVEY, CALM--

HARVEY'S NOT HERE RIGHT NOW!

KILL HER I SHOULD HAVE JUST KILLED HER--

--AND *THEN* YOU'LL HAVE *NOTHING?*

--SHOULD I *KILL* HER, DETECTIVE *LIAR* SHOULD I TAKE *THAT* FROM YOU TOO--

...STOP IT...

227

OH, IT'LL STOP. YES, IT'LL STOP.

ONE WAY OR ANOTHER.

WELL, THEN

LOOKS LIKE I'VE GOT TO *RUN* AN ERRAND.

SHOULDN'T TAKE *TOO* LONG. THE *DOUBLES* WILL LOOK AFTER YOU UNTIL I GET BACK.

TOM! RAY!

WHERE THE *HELL* ARE THEY?

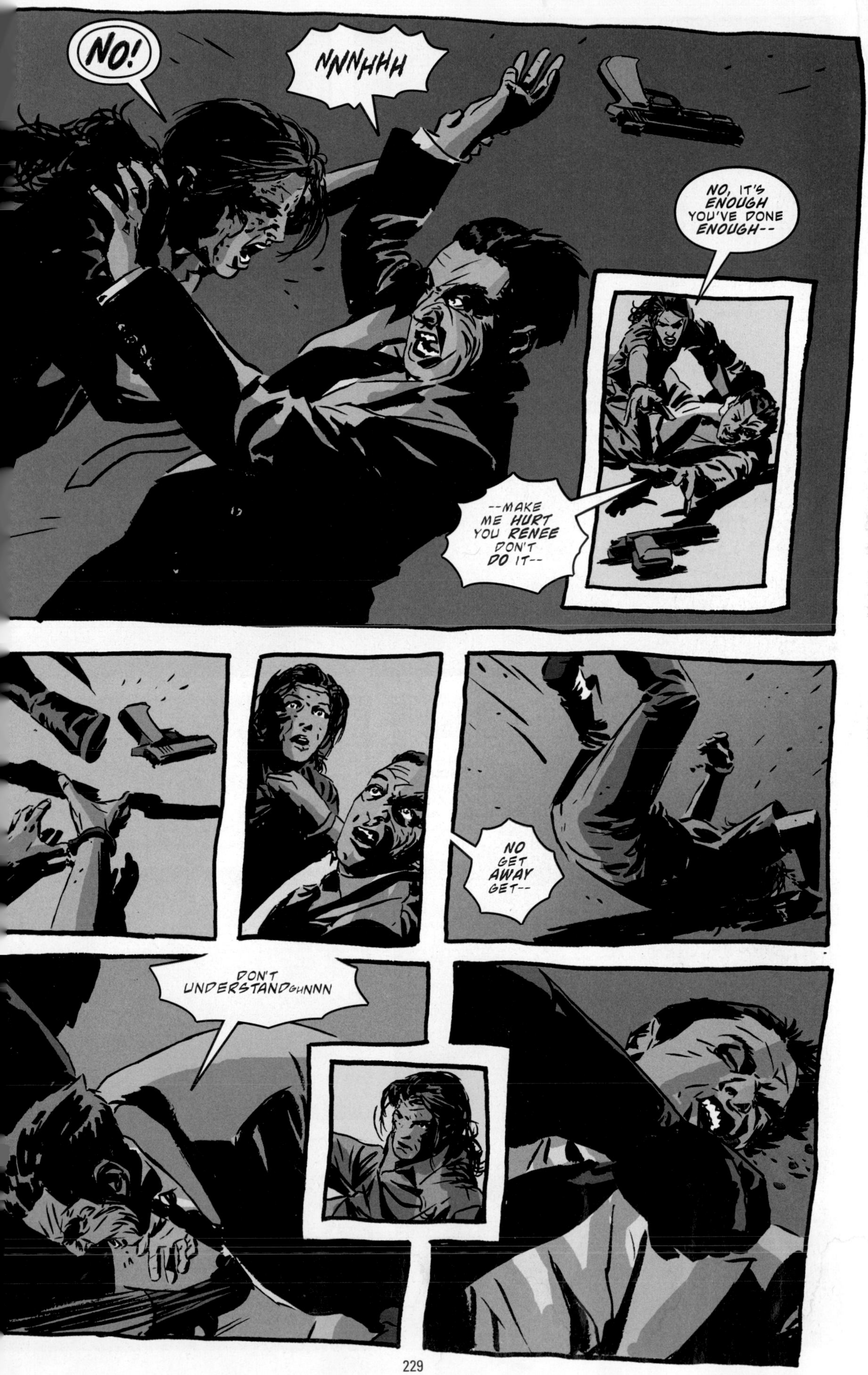
NO!
NNNHHH
NO, IT'S ENOUGH YOU'VE DONE ENOUGH--
--MAKE ME HURT YOU RENEE DON'T DO IT--
NO GET AWAY GET--
DON'T UNDERSTANDGHNNN

ALLEN AND Q.R.T. ARE *THREE* MINUTES BEHIND ME, DETECTIVE...

...TELL THEM THERE ARE *FOUR* MORE CUFFED IN THE *OTHER* ROOM.

I TOOK *CARE* OF IT.

YOU *WHAT?*

YOU TOOK *CARE* OF THIS? SO HE CAN *BREAK* OUT IN ANOTHER YEAR OR TWO, PUT ME THROUGH THIS *AGAIN?*

THAT'S HOW YOU TOOK CARE OF THIS?

YOU WERE FIGHTING FOR THE *GUN.*

EITHER *HE* WOULD HAVE KILLED *YOU,* OR YOU WOULD HAVE KILLED *HIM.*

NEITHER OPTION WAS *ACCEPTABLE.*

YOU'RE *WELCOM...*

HOW'S THE SWELLING?

YOU TELL ME.

UGLY.

THANKS.

THE "W" IS *BUSTED*. I THOUGHT THE M.C.U. HAD *GOOD* EQUIPMENT.

THEN DON'T USE THE "W", ROOKIE.

YOU HAVE *ANOTHER* WAY TO SPELL "TWO-FACE?"

TRY TWO "O"S.

BATMAN ...EAD YOU TO ME?

YEAH. WENT *JUST* SLOW ENOUGH SO MacDONALD AND I COULD KEEP *UP.*

APPARENTLY THE BATMAN DOES A *MEAN* IMPRESSION OF DETECTIVE CROWE.

HE *PROBABLY* ...OES A *MEAN* IMPRESSION OF *ALL* OF US.

NOT *ME.* I'M STILL THE *ROOKIE.*

EVEN *YOU,* ROOKIE.

EXCUSE ME.

TELL HER.

IN LIGHT OF INSPECTOR CONWAY'S *CONFESSION* AND THE EVIDENCE COLLECTED WHEN TWO-FACE WAS APPREHENDED, THE D.A.'S OFFICE IS *DIMISSING* ALL CHARGES.

AND *EXTENDING* APOLOGIES.

WHE IS H

TWO-FACE IS IN *SECURE* HOLDING AT ARKHAM. HE'LL BE *CHARGED* IN THE MORNING.

LET'S HOPE *THIS* TIME THEY THROW *AWAY* THE KEY.

LET'S HOPE.

INSPECTOR ESPERANZA.

CONWAY... HE WAS A *GOOD* COP ONCE, YOU KNOW. TWO-FACE HAS HIS *NUMBER*, THAT'S *ALL*.

SURE.

OKAY, LET'S TALK ABOUT *YOU*.

I'M READY TO *WORK*.

LIKE *HELL* YOU ARE.

YOU'VE GOT *SIX WEEKS* SAVED UP. YOU'RE GONNA TAKE *FOUR* OF THEM. MacDONALD WILL PARTNER WITH ALLEN UNTIL YOU GET BACK.

AND *IF* I SEE YOU IN *MY* SQUADROOM BEFORE FOUR WEEK· ARE *UP*, DETECTIV YOU'LL BE RIDING A DESK FOR THE REST OF YOUR CAREER.

I'M GOING TO *SAY* THIS TO YOU AGAIN, RENEE.

WHAT YOU DO NEXT, YOU GET TO LIVE WITH FOR THE *REST* OF YOUR LIFE.

YES, MA'AM.

NO... PROBABLY *NOT A* GOOD IDEA.

MY *PARENTS* ARE GOING TO FEEL *ATTACKED* AS IT IS...

I'LL COME UP *WITH* YOU IF YOU WANT.

...HAVING MY *LOVER* WITH ME WILL JUST MAKE THAT *WORSE*.

YOU'VE NEVER CALLED E THAT BEFORE.

I LIKE IT. IT SOUNDS *GOOD* WHEN YOU SAY IT.

I KNOW.

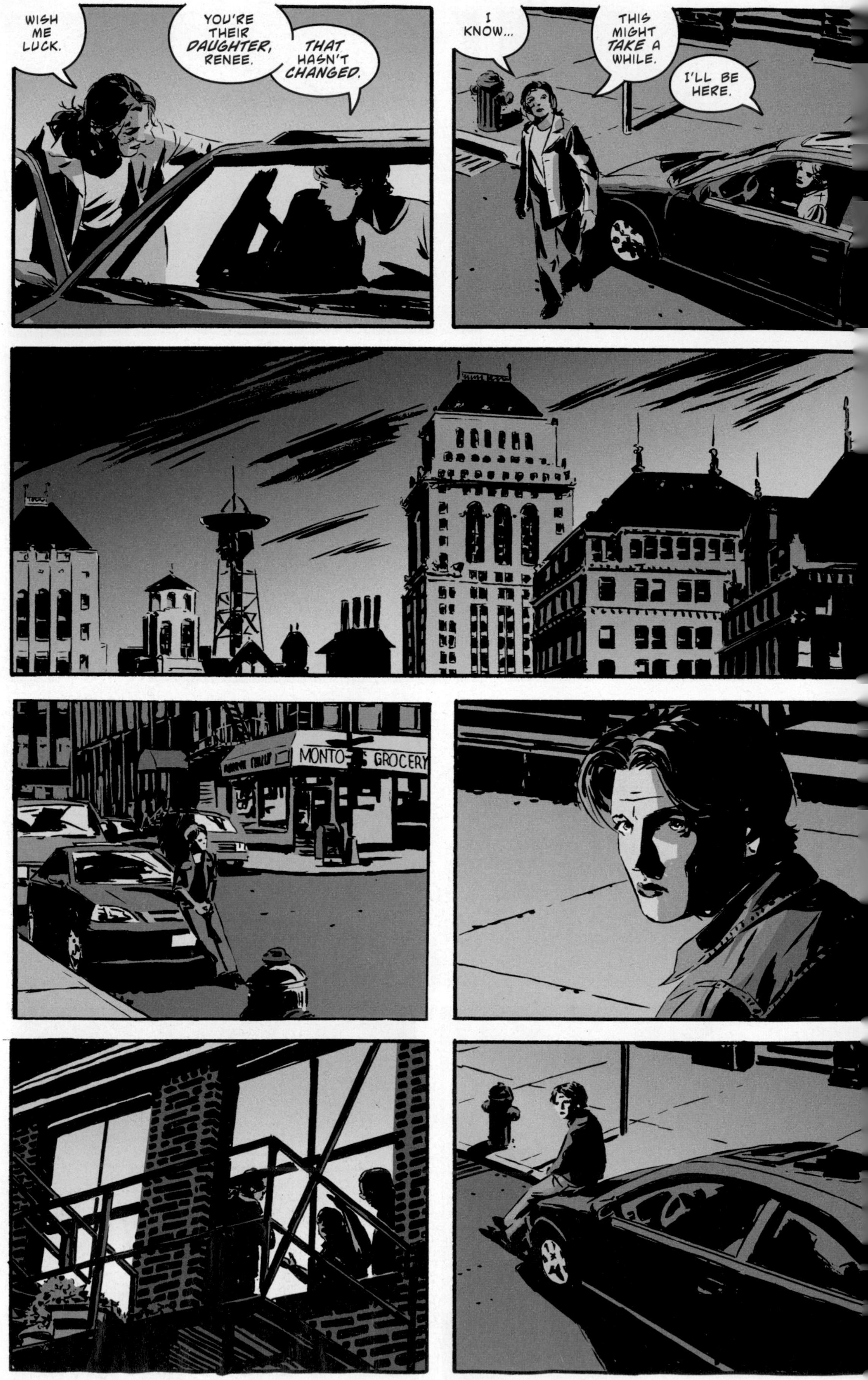
WISH ME LUCK.
YOU'RE THEIR *DAUGHTER*, RENEE.
THAT HASN'T *CHANGED.*
I KNOW...
THIS MIGHT *TAKE* A WHILE.
I'LL BE HERE.
MONTO GROCERY

RENEE?

HOW'D IT GO?

PRETTY MUCH EXACTLY THE WAY I THOUGHT IT WOULD...

MY *MOTHER* TOLD ME I WAS GOING TO *BURN* IN HELL, AND THAT HER *DAUGHTER* WAS *DEAD* TO HER, NOW...

...SO I GUESS WE WERE *WRONG* ABOUT THAT PART, HUH?

MY *FATHER* WOULDN'T *SAY* ANYTHING.

RENEE...

THEY TOLD ME *NOT* TO COME BACK, DEE.

THEY TOLD ME NOT TO *EVER* COME BACK.

...OH GOD...

SHHH, IT'S OKAY, RENEE...

...IT'S OKAY, I'VE GOT YOU...

...OH...

...I'VE GOT YOU...

END

STAFFING THE GCPD

In defining the approach to producing GOTHAM CENTRAL in tandem, writers Greg Rucka and Ed Brubaker divided the cast into the day and night shifts, each masterminding one twelve-hour block. They prepared extensive notes on each of the detectives and uniformed officers for artist Michael Lark. Michael's character designs for the cast are on the following pages.

DETAILED CONCEPT SKETCH OF THE MCU SQUADROOM.

MARKER ROUGHS OF A PAGE FROM ISSUE #4.

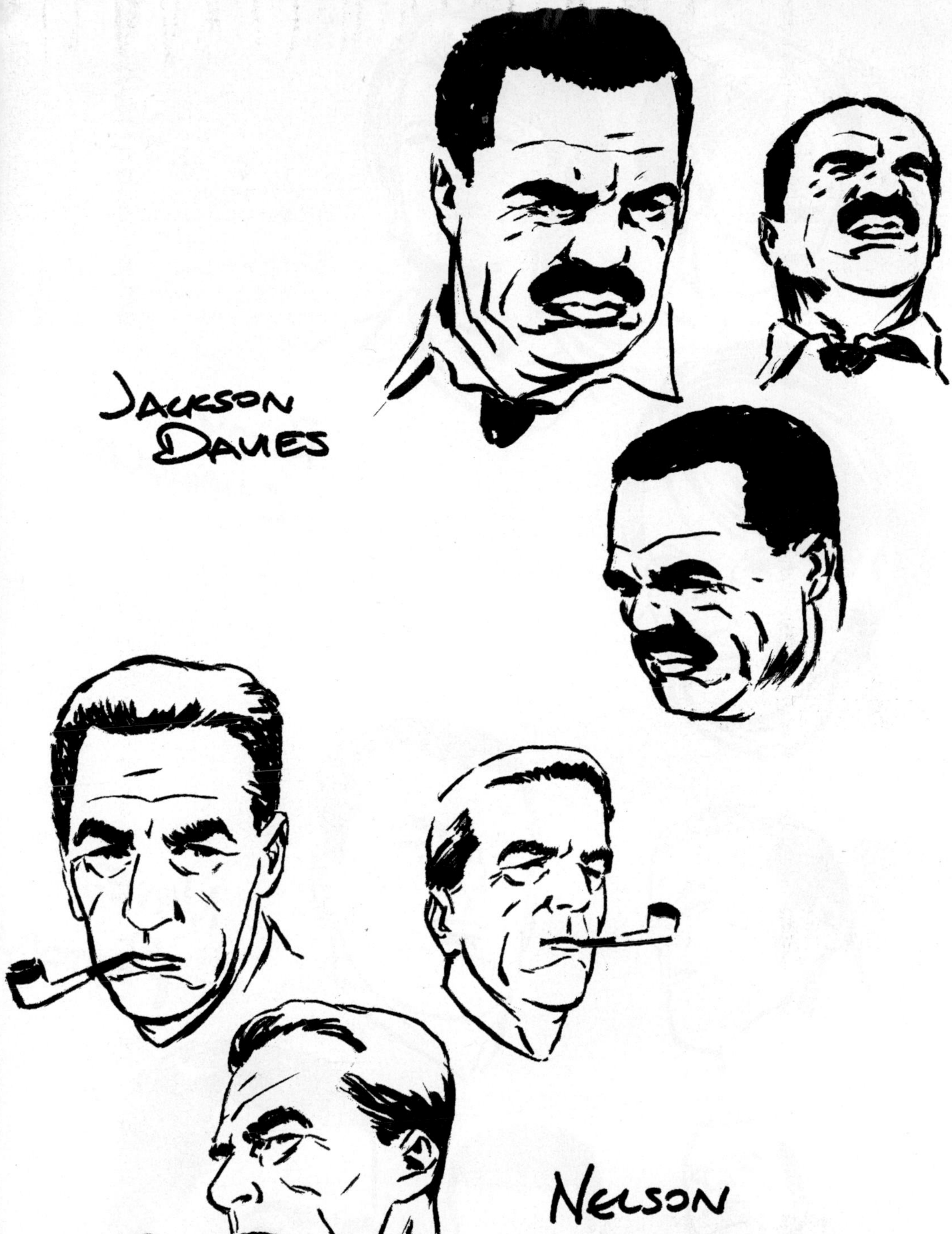
JACKSON DAVIES
NELSON CROWE

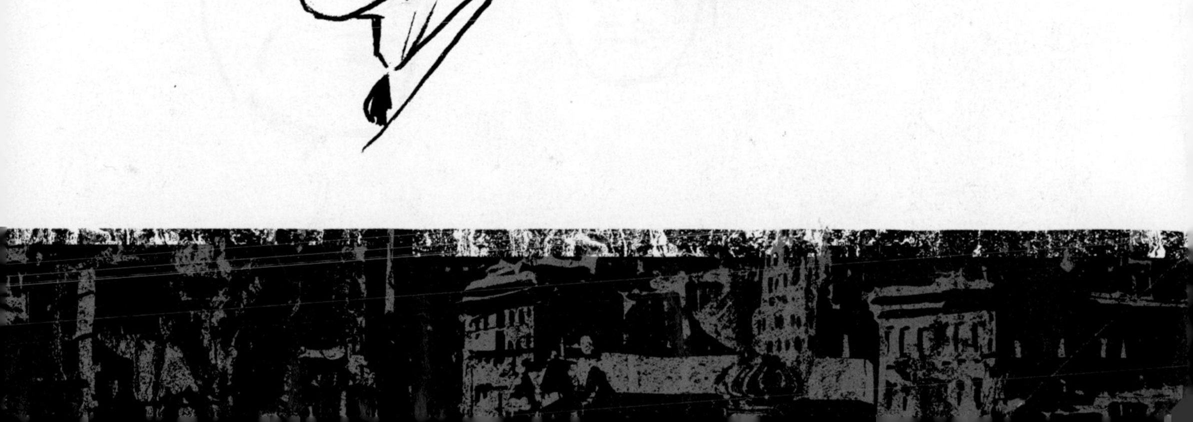

ROMY
CHANDLER

NATE
PATTON

CHARLIE
FIELDS

MARCUS
DRIVER

FIGURE STUDIES FOR
THE COVER OF ISSUE #5.